IMAGES
of America

FARMING IN NORTHERN MACOMB COUNTY

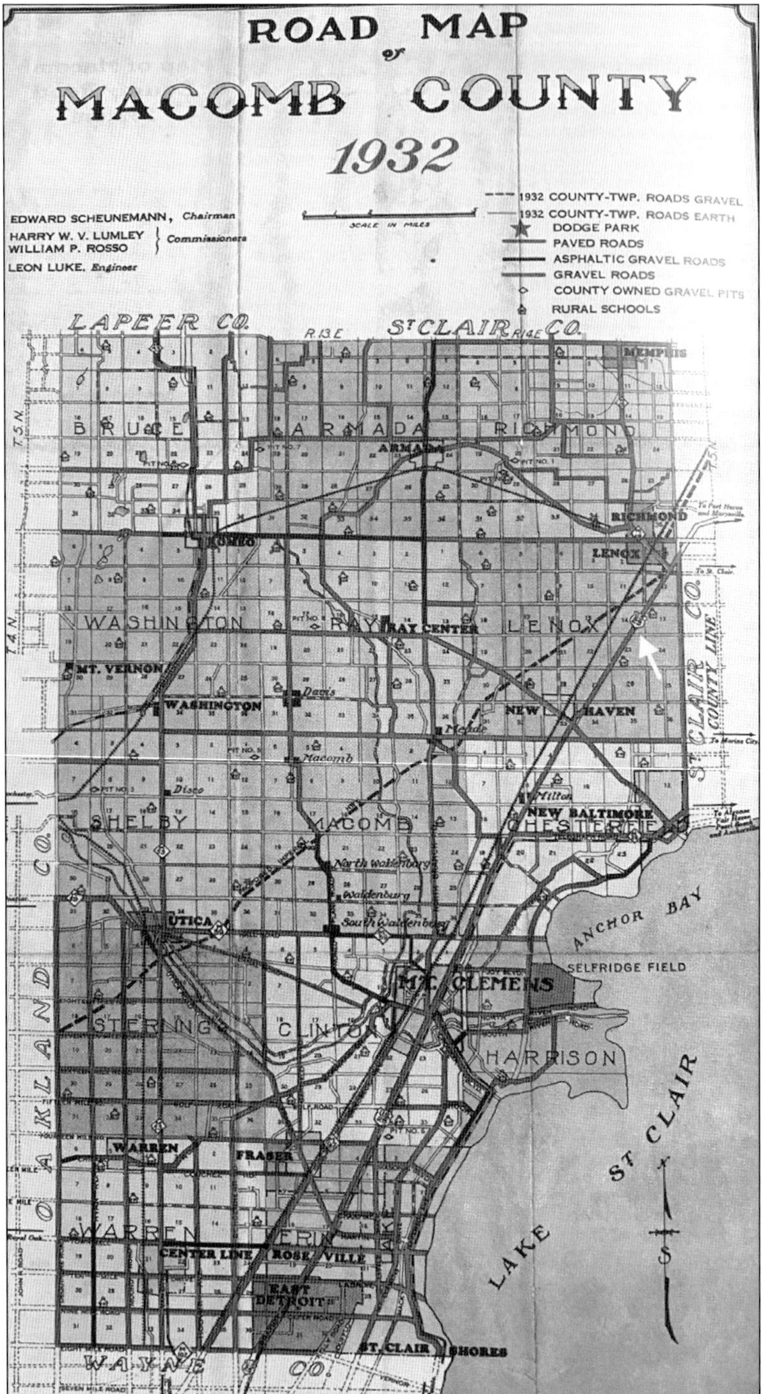

Macomb County, 1932. Michigan highway M-59 divides Northern and Southern Macomb County running along a line where Shelby, Macomb, and Chesterfield Townships start northward, along with Washington, Ray, Lenox, Bruce, Armada, and Richmond. (Courtesy of the Donley family collection.)

On the Cover: Louis Schoenherr is pictured on his new 1953 Golden Jubilee Ford tractor with his youngest son, Pete Schoenherr, who seems to want to take the lead in getting the day's work done. (Courtesy of Pete Schoenherr collection.)

IMAGES
of America

FARMING IN NORTHERN MACOMB COUNTY

Linda Osborne Cynowa

ARCADIA
PUBLISHING

ISBN 978-1-4671-0720-4

Published by Arcadia Publishing
Charleston, South Carolina

Printed in the United States of America

Library of Congress Control Number: 2021935803

For all general information, please contact Arcadia Publishing:
Telephone 843-853-2070
Fax 843-853-0044
E-mail sales@arcadiapublishing.com
For customer service and orders:
Toll-Free 1-888-313-2665

Visit us on the Internet at www.arcadiapublishing.com

This book is dedicated to all the historians and archivists who work so hard to keep the pieces of our past safe for future generations.

"And now let me ask you my friend, whether you do not think, that many of our disappointments and much of our happiness arise from our forming false notions of things and persons."

—*Abigail Adams*

Contents

ACKNOWLEDGMENTS

It is with the greatest appreciation that I once again thank Julie Oparka, certified archivist at the Romeo District Library and Community Archives. Her continued support, unending help, and assistance in producing this project have been invaluable. Thanks go to Stacie Guzzo, branch manager and archivist for the Romeo District Library, for always supporting the project and making the pathways easier and for allowing all the people with submissions to come there for the scanning process; to my dear friend Patty Johnesse for her time in helping me to correct the long sentences and curb too many commas and not enough periods; and to Angel Prohaska, the title manager of this as well as my past two books, for always getting me on the right track and steering me in the right direction.

In Richmond Township, thank you to Christine Rowley and Norm Gibson of the Richmond Historical Society for their help, time, and generous support; Phyllis Fuerstenau; Deborah Leach Doyle; Michael Sullivan; and John Bishop.

In Macomb Township, gratitude goes to former supervisor Janet Dunn, Roy and Joyce Schwark, Jim Schwark, Julie Dosenberger, Marie Leone, the Koss family, Julie Martel, the Klingkammer family, the DeCock family, and Michael Demil.

In Washington Township, thank you to Tim Smith for his wonderful map, Steven LeFever, Gary Kirsh, Barb Colpaert, Richard and Diane Falker, Barbara Clark, Charles Olmstead, Cecil and Steve Schoenherr, and Teri Nickles.

In Armada Township, thanks go to Ross Boelke of the Armada Historical Society, Kathy Dunlop, Steve LeFever, Don Van Houtte, Dale Jenuwine, Blakes Orchard and Cider Mill, and the *Record* newspaper.

In Ray Township, thank you to Christy DeMeulenaere and Terry Goike of the Ray Township Library, Linda Corrion, Judy Gass Lopus, Gary Kirsh, Barbara Clark, Cecil and Steve Schoenherr, Julie Dosenberger, and Betty Youngblood.

In Chesterfield, gratitude goes to Denise Jobe, Randy Walainis, Carol Vance, and Michael Sullivan.

In Lenox Township, thanks to Roy Battestilli, Michael Sullivan, Tina Kacanowski, and John Donley, and special thanks to Lawrence Donley for overnight mailing of pictures and trusting a stranger in another state to return them.

In Shelby Township, gratitude goes to Kathy Goike, the Hessell family, Janet Dunn, Irene Goike, Vikki Papesh, and Steve Diegel.

In Bruce Township, I thank David and Diane Bishop, George Van Houtte, Mark Falker, John Bishop II, Don Van Houtte, Vickie Bower, Nancy Kicinski, and Betty Youngblood.

When I started this book, my intention was to have each chapter or township covered as equally as possible, but as I moved along, I found that to be more difficult than first thought. My sincere apologies if I have slighted any particular community; it was unintended and unavoidable in finishing the book. To John Bishop II, thank you for the image on page 8 of the 1919 Model T. The majority of the images used in this book are individually credited, and to all that I did not mention, I give my heartfelt thanks for permission to use these images to help preserve the history of farming in Northern Macomb County.

INTRODUCTION

Macomb County is located in the eastern portion of the state of Michigan and is considered part of northern Metro Detroit. Macomb County was formally organized on January 15, 1818, as the third county in the Michigan Territory. The county was named in honor of Detroit-born Alexander Macomb Jr., a highly decorated veteran of the War of 1812 and hero of the Battle of Plattsburg. The county at first encompassed a much larger area than it would end up with. As the population grew in the area, the state legislature removed territory in 1819–1820 to form the counties of Oakland, Lapeer, Genesee, and St. Clair.

On April 12, 1827, the county was divided into five townships: Washington, including the present-day Bruce and Washington; Shelby, including the present Shelby and Sterling; Ray, including the present Ray and the west half of Armada; Harrison, including Lenox, Chesterfield, and the present Harrison; and Clinton, including Macomb, Clinton, Warren, and Erin. In 1932, Macomb County was extended to its present size by the addition of the township of Richmond and the east half of Armada. The north portion of Macomb County would end up with nine separate townships.

Historians believe the American township government was modeled after the English system of government. Settlers in New England developed small communities that delivered local services, while a county served as the administrative area of the government. After the Erie Canal opened, many New Yorkers migrated to Michigan and brought their form of government here. Michigan is one of 20 states that use some form of township government.

There are two types of townships: charter and civil. Being a charter township gives certain conditions that leave it exempt from annexation to contiguous cities or villages, whereas civil townships are generally not incorporated, and nearby cities may annex land in adjoining townships with relative ease. Charter townships include Chesterfield Township, Shelby Township, and Washington Township. Civil townships include Armada Township, Bruce Township, Lenox Township, Macomb Township, Ray Township, and Richmond Township.

The M-59 freeway crosses the border between Sterling Heights and Shelby Township and ends at Van Dyke Avenue in Utica, where M-59 becomes a boulevard called Hall Road. The highway crosses the Clinton River and the southern end of the M-53 freeway. This section of the highway is considered somewhat of a "main street," as it runs completely through Macomb County. Hall Road is home to a wide variety of shopping and dining, including Lakeside Mall in Sterling Heights and the Mall at Partridge Creek in Clinton Township. Although it is neither officially designated nor commonly referred to as such, the Hall Road portion of M-59 is considered "20 Mile Road" in the Detroit Mile road system. Although various names are used for M-59, at certain points it will be considered William P. Rosso Highway as it follows the path to Interstate 94 and then continues along the northern edge of Selfridge Air National Guard Base to Lake St. Clair.

Here, we will concentrate on the townships north of the M-59 Hall Road corridor boundary: Shelby Township, Macomb Township, Chesterfield Township, Washington Township, Ray Township, Lenox Township, Bruce Township, Armada Township, and Richmond Township.

Hothouse rhubarb was a very important crop for the farmers in this area from the late 1920s through the 1960s. From January through May 1931, a total of 843,000 pounds were shipped through the Michigan Central Railroad Depot in Warren. Utica came to be called "the Hothouse Rhubarb Capital of the World," producing about 85 percent of the world crop. In 1961, about 300 farmers from Northern Macomb County, in Armada, Washington, Macomb, Shelby, Utica, and across the area, were growing five to six million pounds. At the time, estimates of the year's crop value exceeded more than $1 million. Hothouse rhubarb was discovered by accident in the early 1900s by Ferdinand Schwartz, who lived on a farm in the Harper–Van Dyke Road area. He dumped part of a load of manure on a snowbank when his wagon bogged down in the snow. A few days later, the rhubarb began pushing its way through the fertilizer, and a new industry was born. Ferdinand Schwartz shared his discovery with the neighboring farms, and many farmers found this a good-paying winter crop. The first Rhubarb Festival was held with many of the people and organizations participating, for about 10 years, at the American Legion Hall and sponsored by the Utica Rotary Club and the Wolverine State Growers. There was a Rhubarb Queen, and her court chosen. The growers brought their best to be judged, with prizes awarded for extra fancy, fancy, and choice. An auction was held with the proceeds going to charity.

Today's farmers are dealing with a different set of obstacles in making farming life work. On busy highways instead of country roads, moving their equipment from one property to another can cause motorists upset in their busy lives simply because they are not aware of the importance these farms and the work done on them to our own daily lives. Many farm owners today have their property on the main farm and lease or own property in numerous areas; that equipment needs to be used in those locations also. Many farmers are dealing with townships that would prefer the revenue that development brings to their area as opposed to the local farmer who has spent a lifetime farming in that area along with multiple generations.

Many children might never have seen a cow or a goat, never mind knowing that milk, eggs, apples, cheese, bread, carrots, and honey in their lunch boxes come from a Michigan or, even nearer, a Macomb County farm. From the very start, when the government began selling land in these various areas, farming was the main use for the land because of its soft, loamy features.

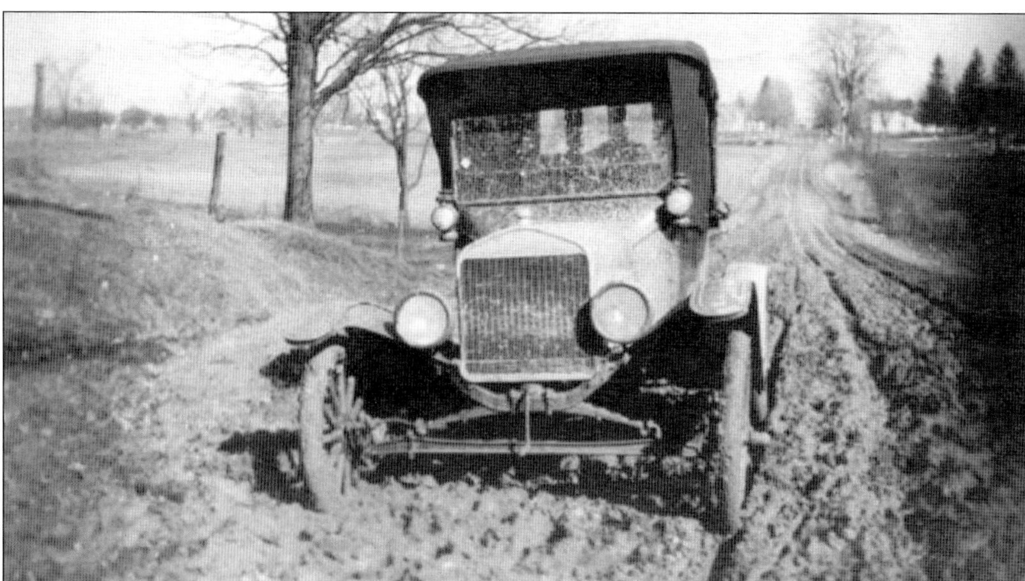

Stuck Car on Boardman Road. I hope you enjoy the ride. (Courtesy of John Bishop II.)

One

Shelby Township

The area now known as Shelby Township was originally a French possession but fell under the control of the British in 1763. It was surrendered to the Americans in 1796 when British rule came to an end in the United States. Treaties were made with various Indian tribes from 1814 to 1819, freeing up much land for future settlement. Early surveyors completed and certified Shelby Township as being correct on February 3, 1818. The area was described as having grassy plains with scarcely any timber. The eastern and extreme northern parts were heavily timbered, with the Clinton River and numerous spring brooks providing enough water.

The first buyer of government land in Shelby was Blake Curtis on May 24, 1818. He purchased the southwest quarter of section 7, now 24 Mile and Dequindre Roads. In 1821, Ezra Burgess bought 250 acres in section 33 for $1.25 per acre. He later sold it at a considerable profit, and it became the site of Utica.

The village now known as Utica was first platted by Joseph Stead in 1829 and given its original name of Harlow, while others preferred the city as it would become, Hogs Hollow. It was finally named Utica by settlers from New York in honor of a city by the same name in that state.

Disco was a village now in Shelby Township and located at the intersection of Whiskey Road (24 Mile Road) and Van Dyke Road. Disco was never incorporated, although the local high school, the Disco Academy, would become well known. A post office named Disco operated there from May 5, 1854, until July 31, 1906. Disco had general stores, a blacksmith shop, harness shops, and a hotel named the Halfway House, as the village was the midpoint between Royal Oak and Almont, Michigan.

Preston Corners is located at the corner of 25 Mile and Schoenherr Roads. Ira and Deborah Preston bought 400 acres from the government in 1826 and settled on it the following year, building a sawmill and picket fence factory. Prestonville Cemetery is still located along 25 Mile Road.

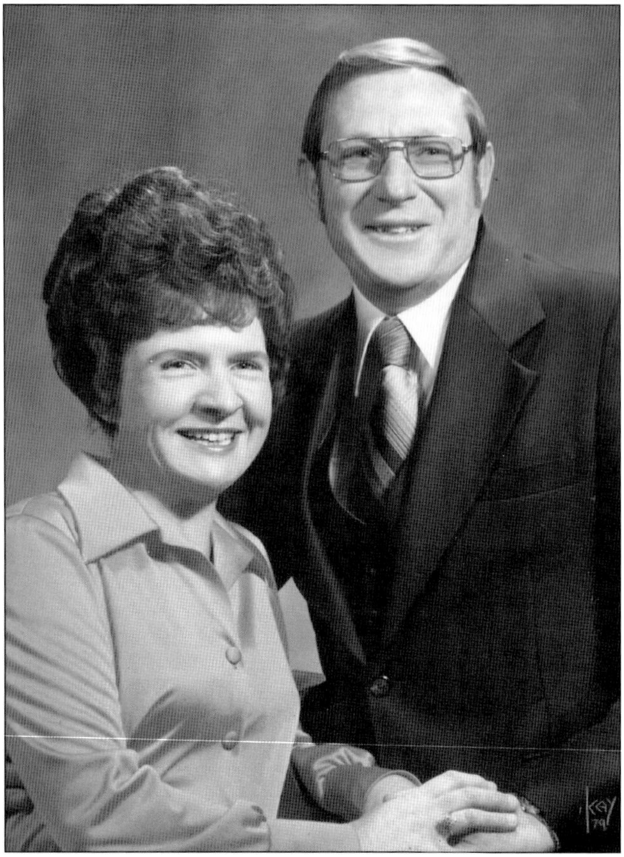

Hessell Farm. Mike Hessell (1929–2001) and his wife, Matilda (1931–), were married in 1950 and raised seven children—three sons and four daughters. The Hessells started a produce stand down in Warren in the 1950s. In 1968, Mike and Matilda moved their family to Shelby Township and started Hessell's Greenhouse in the location it still inhabits today. The original farm consisted of 35-plus acres of land. In 1991, their son Edwin Hessell and his wife, Karen, took over the business from Mike and Matilda. During the transition, the 30-plus acres of farmland behind the greenhouse were sold, leaving just over five acres that the greenhouse uses today. Ed and Karen ran and grew the business while raising their family of four daughters until 2020, when the business was taken over by two of the Hessell girls—Christine and her husband, Jonathan Currie, and Julie and her husband, Justin Ploetz. (Both, courtesy of the Hessell family collection.)

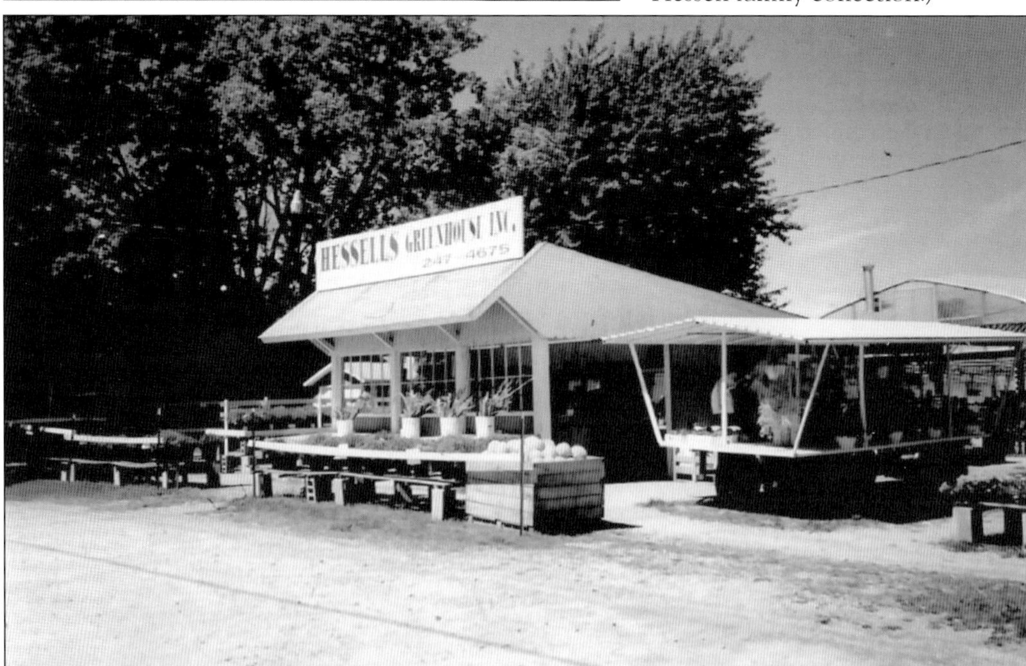

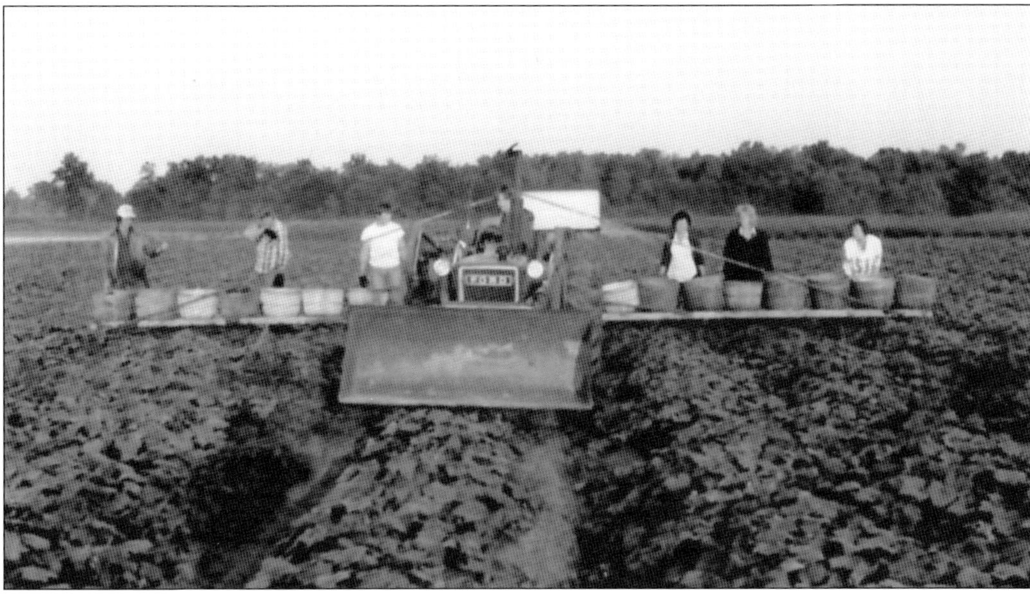

The Hessell Family. Pictured above is the family picking cucumbers around the late 1970s; from left to right are Ed Hessell, Ken Hessell, Mike Hessell (Ed's brother), Karen Hessell (on the tractor), Matilda Hessell, Jackie Lasuer, and Mary Hessell Rogers. Below, Hessell's Greenhouse is a third-generation family-owned business. The business started out as a farm and fresh produce stand and has become the retail garden center that is seen here today. It has 35-plus greenhouse structures and currently specializes in the production of spring annuals, vegetable plants, perennials, fall mums, poinsettias, and handmade Christmas decor, including grave blankets, wreaths, and patio pots. Matilda still stops by the greenhouse to look over what she and Mike had envisioned. (Both, courtesy of the Hessell family collection.)

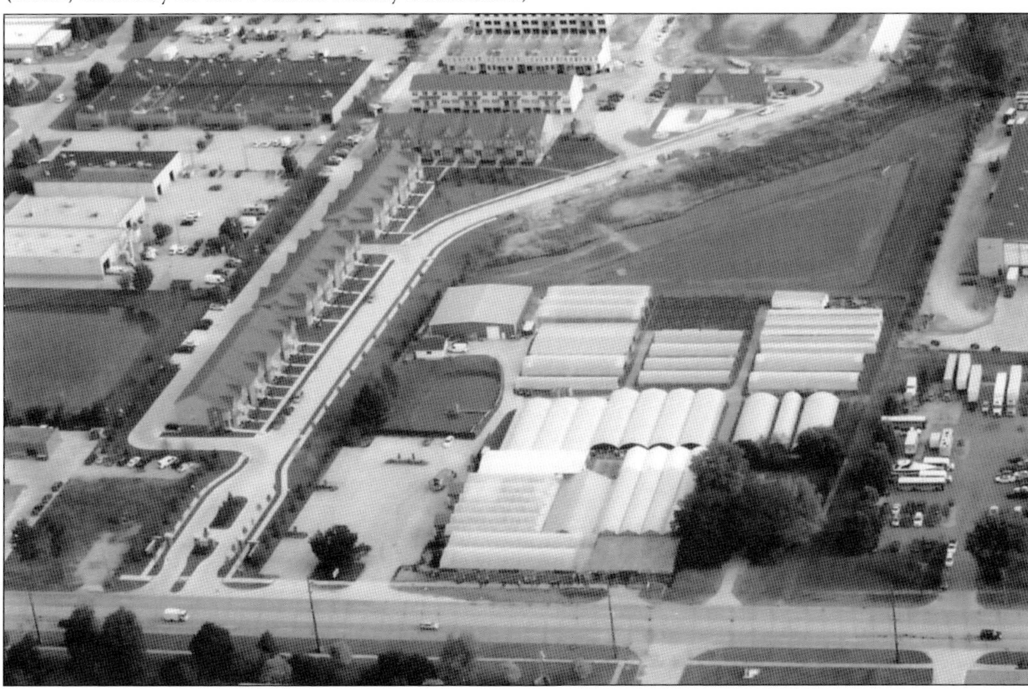

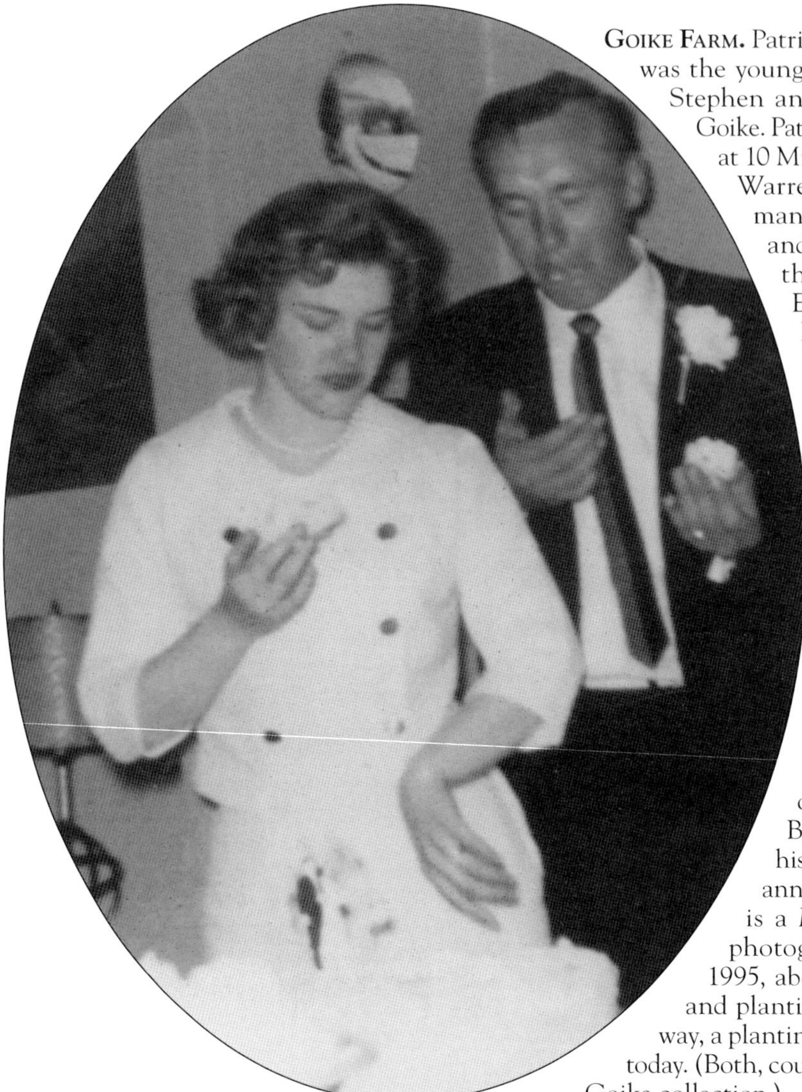

GOIKE FARM. Patrick Goike (1935–2017) was the youngest of 12 children of Stephen and Irene Dobblestein Goike. Patrick's family had a farm at 10 Mile and Ryan Roads in Warren where they raised many types of vegetables and strawberries, which they took to Detroit's Eastern Market. Patrick opened a roadside stand in the mid-1950s on the homestead in Warren, but by the early 1960s, Patrick and his wife, Barbara, bought a farm out in Shelby Township, and they moved the family there in 1972. He expanded his farm in the early 1980s by buying additional land adjacent to his on Schoenherr Road. By 1986, he expanded his greenhouse to include annual flowers also. Below is a *Detroit News* article photograph from June 23, 1995, about the Goikes' farm and planting the old-fashioned way, a planting technique still used today. (Both, courtesy of the Katherine Goike collection.)

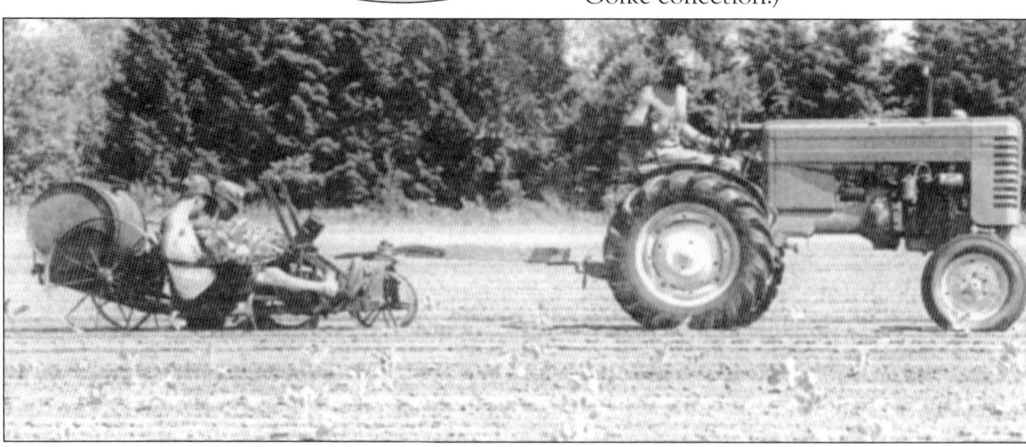

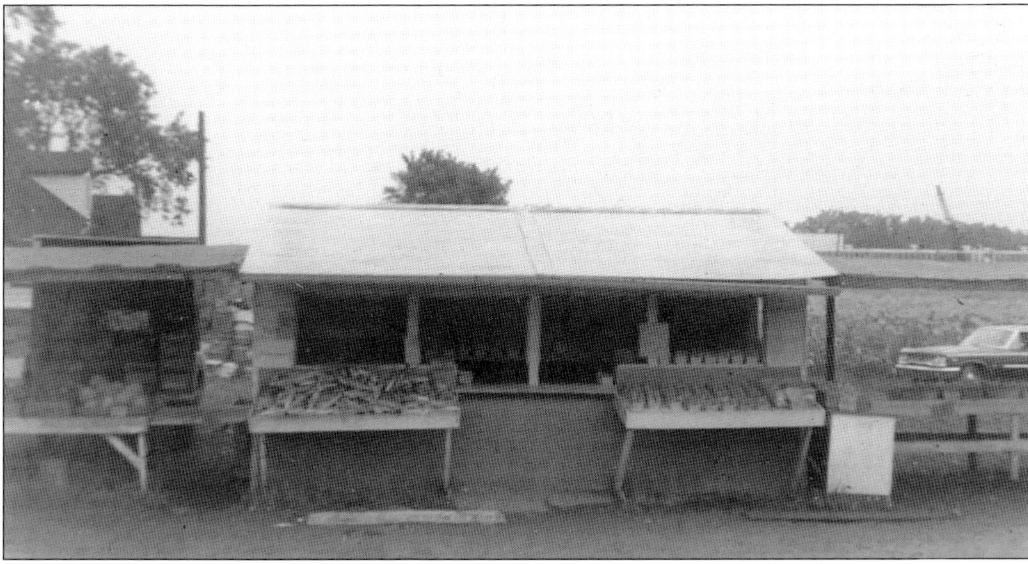

Goike's Opens a Roadside Stand. At the farm on 26 Mile Road, Patrick's daughter Katherine and his son Patrick Jr. worked alongside him. Patrick Goike raised tomatoes, strawberries, asparagus, melons, and peppers, and he was famous for his sweet corn. In 2005, Patrick sold the 26 Mile Road farm, as well as the roadside stand on 10 Mile Road, due to road improvements. He bought another farm in Richmond Township from Nelson Leach and started raising soybeans, field corn, and wheat. Both father and son continued to work the Leach property, and Patrick Jr. purchased a farm on 27 Mile Road in Ray Township in 1994. Many hardships go along with farming, but Patrick Goike never lost his love for it. (Both, courtesy of the Katherine Goike collection.)

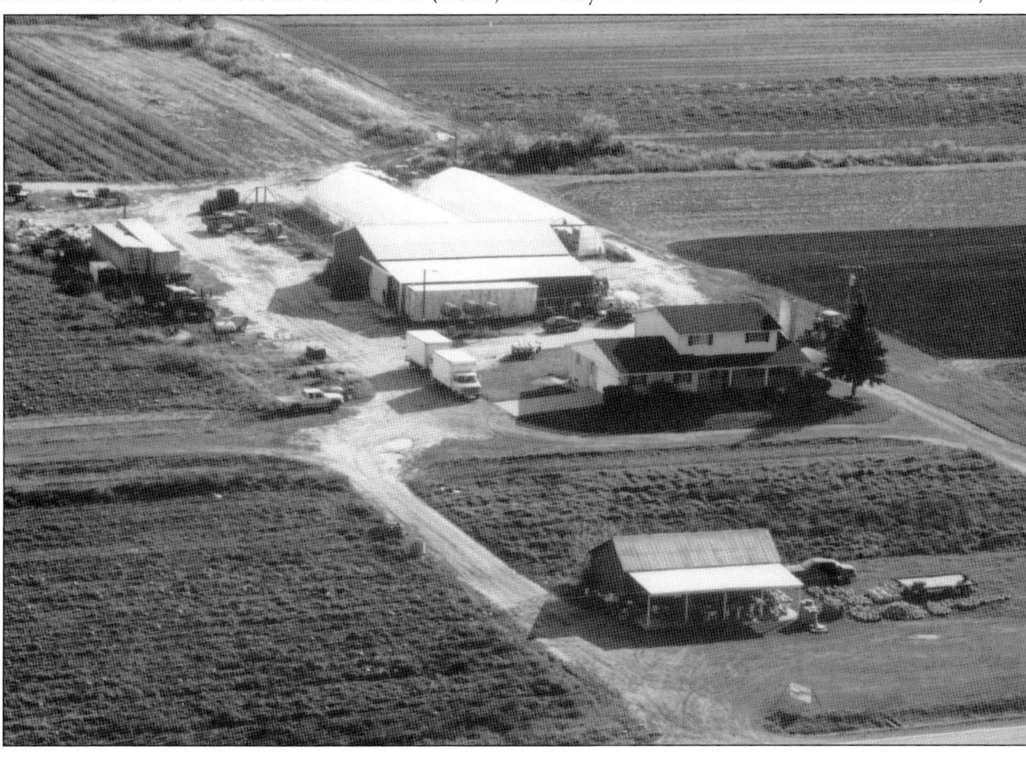

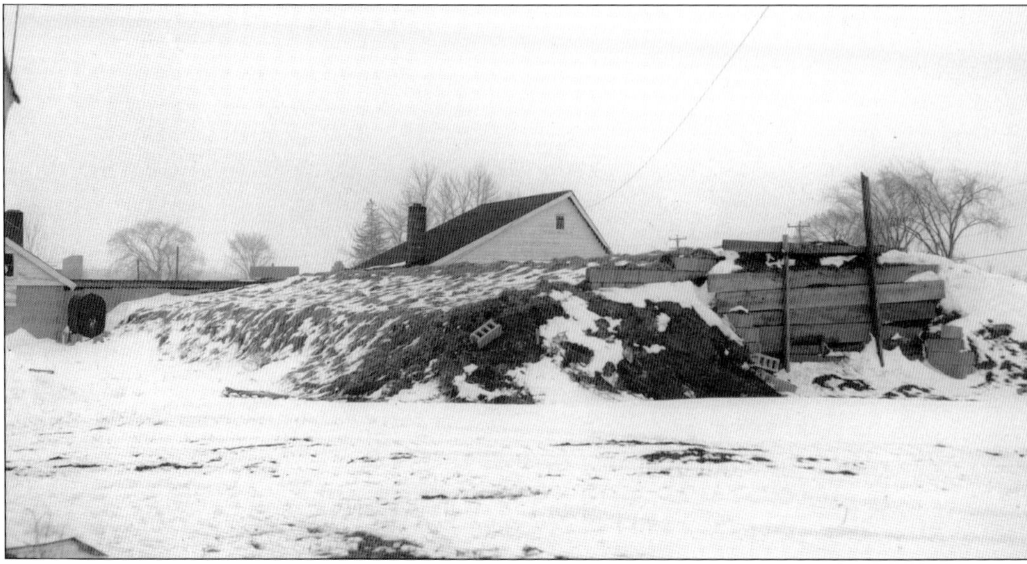

LAMBERT FARM. Arthur (1913–1996) and Goddelove (1915–2010) Lambert married in 1934. They purchased 60 acres of property on the north side of 21 Mile Road between Schoenherr Road and Hayes Road. Lambert's farm was one of many that grew rhubarb in the area. They had two 100-by-25-foot hothouses with a boiler between them. They could grow approximately 22,000 pounds of rhubarb in these hothouses while covered in straw as their winter crop. During other growing times, they grew sugar beets, which were taken to a processing plant in nearby Mount Clemens. As seen below, care had to be taken in packaging and shipping the rhubarb, which had grown to approximately 24 inches long. For convenience, after the crop was packaged in five-pound boxes, 10 of those boxes were put into a carton before being shipped in long-haul trailers to markets. (Both, courtesy of the Janet Dunn family collection.)

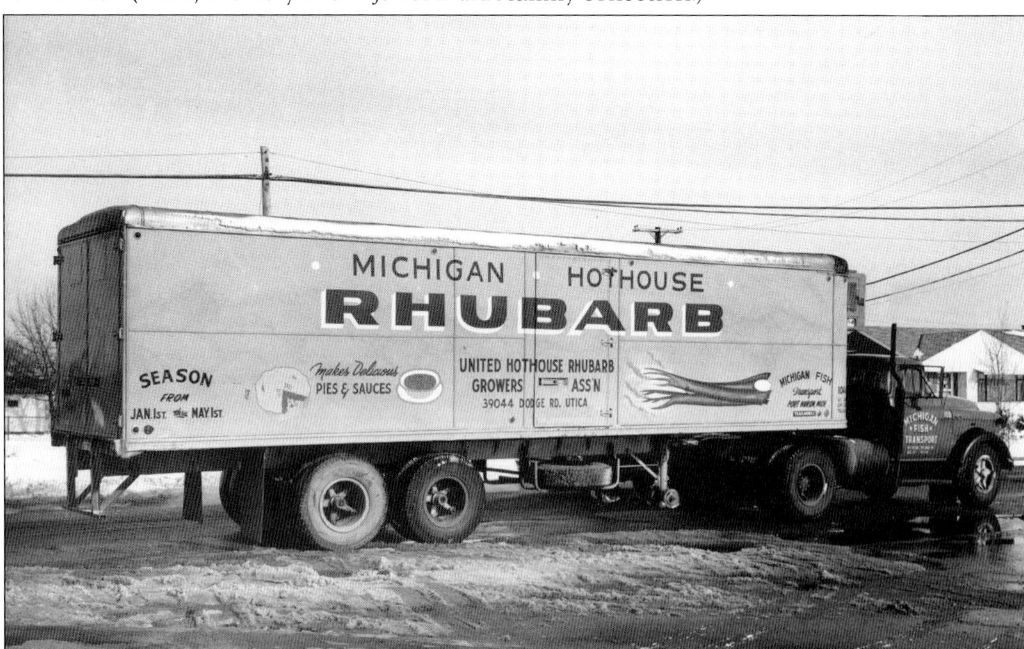

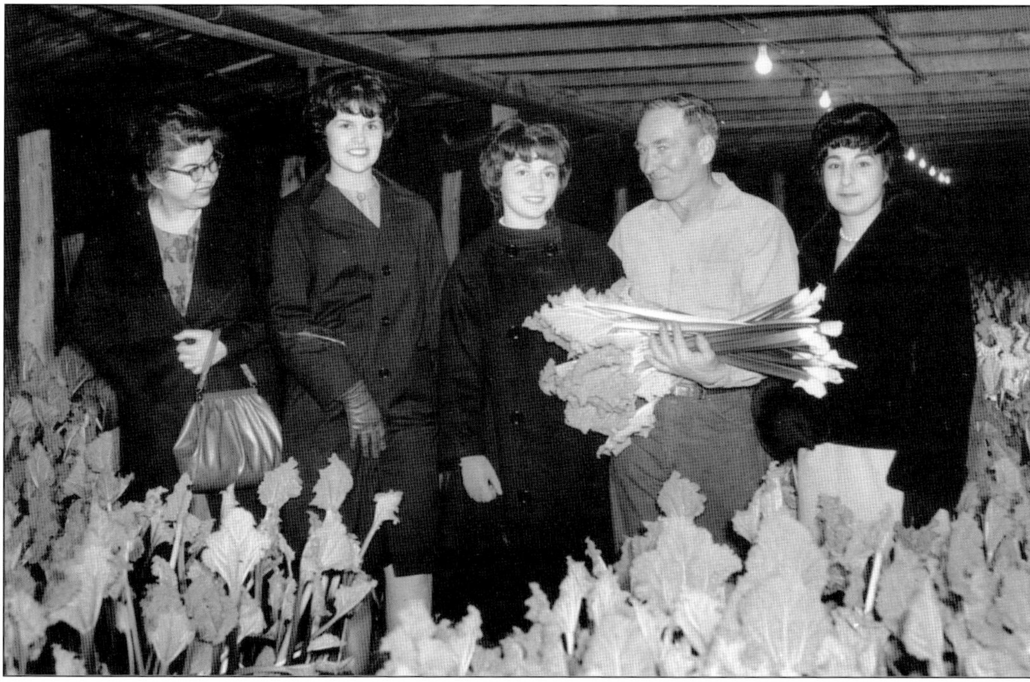

Rhubarb Growers Association. Seen above from left to right in the hothouse, chaperone Ann Kay, 1962 Rhubarb Court member Diane Van Haverbeck, queen Kathy Fletmeier, grower Art Lambert, and court member Pat Smigelski pose for a publicity shot to promote the Rhubarb Growers Association. The image below was taken at the sale of the five-pound box of first-place rhubarb. From left to right are Jack Prescott, agricultural director of Macomb County; Art Lambert, festival chairman; Clem Brinker, Rhubarb King of 1963; Dick Bracco, rhubarb distributor and buyer of the rhubarb box for $500; and Joe Koss, the auctioneer. (Both, courtesy of the Janet Dunn collection.)

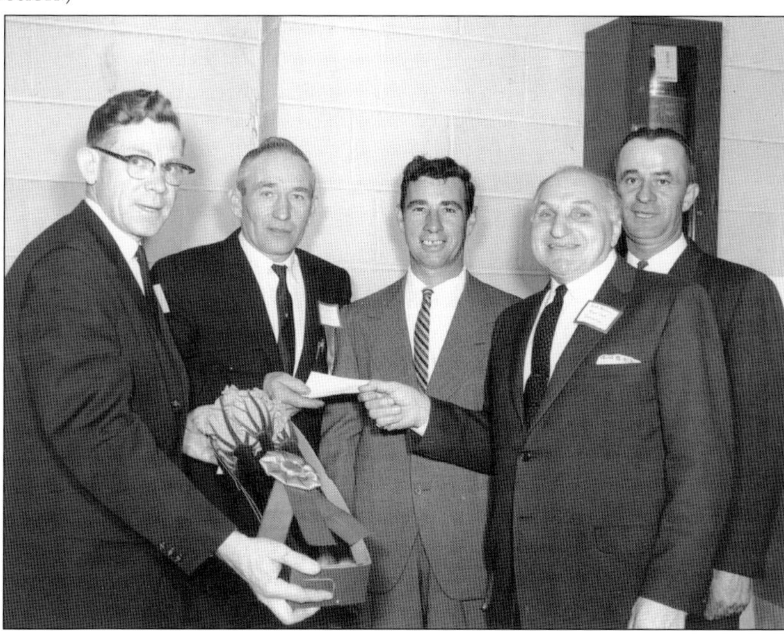

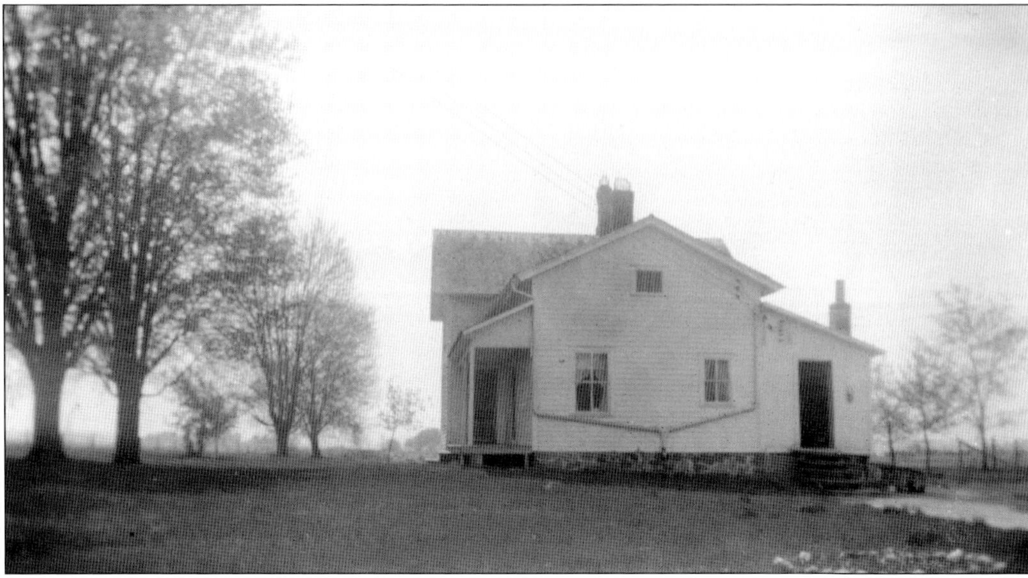

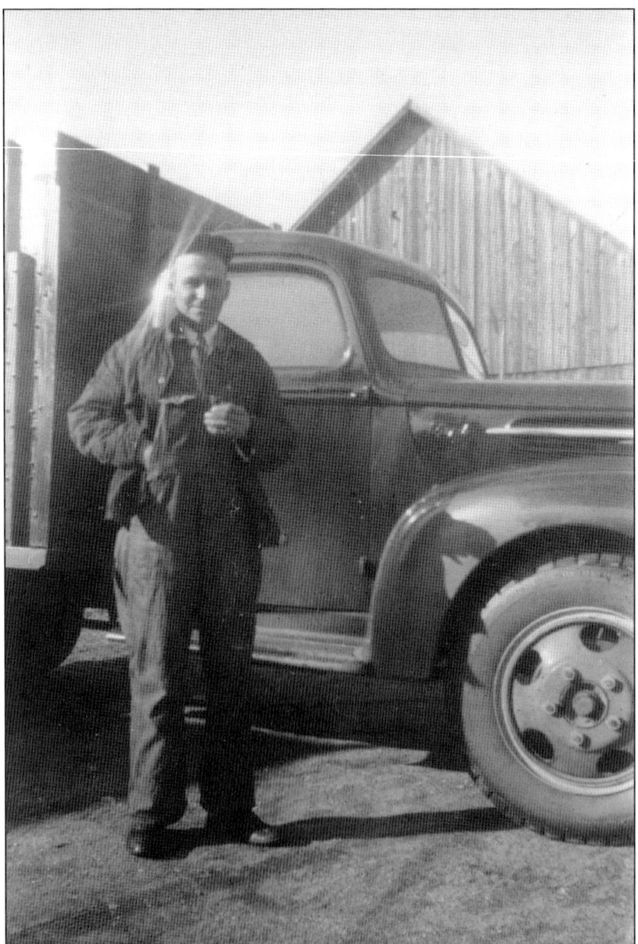

Joseph Goike Farm. Joseph (1910–2003) and Rosalie Goike (1916–2003) bought 20 acres on the west side of Hayes Road between 24 and 25 Mile Roads in the late 1930s. They raised two children, Irene and William. Joseph was known for his hothouse rhubarb, along with raspberries, strawberries, and most cash crops, like cauliflower and cabbage, which he would take to Detroit's Eastern Market. To the left, Joseph stands with his farm truck. (Both, courtesy of the Irene Goike collection.)

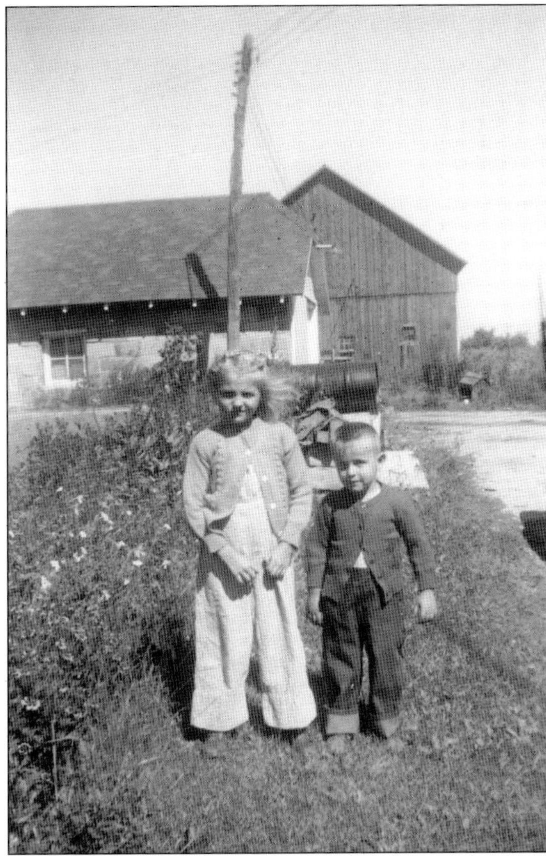

Irene and William on the Farm, c. 1950. Joseph leased out the farm in his later years and, in the mid-1980s, sold the property to developers for a subdivision of homes. Seen below is the house as it sits today, surrounded by progress. (Both, courtesy of the Irene Goike collection.)

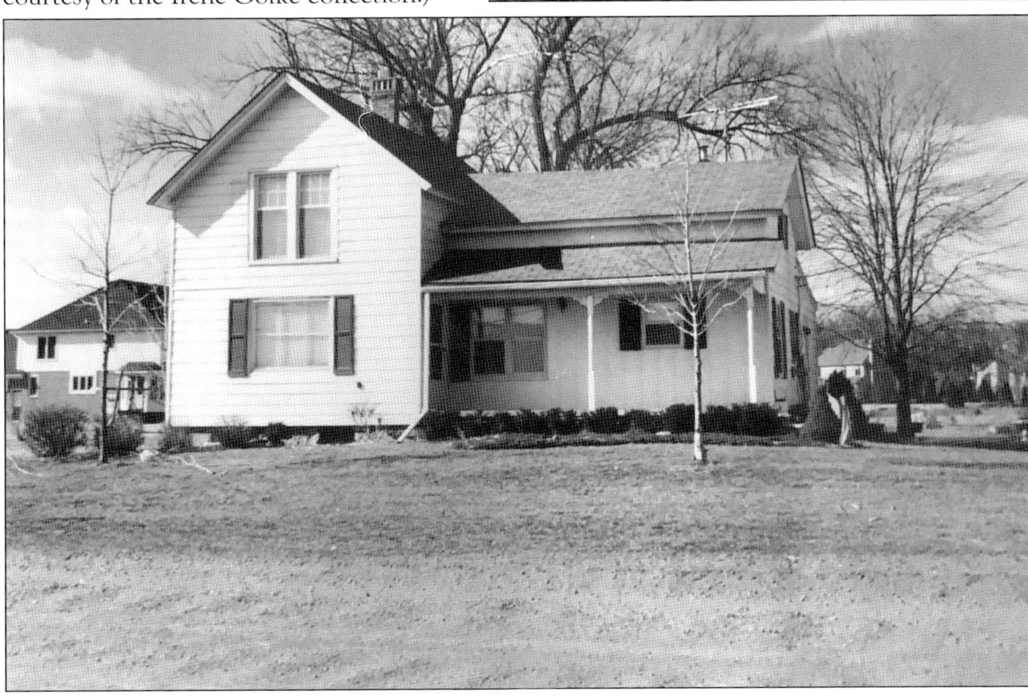

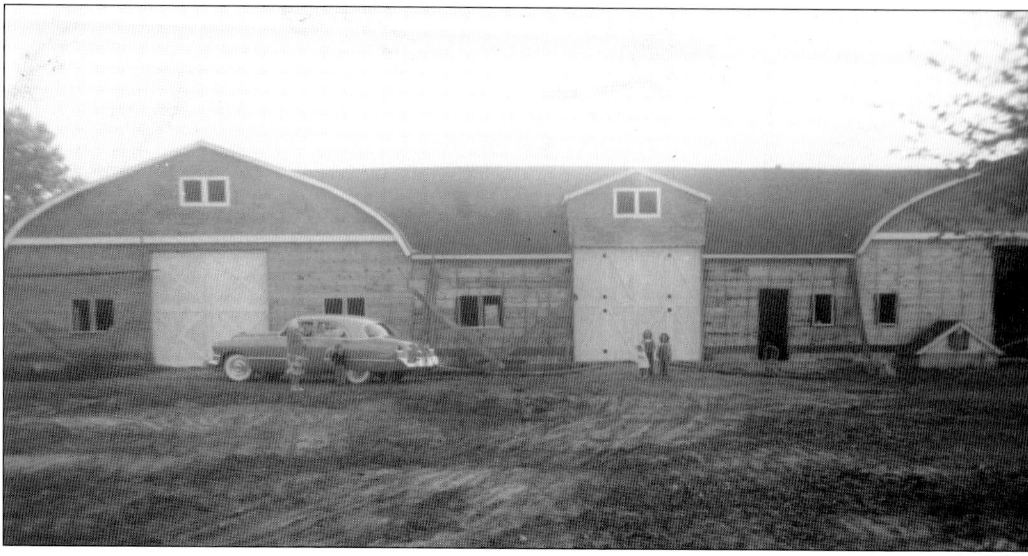

Diegel Greenhouse. Arthur and Genevieve Diegel started farming the all-wooded 96-acre property on Schoenherr Road at 25 Mile Road in 1947. They milled the logs off the property to build the barn, pictured here. As truck farmers, the Diegels loaded up the produce of corn, cabbage, lettuce, and tomatoes, and on Mondays, Wednesdays, and Fridays, they drove to Detroit's Eastern Market to sell the produce. Pictured below are Earl Diegel Sr. (top left in the truck) and Arthur Diegel (standing on right) with Arthur's three grandchildren—from left to right, Earl Jr., Laura, and Nora—while still farming on Schoenherr Road in 1953. (Both, courtesy of the Diegel family collection.)

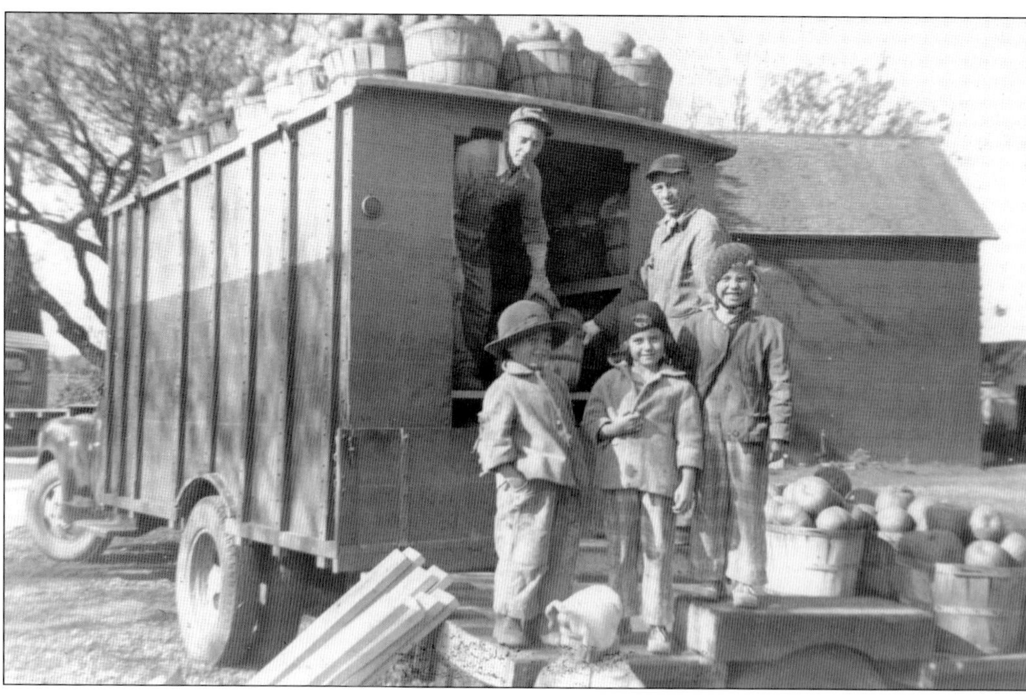

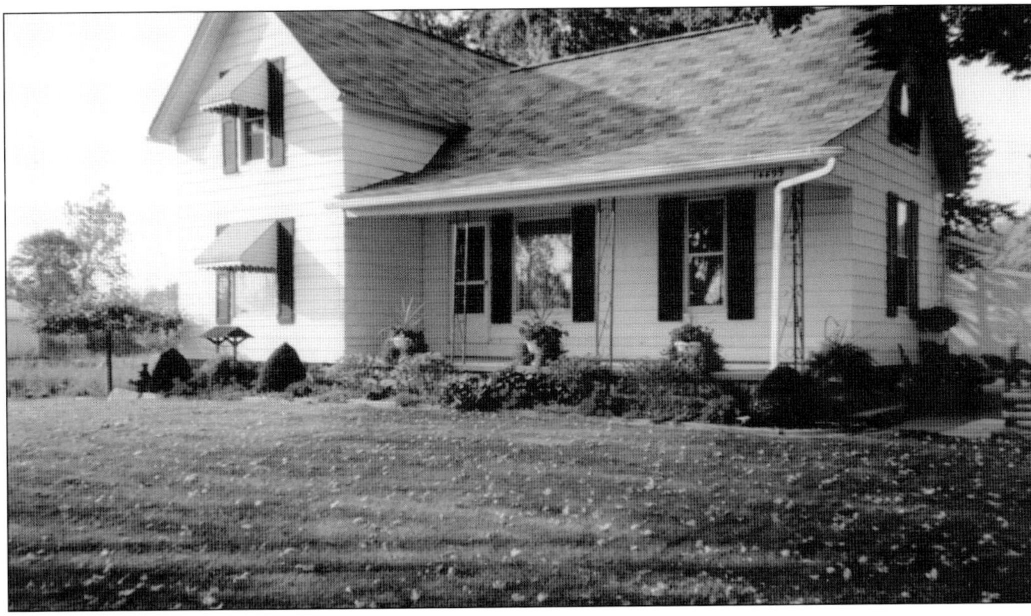

Diegel House and Greenhouses. Over the years, with taxes getting harder to satisfy with the township, the farm was sold to developers in three different phases by 1992. In 1993, Earl Jr. and his wife, Linda Diegel, bought a home and a few greenhouses with 10 acres of property from relatives Ed and Joan Beste on 25 Mile Road between Schoenherr and Hayes Roads. Over the years, they expanded their business and added many more greenhouses, with flowers and plants being sold from the storefront on 25 Mile Road. In 2012, Earl and Linda's son Steve and his wife, Sarah, bought the family business, which they continue to run. (Both, courtesy of the Diegel family collection.)

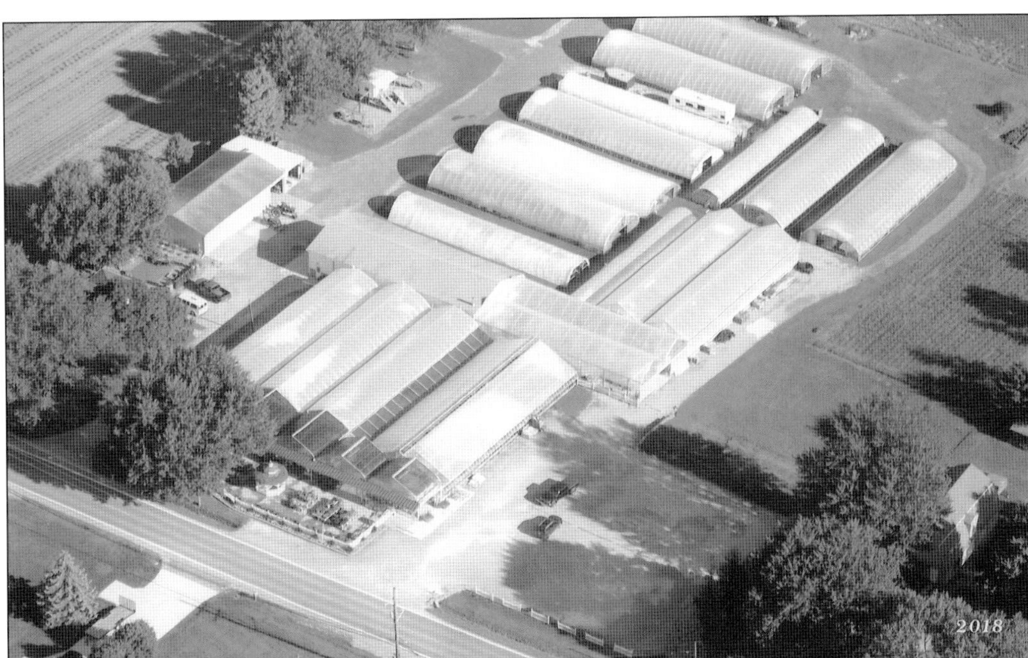

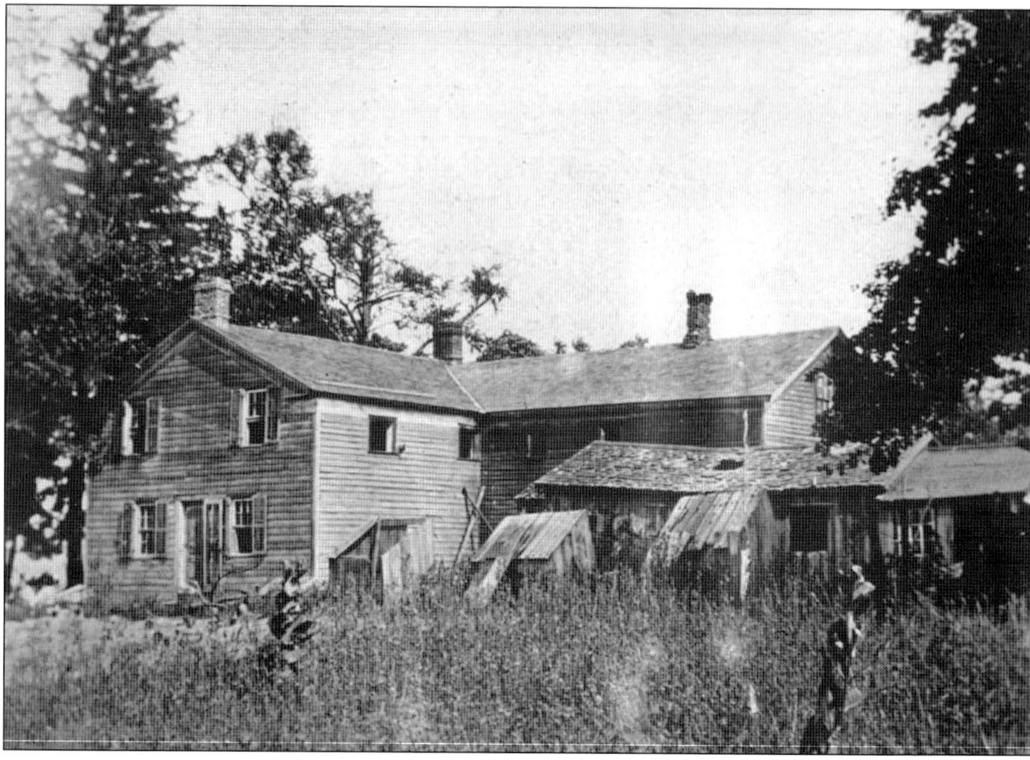

Burgess Farm. The homestead of Ezra Burgess (1788–1853) and his wife, Sally Loomis, was one of the oldest in the northwest corner of Shelby Township. Ezra's first parcel of land was in Utica, but here, he had his homestead of 84 acres. The land patent was signed May 22, 1822, by Pres. James Monroe. The home built was a 24-by-28-foot hewn timber frame house and still retains much of the original integrity, including wood windows and glass from 1822 and electrical and plumbing fixtures dating back to 1915–1925. Additions were made to the home in 1840 and 1915. Pictured above is the house in 1880, during the time of Ezra Burgess Jr. Below is a 1949 aerial image of the farmhouse and surrounding property. (Both, courtesy of the Vikki Papesh collection.)

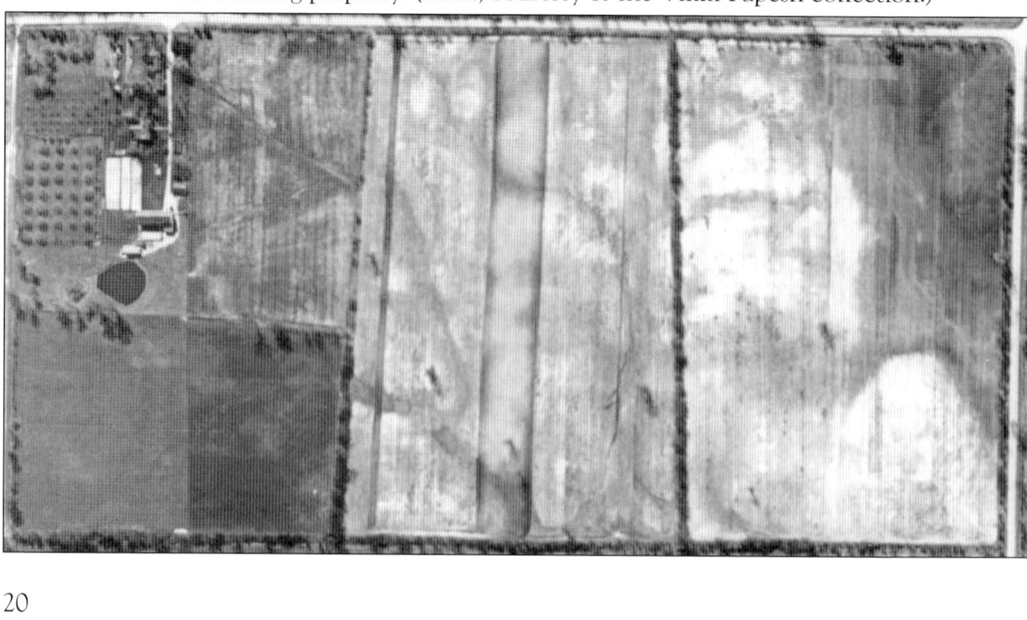

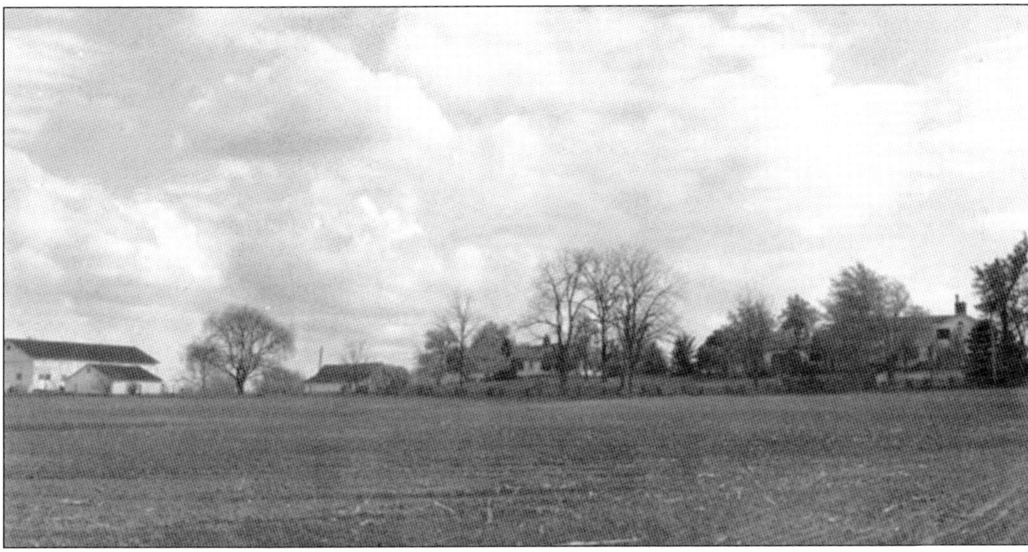

Burgess House and Property. Pictured is the farmhouse on the right and the barns to the left. The agriculture on the farm varied over the years but included cattle, chickens, horses, and produce, such as corn, apples, cherries, and black walnuts, along with many other items the present owners are not aware of yet. The farm was sold to Oscar and Nelson Price in 1873, not long before the death of Sally Burgess. When Nelson died, the property had probate inventory, and it was not until 1935 when it was again sold to Raphael Lawler. In 1944, Raphael sold the property to Robert and Ina Waugh. (Both, courtesy of the Vikki Papesh collection.)

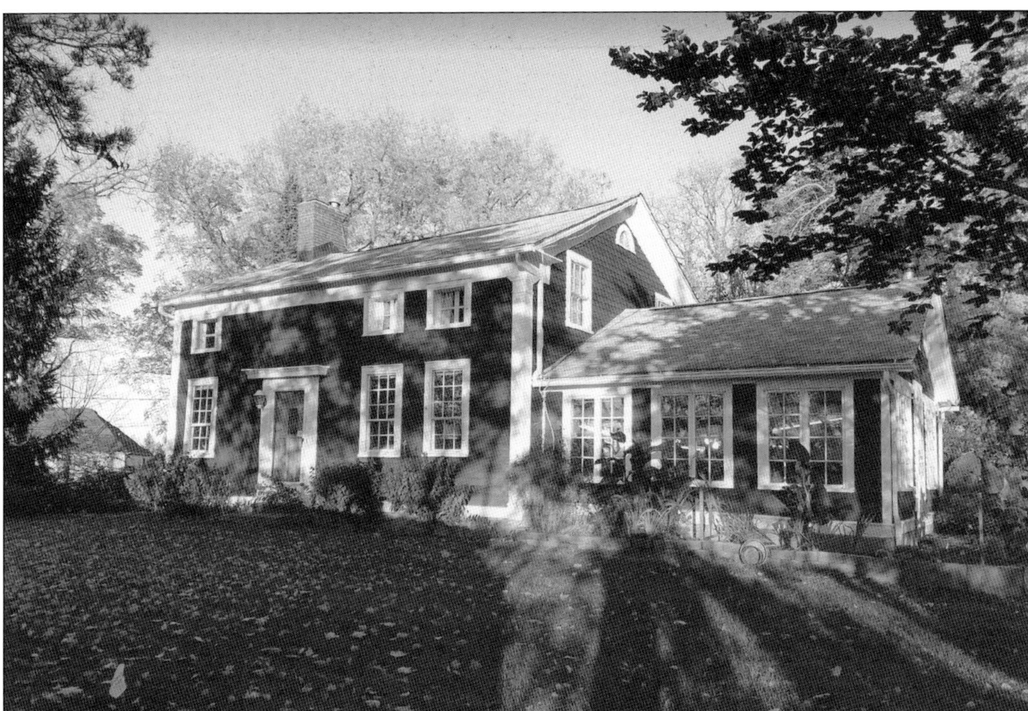

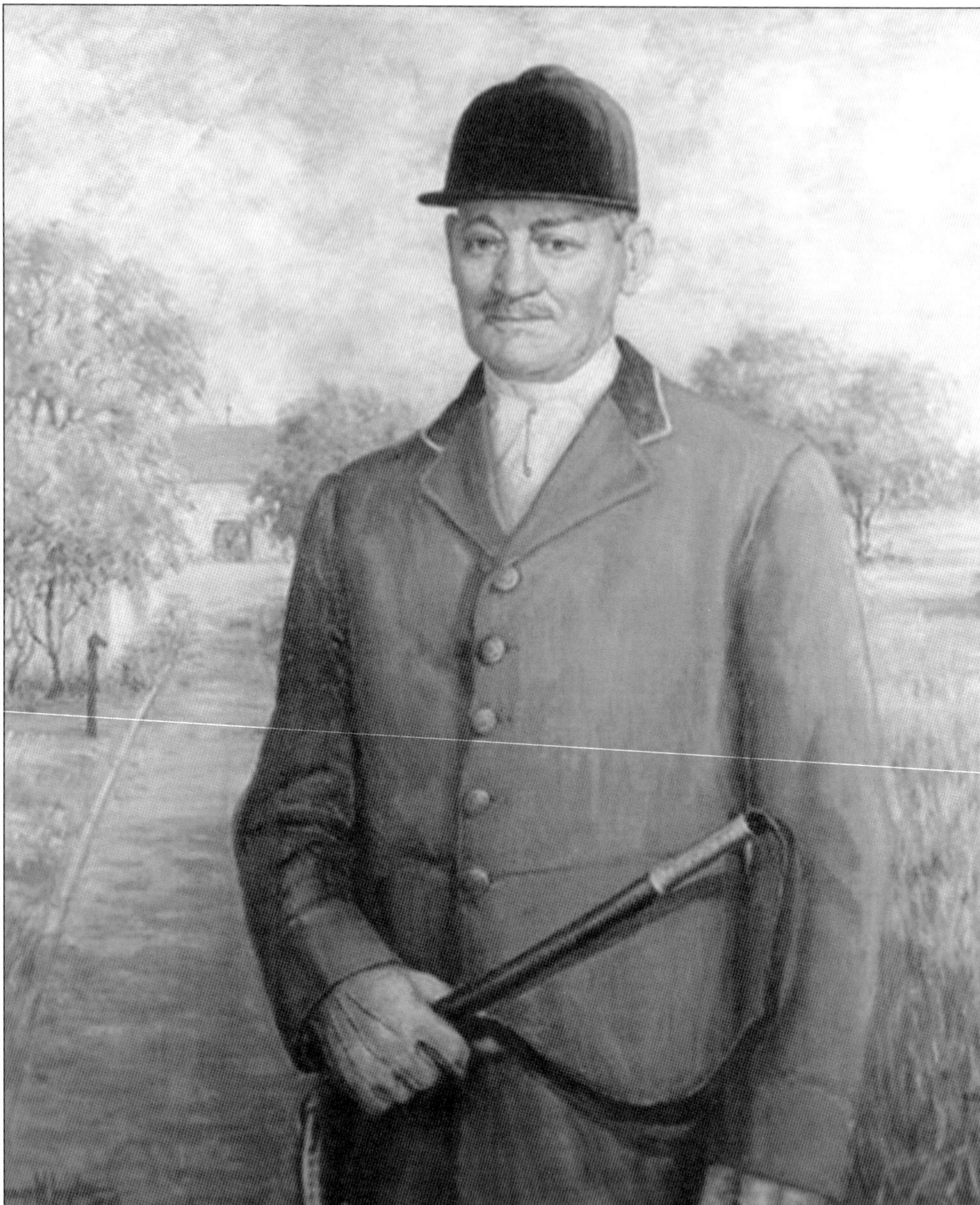

Robert Waugh. Pictured above in the painting with the property barn in the background, Robert Waugh did not live in the house. He was a member of the Bloomfield Open Hunt Club. The Burgess farm was where the horses were raised and kept for the hunt club. Robert and Ina Waugh resided in Bloomfield Township, although they retained ownership of the farm from 1935 to 1944. Robert was the grandson of Freeman Waugh, a Bloomfield Township pioneer. The Burgess house was used over the years as a boardinghouse and antique store and was even a proposed day-care center. In 1995, Marty and Vikki Papesh purchased the Ezra Burgess house, became the 15th title owners, and eventually were honored by the Charter Township of Shelby Historical Committee for owning the oldest home in the township. They received a historical marker to be placed near the entrance to the house commemorating the date of its construction. Today, the Dequindre Road property is called the Walnut Hill Farm. (Courtesy of the Vikki Papesh collection.)

Two

Macomb Township

The founders of Macomb Township came in the early 19th century to find flat and fertile farmland along the Clinton River. On March 17, 1834, the Township of Macomb was organized by an act of the territorial legislature. As it was first organized, it was composed of what now are the townships of Chesterfield and Macomb. In 1842, Macomb became territorially independent, and sales of property were very rapid after the split. The township was named in honor of Gen. Alexander Macomb, who was a highly decorated veteran of the War of 1812. His successful mercantile family owned most of the area in Macomb County during this time. Macomb Township was also a large part of the lumber and logging industry of this part of Michigan, with a large part of the township flat futile land and swampy wetlands.

Macomb has always ranked among the foremost townships in the county in respect to agriculture. In the early days, a general immigration of German settlers of the industrious and economical class came to farm the land. Renowned names in early Macomb Township were Daniel Kniffin, Daniel Miller, Noble Robert Sutton, Lester Giddings, Samuel Whitney, and Chauncey Church, to only mention a few.

Three unincorporated villages are still a part of Macomb Township. Macomb Corners is located in the northeast part of the township on Romeo Plank Road at 25 Mile Road, near the middle branch of the Clinton River. Waldenburg is located in the central portion of the township a few miles south of Macomb on Romeo Plank Road, mainly in the 22 Mile Road area. Meade is located in the northeast portion of the township on the boundary of Ray Township at 26 Mile Road and North Avenue. Meade was originally called the Crawford Settlement, and after the Civil War, it changed its name to honor Gen. George Gordon Meade.

The farming communities of Macomb Township grew exponentially as the 1970s began, with many parcels of land and family farms becoming new subdivisions filled with homes and new families. Some would hang on and become as popular today as they were yesterday.

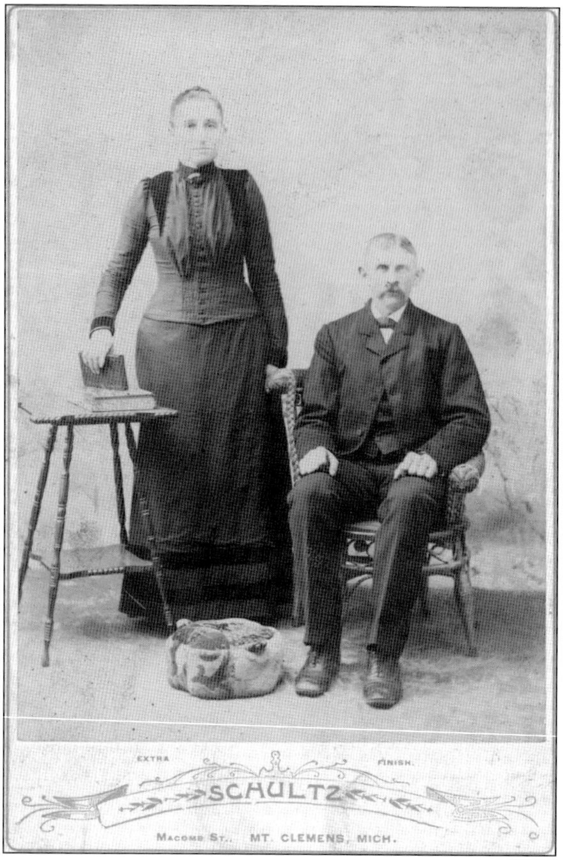

GETTGEN FARM. Henry Rocker, the father of Anna Rocker Gettgen, came to the United States from Germany and worked in the steel mills in Pennsylvania to get enough money to come to Michigan to buy a farm in 1853. Nicolaus Gettgen (c. 1821–1896) and Anna Rocker (c. 1832–1898) were married on April 4, 1853, in St. John's Church in Detroit, Michigan. Nicolaus was 30 years old, and Anna was just 20. A log cabin was built on the 80-acre property at 19961 Hall Road in Macomb Township. Pictured here, their son William I (1857–1911) and his wife, Louise Kling Gettgen (1861–1932), built the big white farmhouse and the barns on the same property. William and Louise had three children: William II, Anna, and Elizabeth. Pictured below are William I and Charles Wolf, a young man who helped around the farm with the horses. (Both, courtesy of the Julie Dosenberger collection.)

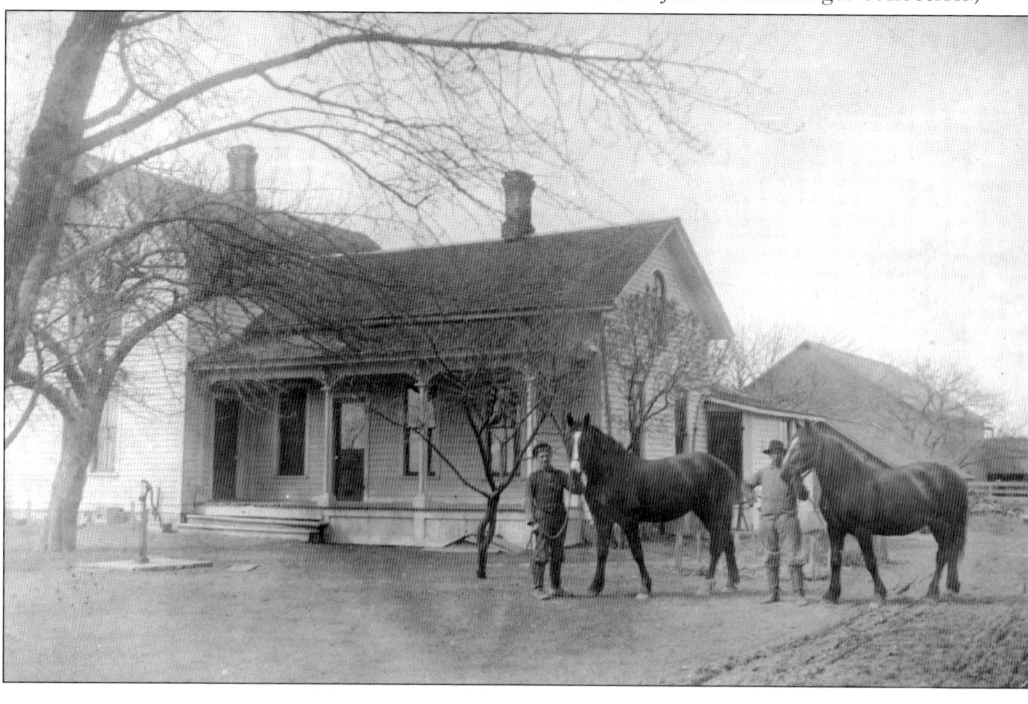

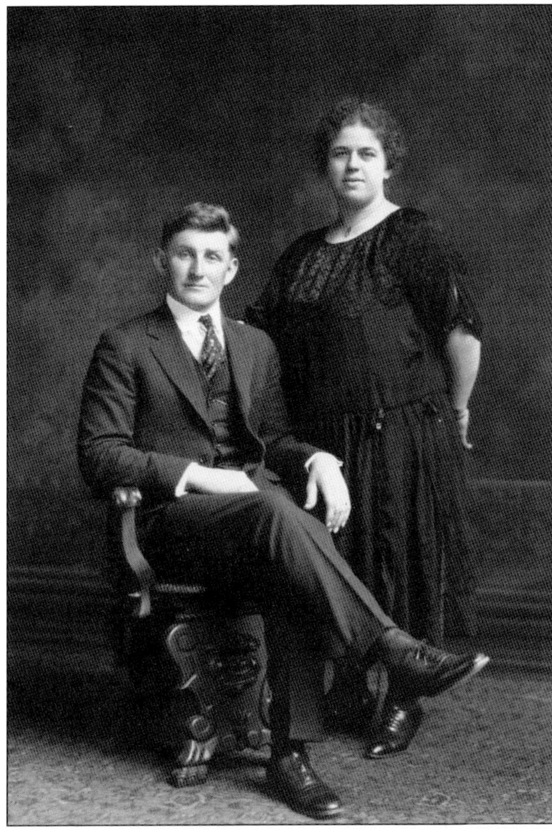

A Centennial Farm. William Gettgen II (1896–1982) married Delia Hintz (1895–1982) in 1920 and had three children: Henry (who died at birth), William III, and daughter Ruth. In 1937, they raised the farmhouse and added a basement. In 1956, a second home was built on the property. Listed as 20009 Hall Road, this home was built by William and Delia's granddaughter Cheryl and her husband, Joe Ballor. This Centennial Farm, seen here around 1980, was sold in 1992 for the expansion of Hall Road (M-59). (Both, courtesy of the Julie Dosenberger collection.)

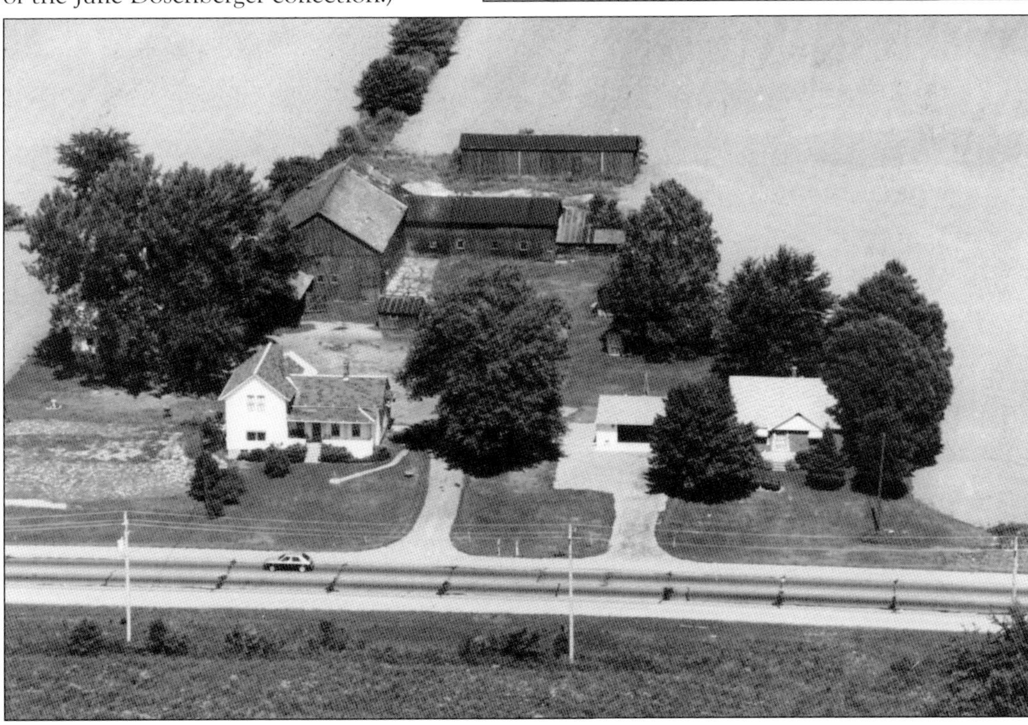

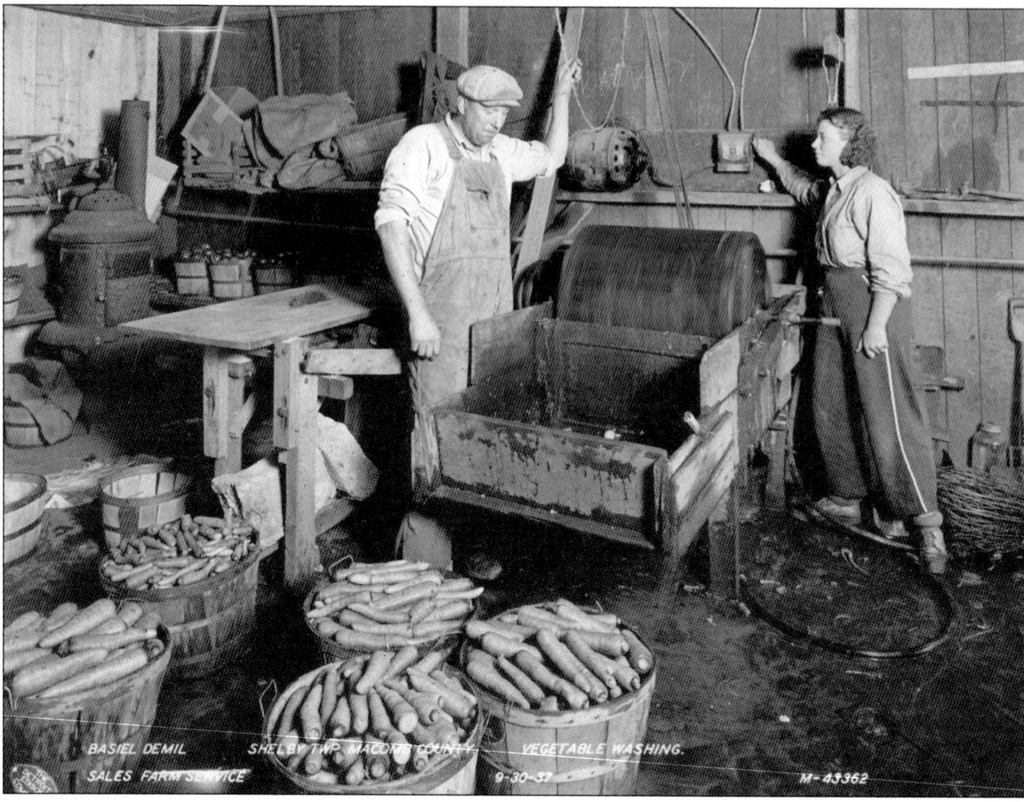

Koss Farm. Basil Demil (1893–1970) and Mary Valckenaeree Demil (1895–1980) were married in Belgium in 1921. Basil made his first trip to the United States in 1910 and traveled back and forth to Belgium a few times before settling in the United States for good. Their daughter, Yvonne, was born in 1921. Basil leased farmland in Shelby at 23 Mile and Schoenherr Roads for a time until he purchased 60 acres on 23 Mile Road in the 1930s. Yvonne married Joseph "Joe" Koss (1921–1977) in 1946, and at that time, Basil and Mary sold 40 acres to the young couple. Joe also had a family history in farming. Basil and Mary continued to farm the east 20 acres where the house was located. They raised vegetables, corn, poultry eggs, and rhubarb. Pictured above are Basil and his daughter, Yvonne, on the leased property in Shelby Township. Below is the farm on 23 Mile Road. (Both, courtesy of the Koss family collection.)

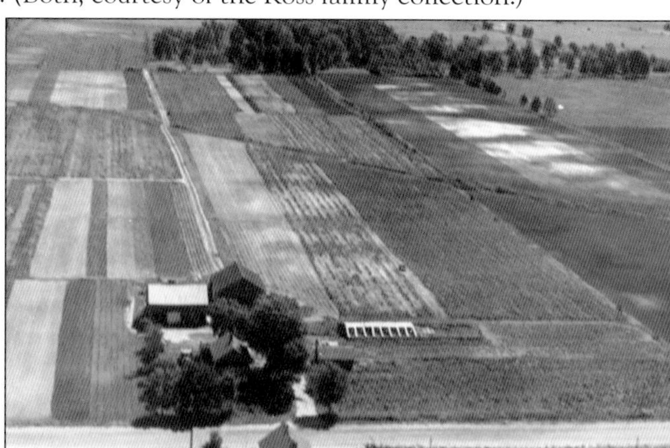

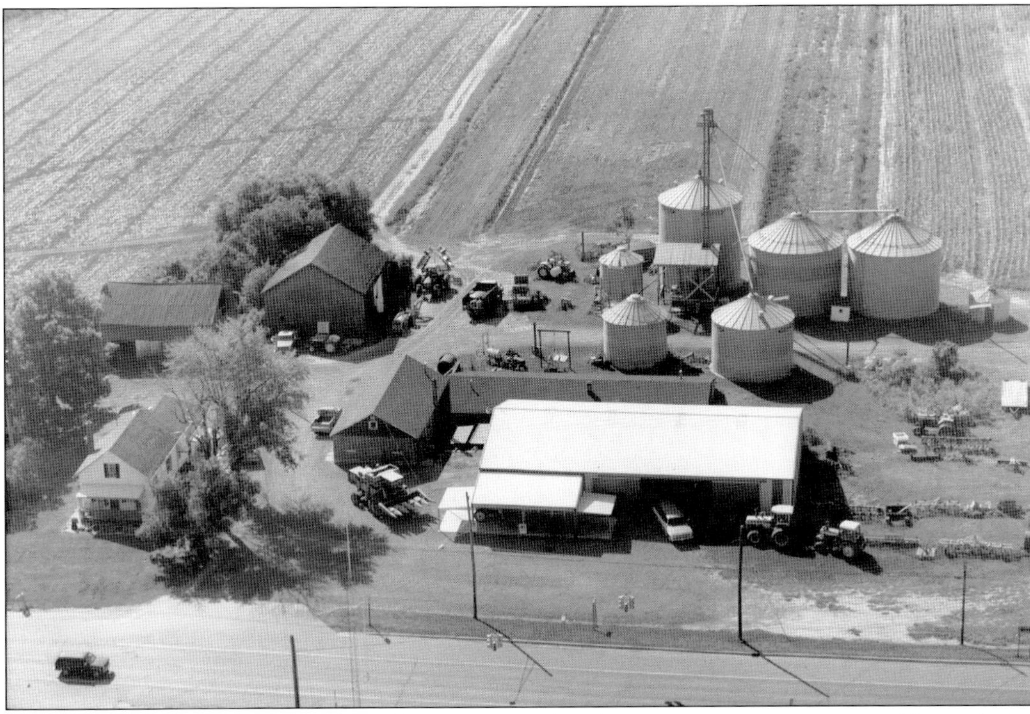

New Subdivision. Joe and Yvonne Koss were garden farmers, raising many vegetables and vine crops in the summer and selling them at the Detroit Eastern Market as well as growing cabbage and hothouse rhubarb in the winter. Joe and Yvonne had three sons: James "Jim," Richard, and David. Joe was an auctioneer and the Macomb Township fire chief from 1955 until his death in 1977. After Joe's death, the farm turned to sweet corn and general farming and became known as Koss Farms. Jim and David headed the farming operation, raising as much as 1,200 acres of general crops and vegetables, which were all sold at the 23 Mile Road stand. With the expansion of 23 Mile Road, most of the farm was sold in 2000. The family legacy still lives on, as the subdivision streets were named in their honor. (Both, courtesy of the Koss family collection.)

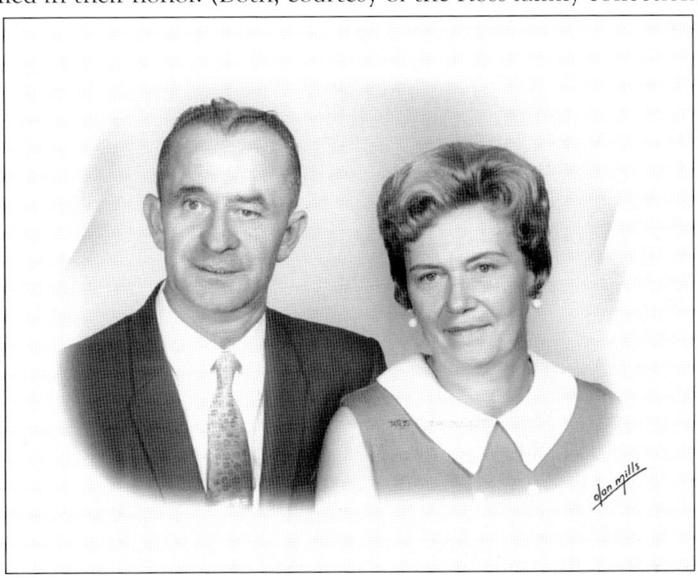

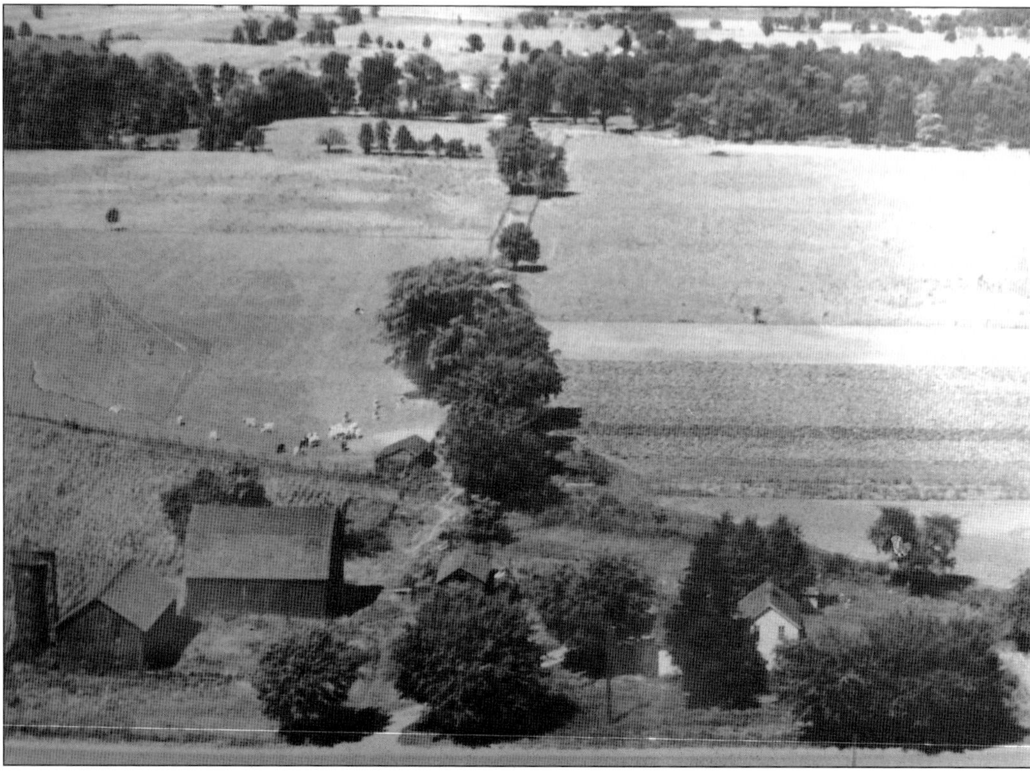

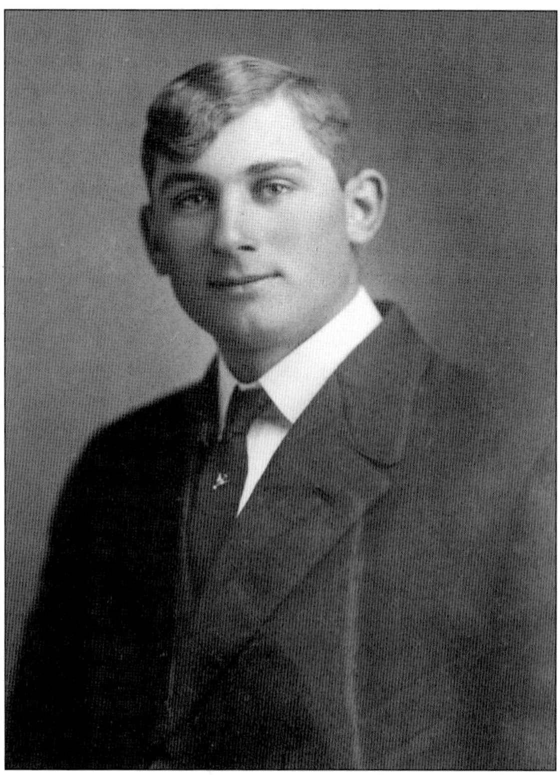

RACHOW FARM. John (1879–1957) and Emma (Krueger) Rachow (1882–1946) owned their farm at 21139 23 Mile Road in Macomb Township, on the north side of the road between Card Road and their neighbors, Boyka's Farm and Greenhouse. John farmed on that property his entire life, up until his death. John was a lifelong and active member of St. Peter Lutheran Church, where he served as a trustee and elder. He was also a member of the Macomb Township District No. 10 School Board and served as treasurer for more than 30 years. Through his wife, Emma, they had connections with the Krueger and Luchtman families of Macomb Township. (Both, courtesy of the Joyce Schwark collection.)

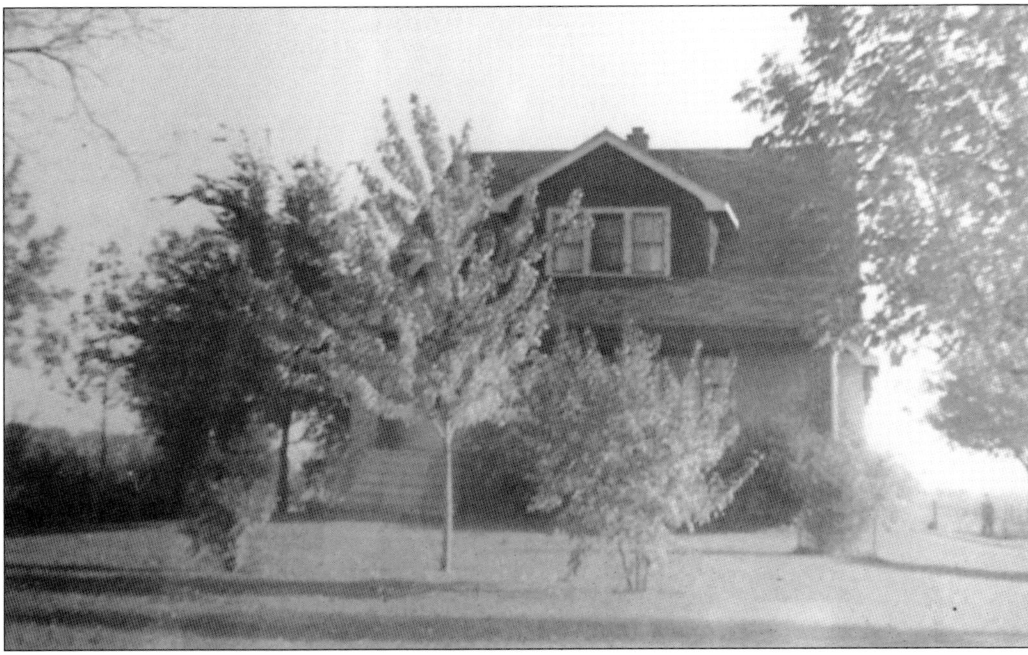

Bock Farm. Paul Bock (1891–1967) and Lillian Puffpaff (1895–1981) married in 1916 in East Detroit, where Paul was born and raised. The couple moved to Fraser in 1926 and purchased their farm in Macomb Township at 15700 24 Mile Road in 1931. The farm was about three-fourths of a mile west of St. Peter Church, just before Hayes Road, on the south side of the road. To their large family, the home was always referred to as "Grandma and Grandpa Bock's house." They were members of St. Peter Lutheran Church, and Paul was also a member of the Lutheran Fraternities of America and a former supervisor and treasurer of Macomb Township. (Both, courtesy of the Joyce Schwark collection.)

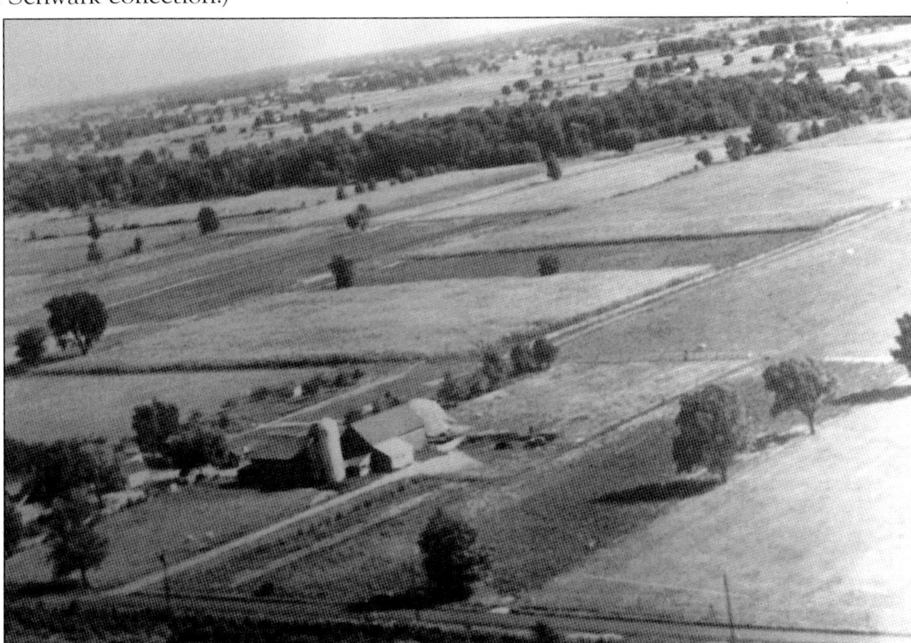

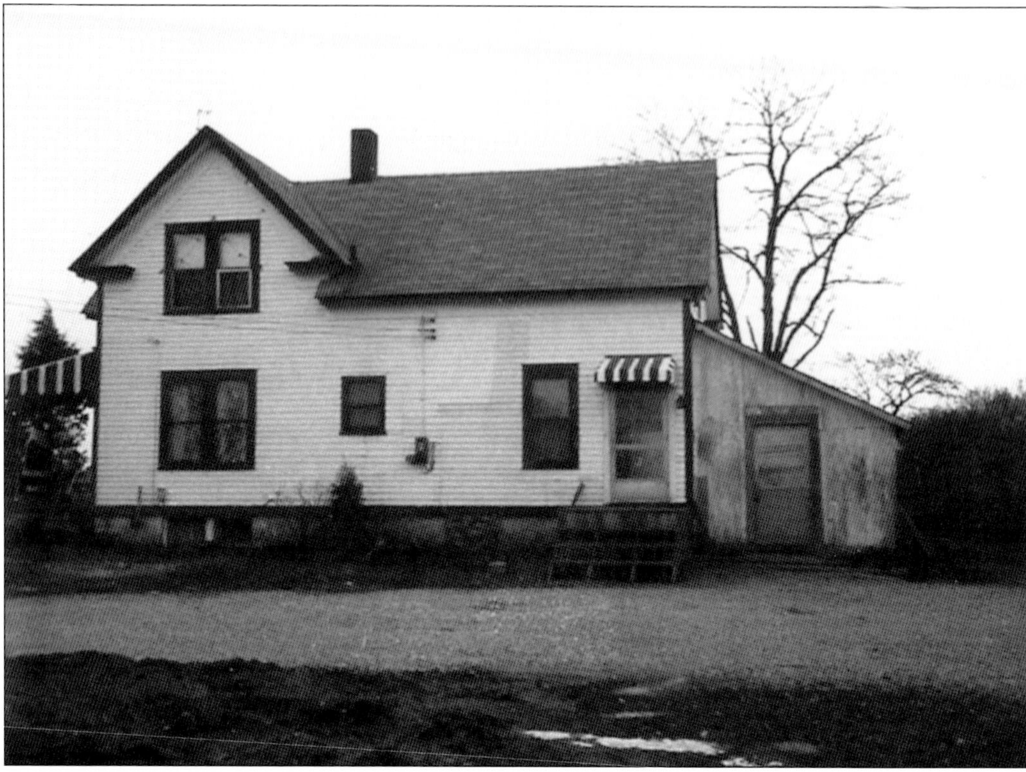

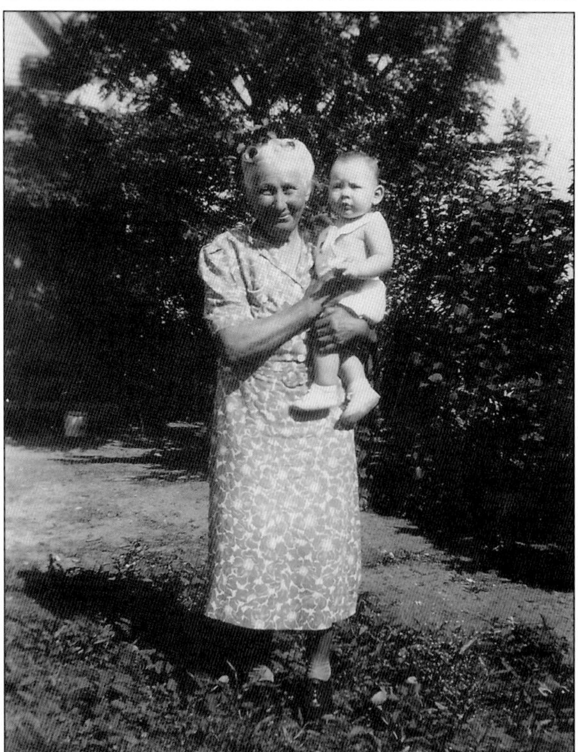

Grala Farm. Joseph Grala (c. 1886–1958) and Mary Majewski Grala (1887–1968) purchased their farm on Card Road in Macomb Township in June 1925. This became home to Joseph and Mary and their five children. Their son Wallace (1910–1955) and his wife, Phyllis (Jakubiak) Grala, had married in 1937, and with their four children, they moved into the family farm to help with the running of it. Cattle farming and truck farming were the two dominant forms of farming before sod farming took over. Over the years, the farm went from 40 acres to a manageable 20 acres. In the early days on the farm, when it came to harvesting the food, it would become a community affair, with neighbors helping each other out. Everyone in the family had a part to play. To the left, Mary Grala holds her grandson Wallace Grala II behind the house on the farm. (Both, courtesy of the Julie Martel collection.)

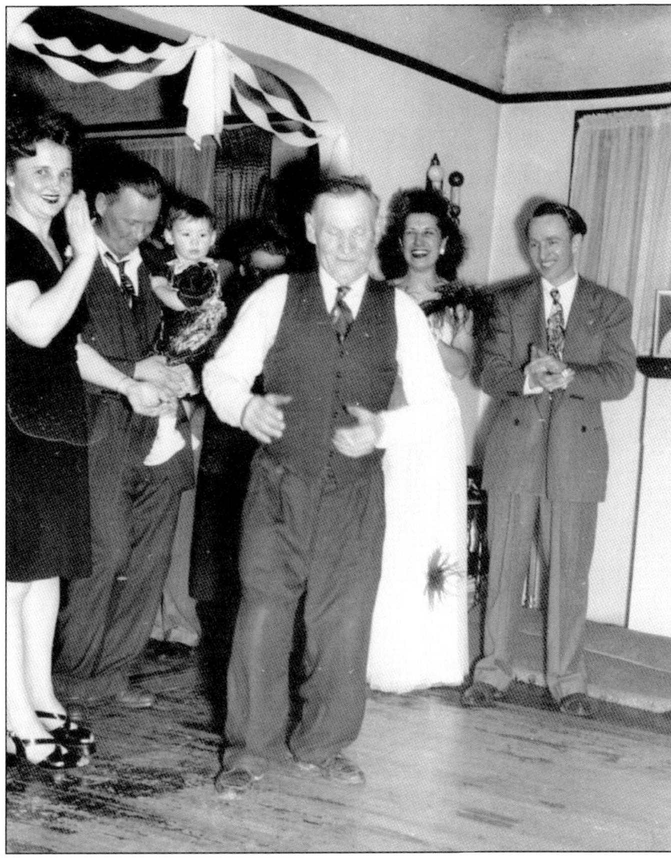

Grala Family. To the right, Joseph Grala dances at his son Ted's wedding in 1947, with another son, Wallace Sr., holding his daughter Gloria while watching the fun. Below, at the side of the family home, the third-generation Gralas are pictured on the family farm around 1955; from left to right are Richard, Gloria, Wallace, and Patty. Over time, three of these four children each built a home on an acre of the property, with a great-granddaughter moving into the family home after the death of her grandmother in 1991. (Both, courtesy of the Julie Martel collection.)

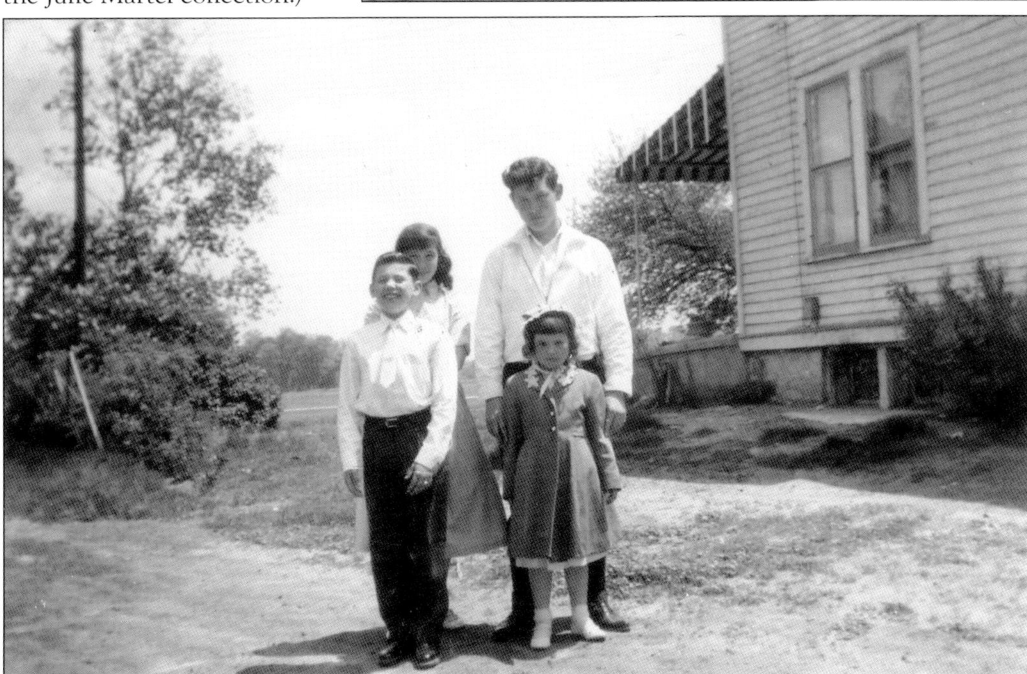

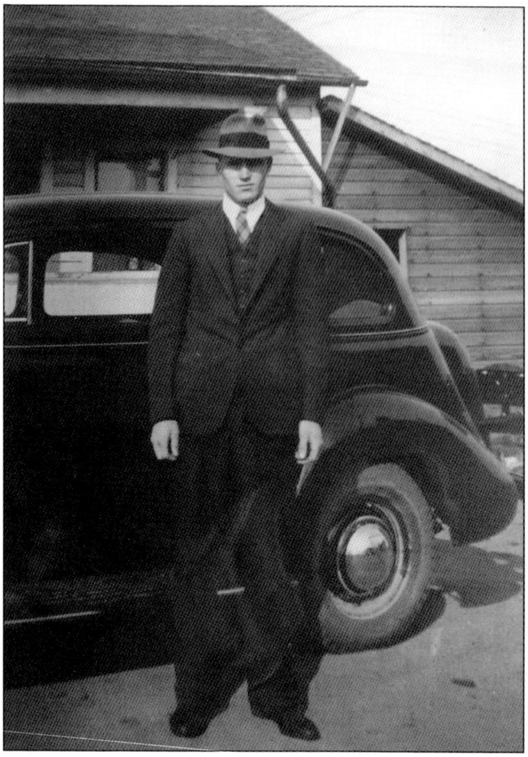

Schwark Farm. Arthur Schwark (1913–1978) was born on a farm and farmed all of his life. Arthur met Elsie Elizabeth Engelbrecht at their church, St. Peter Lutheran, and on October 2, 1937, they married at the little white church that stood on the southeast corner of 24 Mile and Romeo Plank Roads in front of the church cemetery. When not working on the farm, Arthur loved hunting and fishing. (Courtesy of the Schwark family collection.)

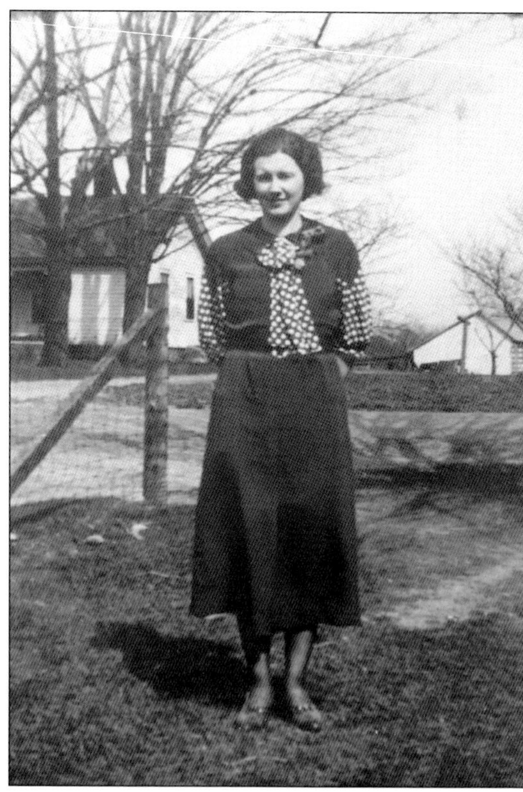

A Well-Remembered Lady. Elsie Elizabeth Engelbrecht (1916–1989) grew up in the Davis area of Ray Township. In the years after her marriage, she raised five sons and helped Arthur work their farm. She picked vegetables on the farm and went to Detroit's Eastern Market every Saturday to sell their produce. She tended her chickens and had an egg route, where she would drive to Mount Clemens every other week to sell the eggs to families there. She is remembered for the cookies that she baked each Christmas. (Courtesy of the Schwark family collection.)

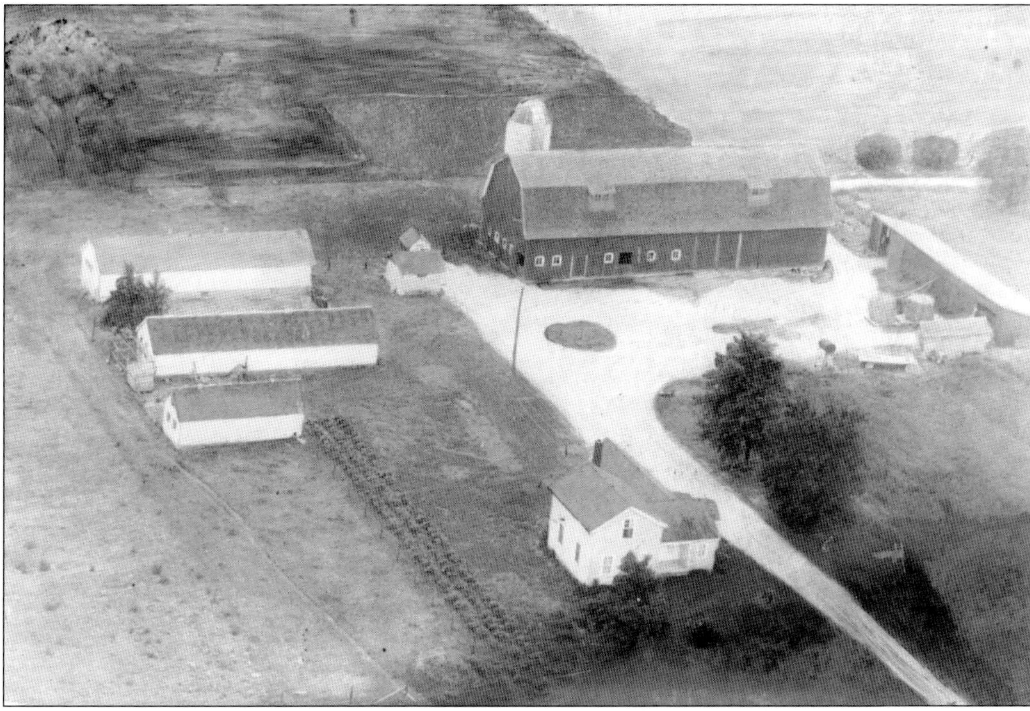

Leading the Horses. The Schwark farm on 24 Mile Road in Macomb Township was worked as a dairy farm. The farm grew vegetables as a cash crop, with Arthur Schwark's favorite being the green beans. At right, Roy Schwark, the oldest son of Art and Elsie, at five years old, leads a team of horses up to the barn around 1943. The Schwarks had a marriage of 40 years on the farm in Macomb Township. (Both, courtesy of the Schwark family collection.)

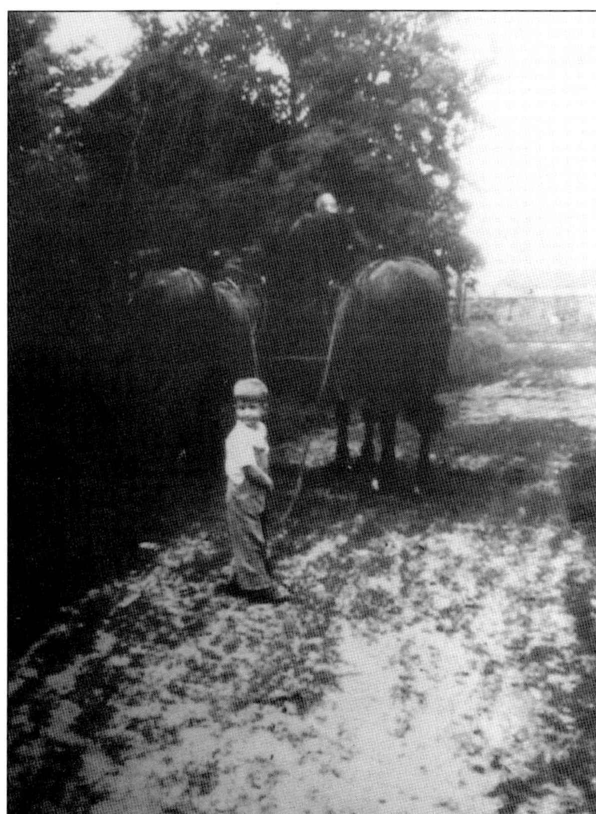

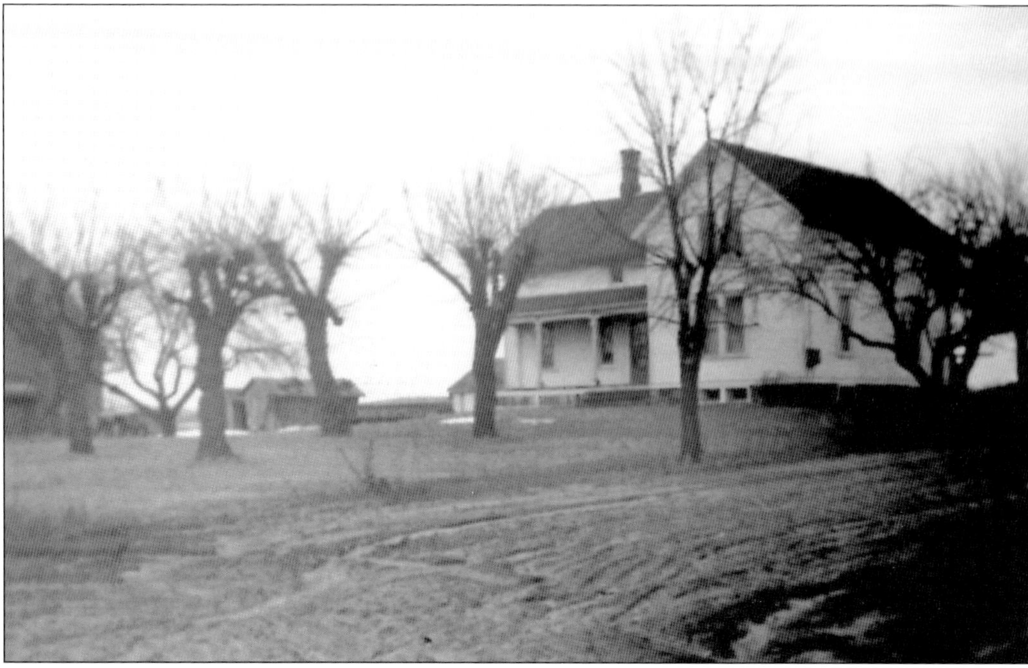

Klingkammer Farm. The Stark homestead, on the south side of 24 Mile Road, was purchased in 1953 by Joe and Leona Klingkammer. It was a dairy farm until the Klingkammers purchased it and transformed it into a produce and vegetable farm. The winter crop was hothouse rhubarb, and it was shipped to several states. The main spring crop was "hardy" outdoor-grown pansies that could be found in Frank's Nursery stores all around the Detroit Metro area. The fall harvest would see many trips to Detroit's Eastern Market with more produce. Below, the 1946 GMC truck is loaded with sweet banana peppers going to the Safie Brothers Canning Factory. (Both, courtesy of the Klingkammer family collection.)

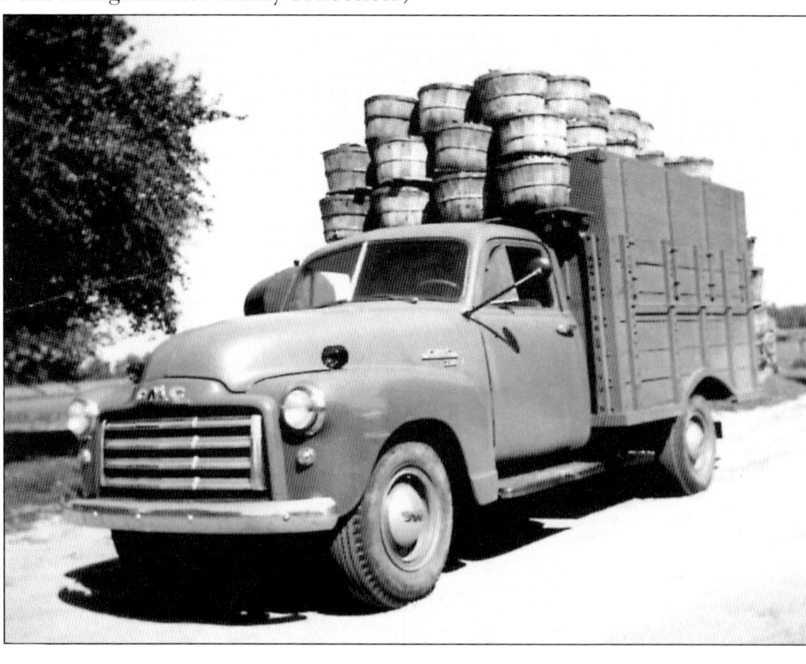

The Start of St. Isidore's. In the image to the right, Joe Klingkammer and his son Gary clear snow after another large snowfall in 1965. Below, a team takes the garage doors off while getting ready to put an addition on the front of the building to prepare for Sunday Mass to be held that summer for St. Isidore Church. Frank Van Thomme made a large wooden cross that was later added to the front of the entrance. The Klingkammer building was used during the summer and fall months of 1957, until the new church building was established at 23 Mile and Romeo Plank Roads. (Both, courtesy of the Klingkammer family collection.)

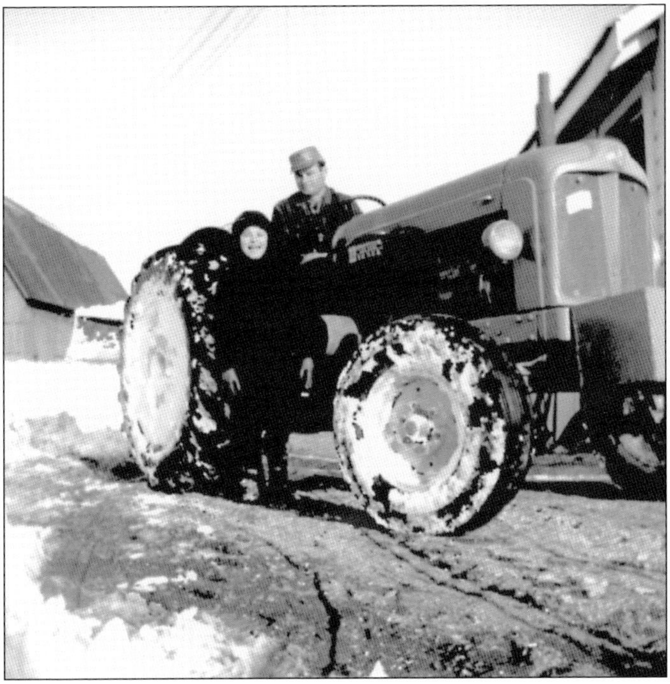

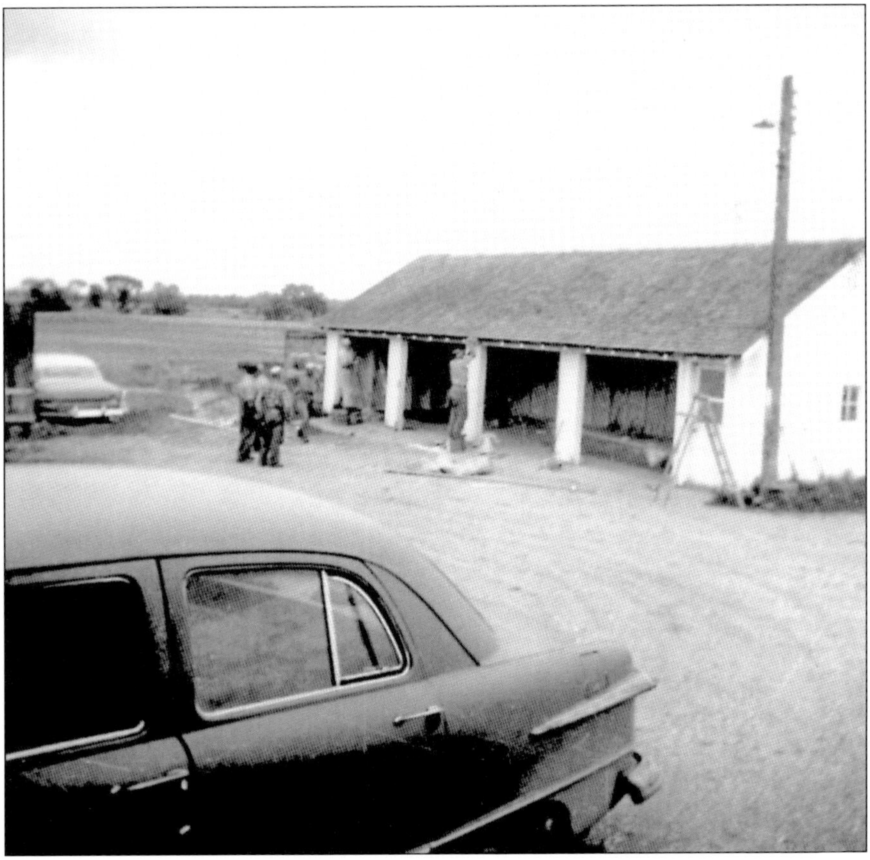

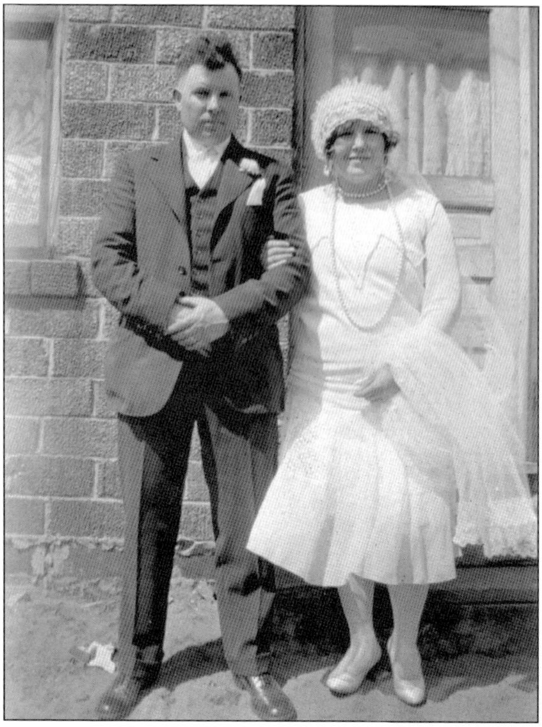

DUNN FARM. Frank Dunn (1897–1985) and his wife, Grace, married on May 1, 1928, and raised five children on the farm at 21130 22 Mile Road in Macomb Township. In 1998, their son Jay Dunn took over the care of the farm until it was sold that year to developers coming into the area. The main crops on the farm were corn, wheat, and soybeans. (Both, courtesy of the Janet Dunn collection.)

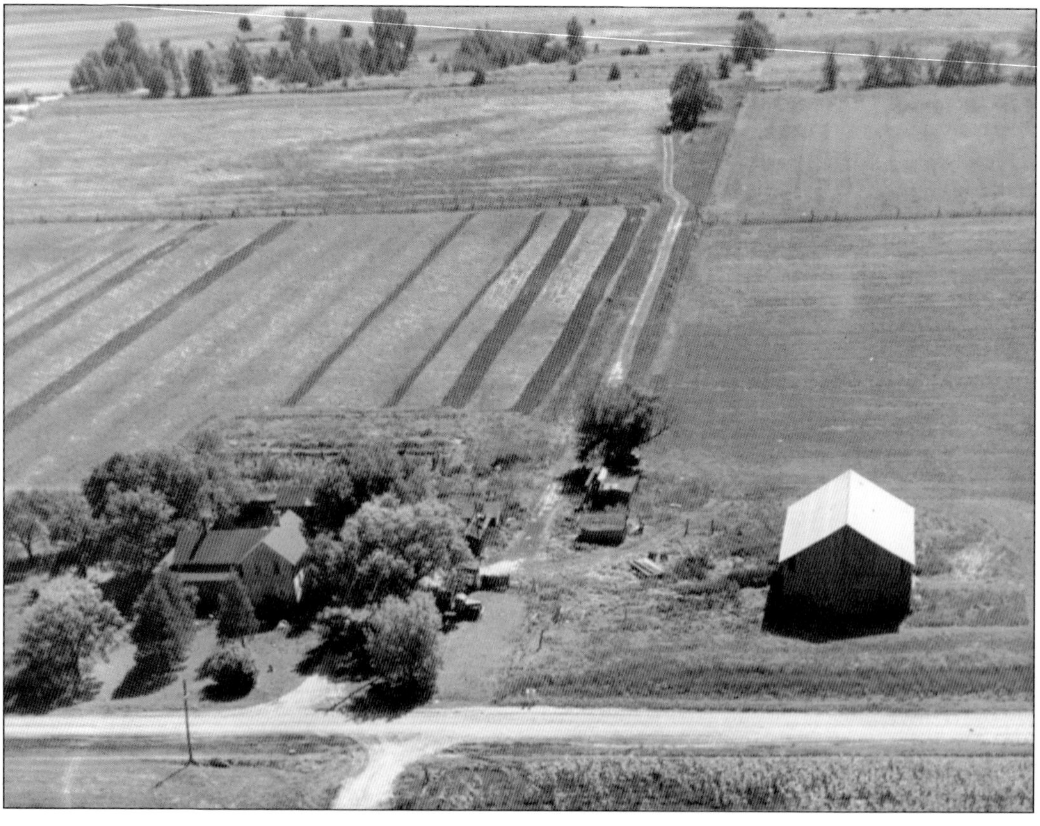

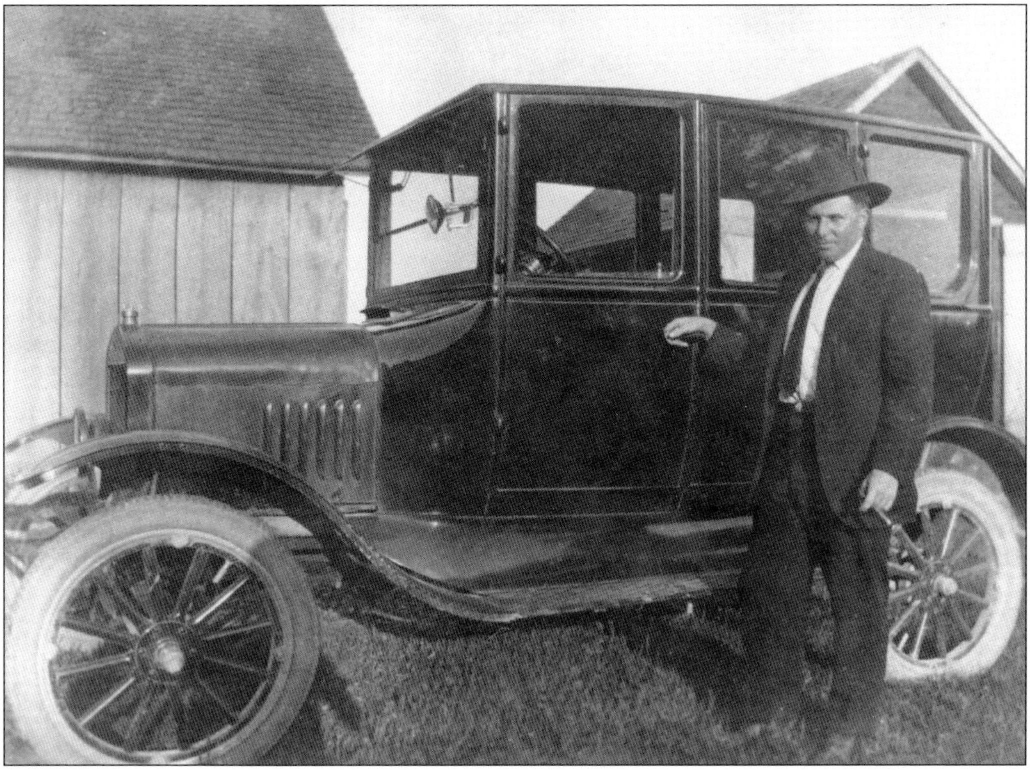

Mount Clemens Rose Gardens. Frank worked for a time at the Mount Clemens Rose Gardens. Here, he is standing next to his car. Grace received a letter from the state representative at the time, Charles R. Towner, making her aware that she had won the cooking contest in the Annual Rhubarb Festival in 1964. Frank filled his time when retired, belonging to the Jolly Seniors of Macomb Township, Waldenburg Seniors, Senior Citizens Inter-Faith of New Baltimore, and St. Isadore Catholic Church. (Both, courtesy of the Janet Dunn collection.)

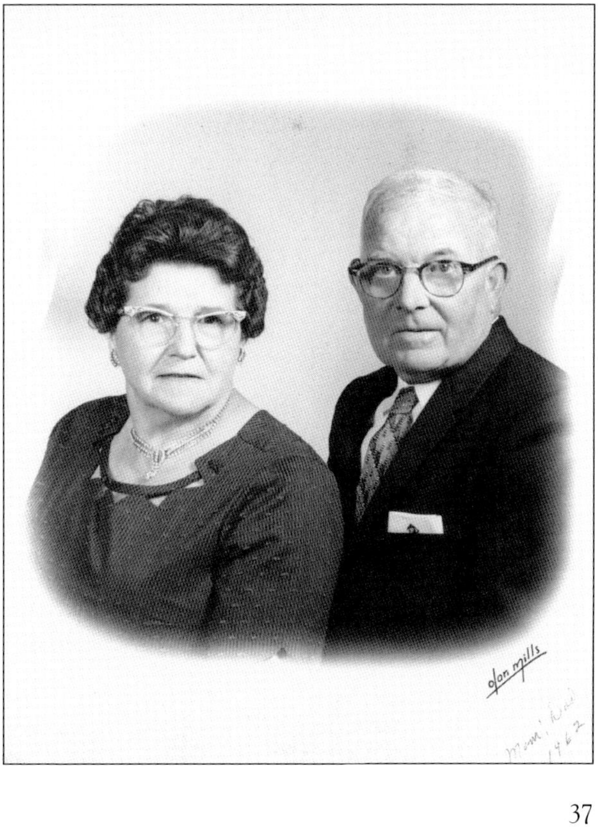

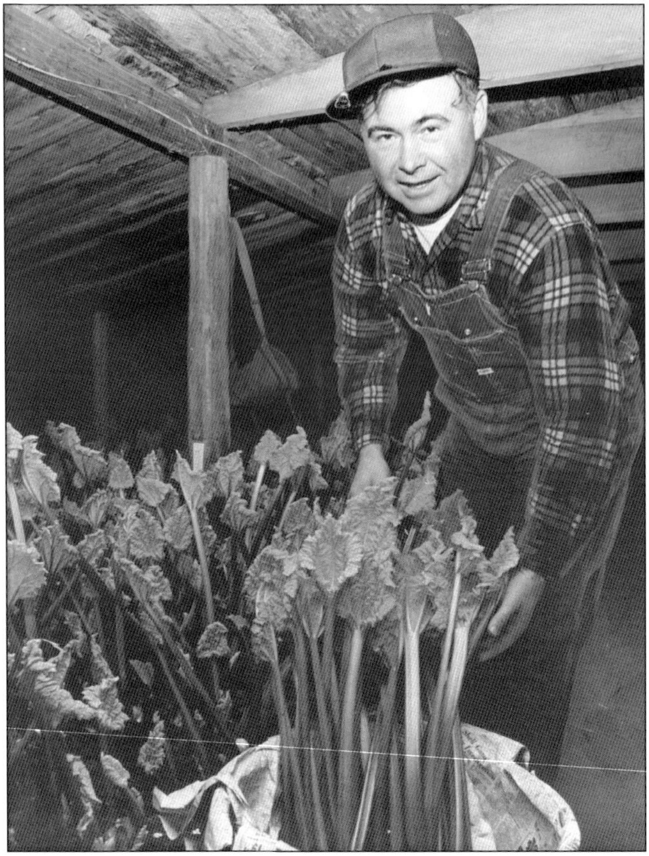

Boyka Farm. Boyka's Farm Market is named after Sylvester DeCock. *Boyka* is Flemish for "little boy" and was Sylvester's nickname throughout his life. Sylvester was the oldest of the three sons of Hilaire (1897–1980) and Mary DeCock (1903–1994). Hilaire's parents, August (1868–1949) and Marie (1871–1942), were both born in Belgium. Because of the chaos during World War I, they decided to start the process of immigrating to America. Although they would have to travel separately, by 1918, the family was together in America, and farming was to be their future. Pictured here around 1970, Sylvester is seen with his prize hothouse rhubarb. Below in the c. 1960 photograph is the construction of the brick barn, with rafters from the elm trees on the property during a cold winter. (Both, courtesy of the Virginia DeCock and Ken DeCock family collection.)

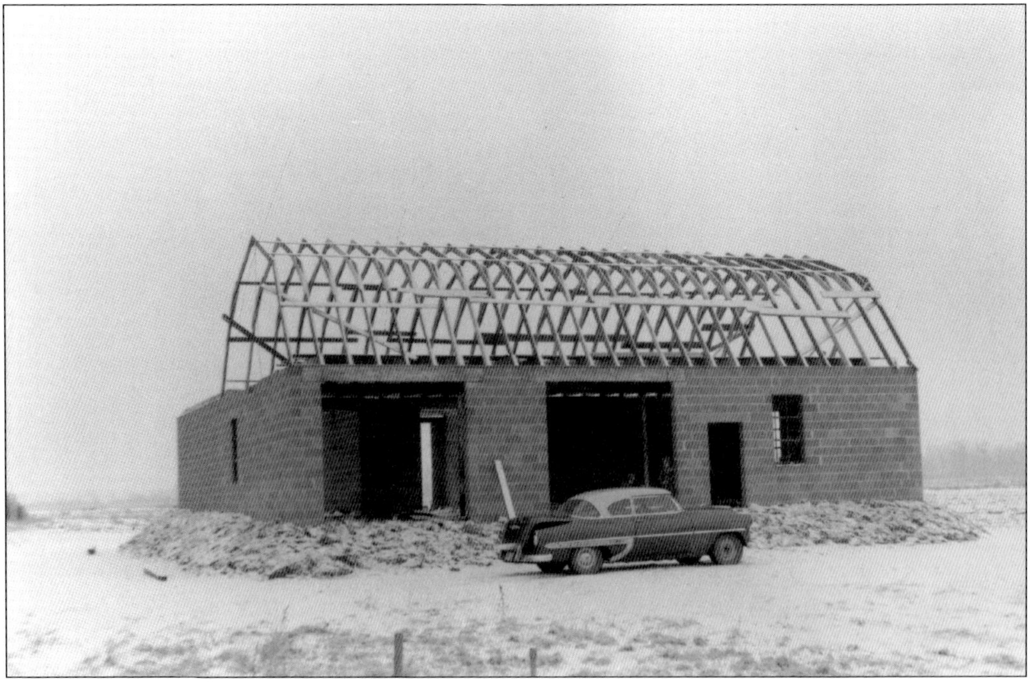

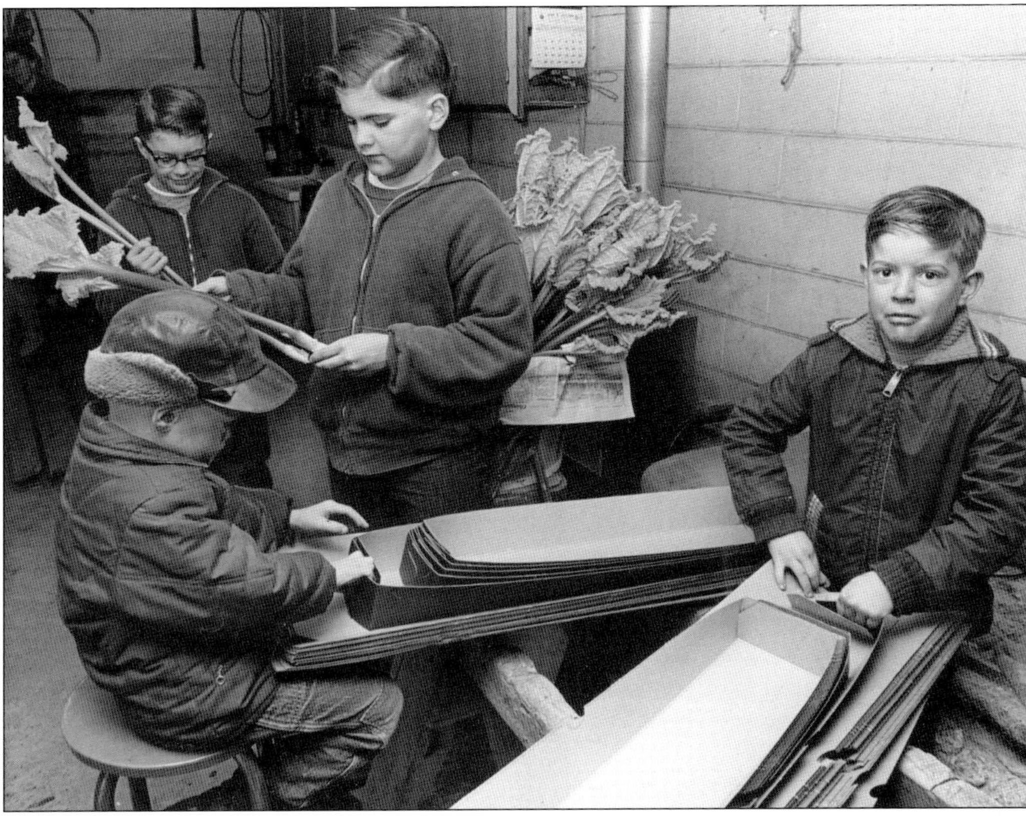

Folding Rhubarb Boxes. In 1981, Sylvester and Virginia began selling fruits and vegetables off wagons on the 23 Mile Road property. By 1984, they were growing and selling bedding plants and hanging baskets of flowers. Depending on the time of the season, the DeCocks had their produce and plants ready for the public. Getting ready to ship the rhubarb is Robert (sitting), while, from left to right, Larry, Ken, and Jim put together the boxes needed for shipping around 1970. To the right are Virginia and Sylvester DeCock in about 1997. (Both, courtesy of the Virginia DeCock and the Ken DeCock family collection.)

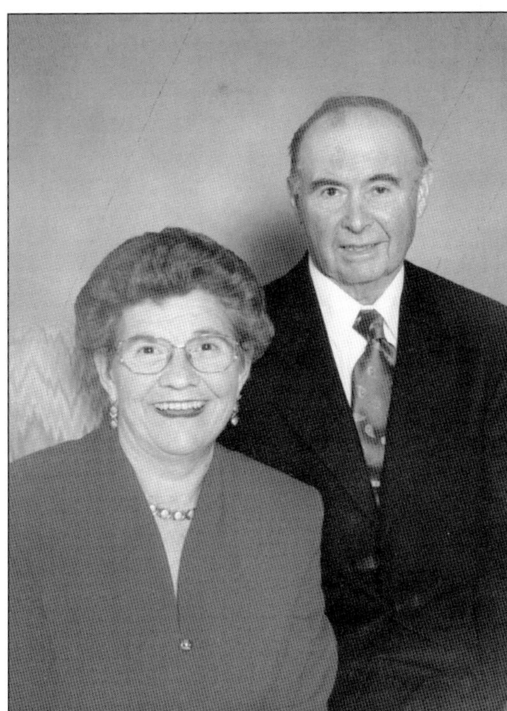

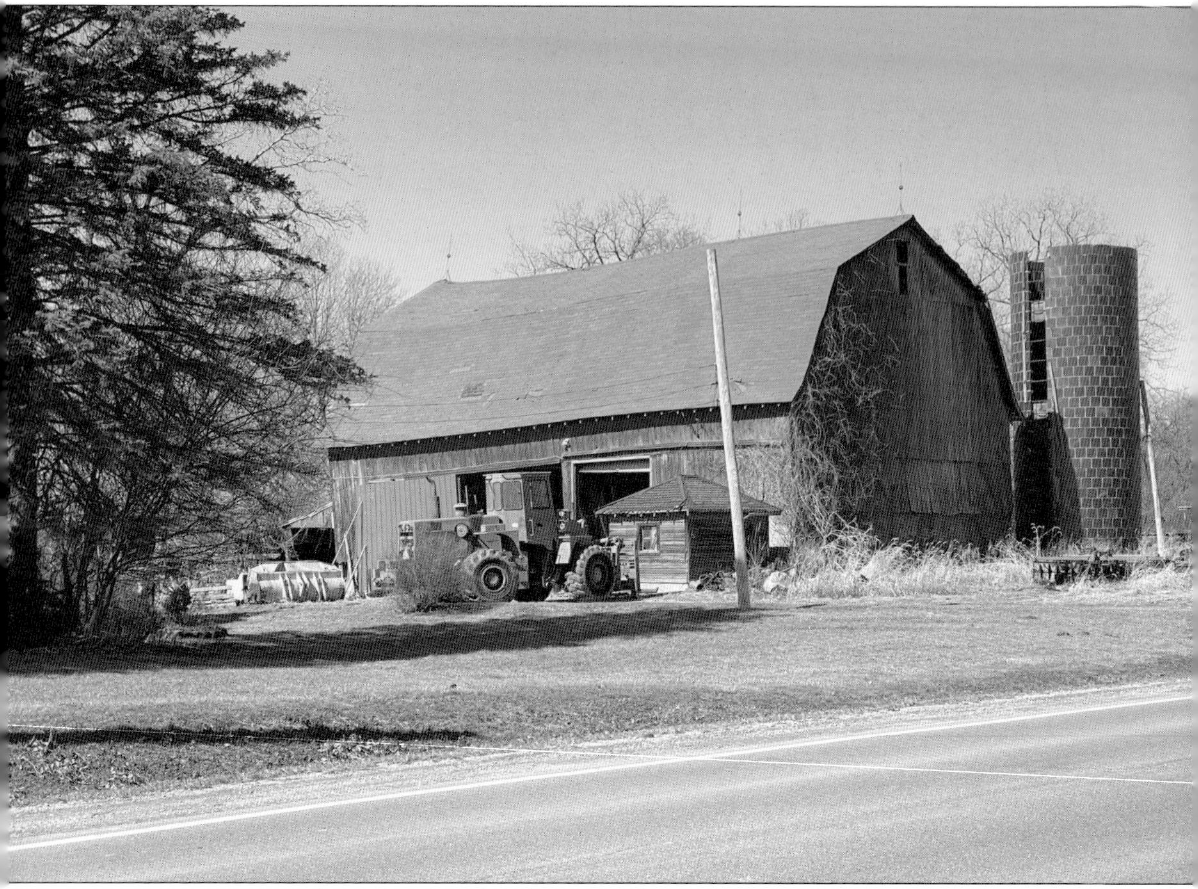

Demil Farm. Henri (1930–2020) and Delores Demil (1935–) raised three children on the 200-acre farm located on Fairchild and 25 Mile Roads in what is left of the rural area of Macomb Township. Henri started farming rhubarb just a year after arriving here from Belgium. The Demils started growing rhubarb in 1951, and by May, they cleaned out their fourth and final hothouse for the season, where people often stopped and asked what was being grown in the old-fashioned straw-covered hothouses. Hothouse rhubarb is more tender and less stringy than field rhubarb and grows without the large dark green leaves when planted outside. Botanically a vegetable but eaten as a fruit, rhubarb is still what people think of in spring. Each summer, the Demils plant between 25,000 and 30,000 rhubarb plants in the field. Two years later, in November, the root system of the plants is large enough to be removed from the soil. They are then carted into the hothouse and planted in rows. The process is similar to forcing spring flower bulbs indoors. Using a wood-burning stove, the hothouse is kept at a constant temperature of 55 degrees. In mid-January, the Demils' hands start showing the staining that comes when they start picking the rhubarb. They found growing the rhubarb more lucrative than their other crops of soybeans, greens, wheat, oats, and hay. (Courtesy of the *Detroit Free Press*, Michael Demil, and the author.)

Three

Chesterfield Township

"Throughout the state, there cannot be found a more beautifully located township than Chesterfield," according to *History of Macomb County, Michigan*, by M.A. Leeson & Co., published in 1882. Early on, the lake and streams of the township offered the Native Americans their wealth of fish; the forest, its game; and the soil, the wild fruits, herbs, and in many cases, corn. The first exodus of the Native Americans of the Macompte tribe took place between 1830 and 1838, and soon, they would all have reason to leave. Among the earliest and most prominent settlers to Chesterfield Township were Alfred Ashley, the LaForges, the Miltons, John Horriman, Robert W. Knight, William Little, Elisha Weller, John and Stephen Fairchilds, Zephaniah Campbell, Zara Granger, Joseph Horriman, and John Lusk.

The first post office in Chesterfield was established in 1837 with Robert O. Milton as the postmaster. The office was kept in his house and named the New Haven Post Office until it was moved to New Haven. Another post office was started in Milton, where it would operate until 1904. The fractional township of Chesterfield was created in 1842 by the Public Act 57 from the Michigan Legislature, in which the separation with Macomb Township would take place. The first election was ordered to be held at the schoolhouse near the residence of Charles Mathews.

Chesterfield sits between the two old Michigan cities of New Baltimore and Mount Clemens but seems more closely tied to New Baltimore. Alfred Ashley, with 60 acres of land, established the village of Ashley, as it would be called originally, and started a post office in 1851 called Ashleyville. By 1855, the name became New Baltimore; it was incorporated as a village in 1867 and became a city in 1931.

Chesterfield is just over 30 square miles, with 27.9 square miles of land and 2.8 square miles of water. The township is bordered on the north by Lenox Township, on the east by Ira Township and New Baltimore, on the southeast by Anchor Bay (which is part of Lake St. Clair), on the south by Harrison Township, and on the west by Macomb Township.

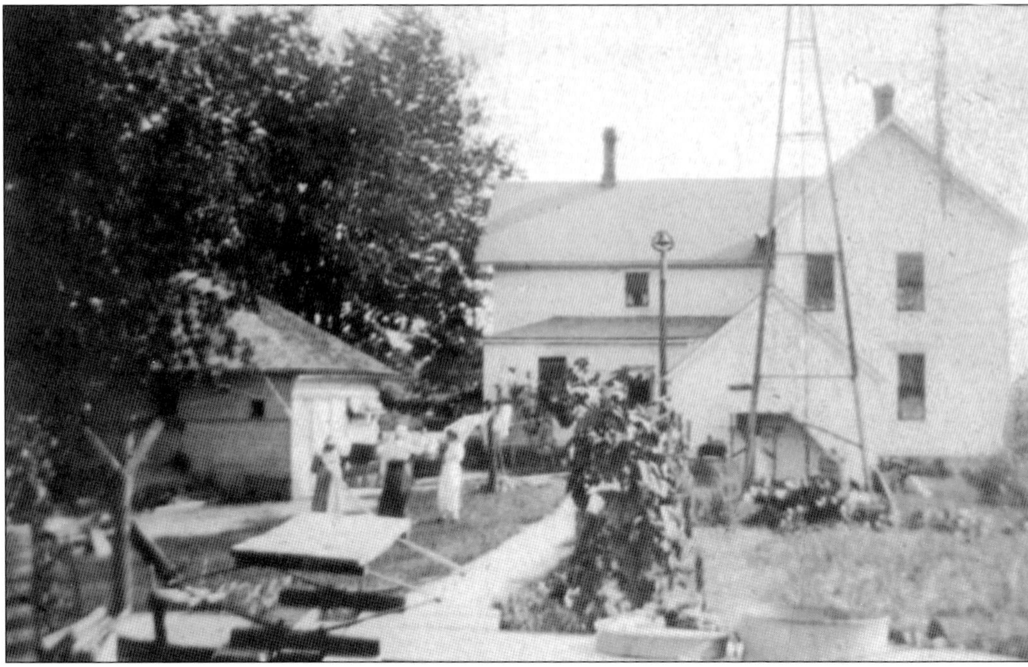

Collins Farm. August Collins (1859–1937) and Minnie Brower (1863–1944) were married on October 28, 1893, in Detroit. They raised four sons and four daughters on a ribbon farm rented from Henry Joy in Harrison Township. In the years around World War I, lobbying began in Washington to place a military airfield in Harrison Township, and the Collins family found a new farm of 80 acres in Chesterfield at 23 Mile Road and Old Telegraph Road. August was called a "gentleman farmer," as he hired out help to do the farming for him. Below is a picture of the transportation around the farm and their young son waiting to make a trip into town. (Both, courtesy of the Denise Jobe collection.)

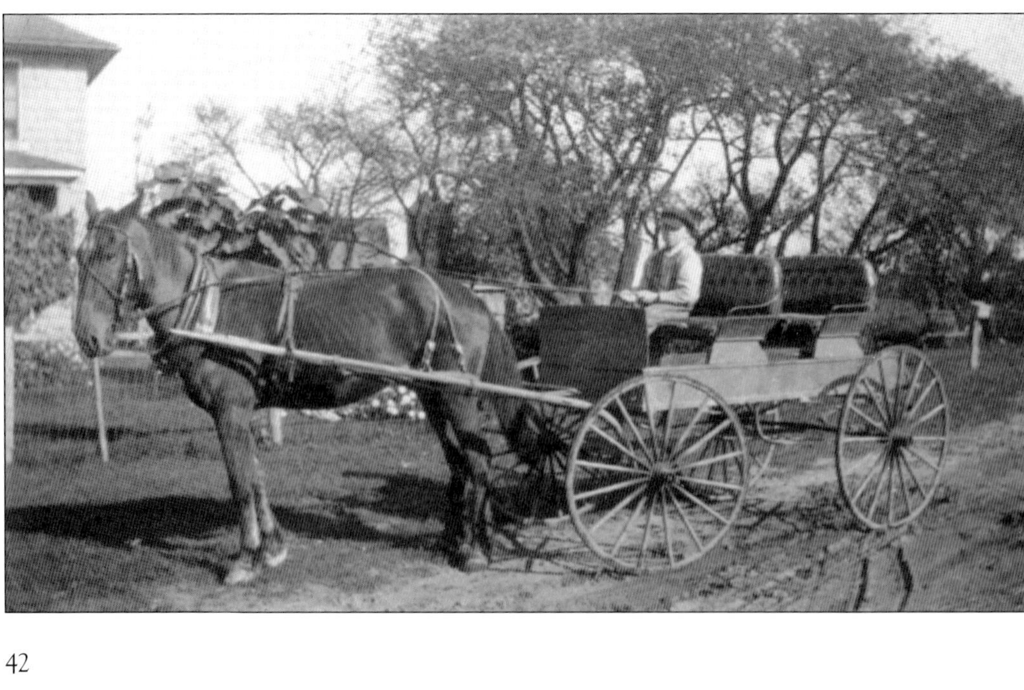

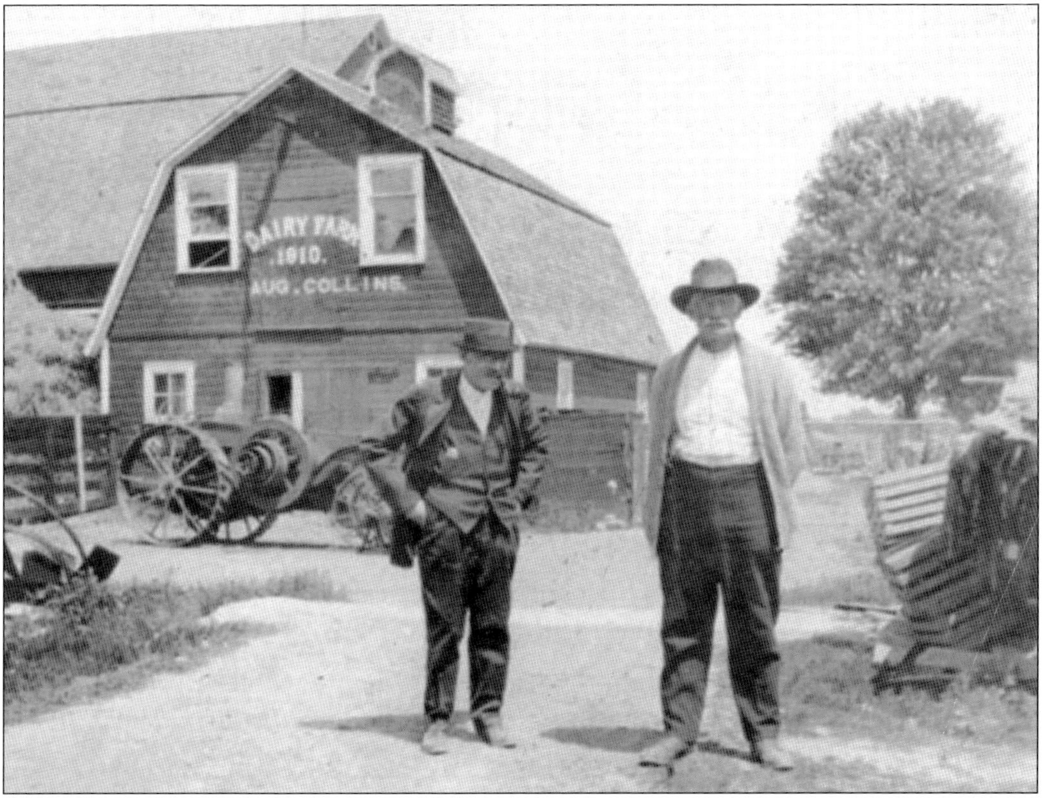

A Very Proud Couple. When August Collins started his farm, he was raising horses, but dairy farming was where he would start again once he settled in Chesterfield. The dairy farm was worked by the family until August's death in 1937, and with Minnie's death a few years later, the farm was sold to Alfred Foerster. Progress once again disrupted farm life by having the Interstate 94 corridor pass through the land. Below, in this c. 1920 image, August and Minnie stand proudly with their car, thought to be a 1918–1920 Buick Model K or H. (Both, courtesy of the Denise Jobe collection.)

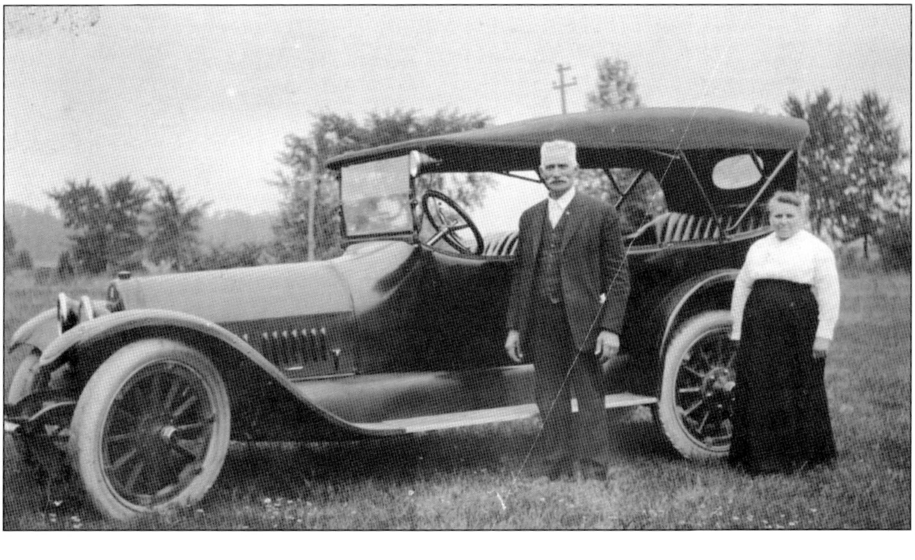

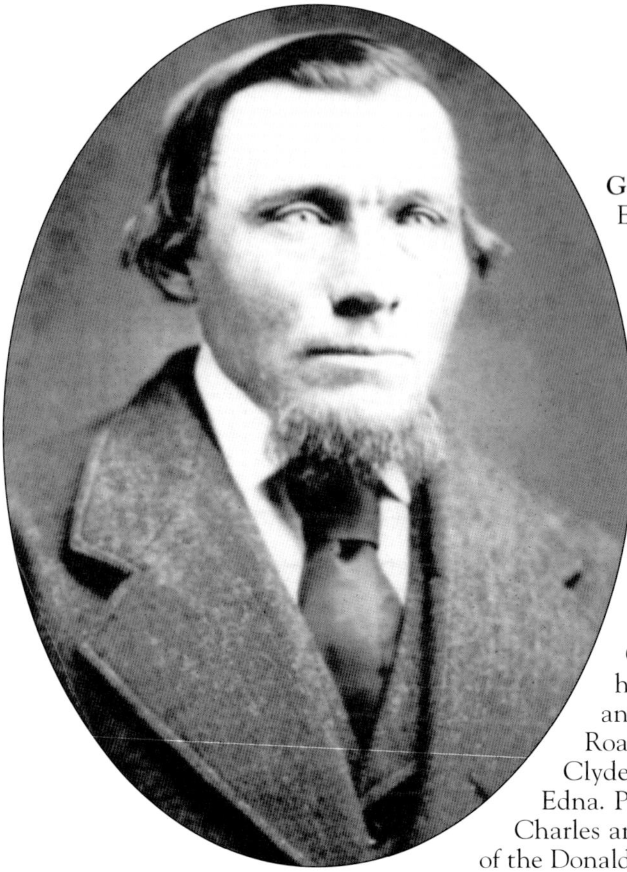

Gundlach Granzow Farm. Theodore Ernst Frederick Gundlach (1831–1915) was born in Ankershagen, Mecklenburg-Schwerin, Germany. Theodore came to America in 1857 with his parents and siblings, and he bought a farm on Quick Road (25 Mile Road) east of Gratiot Avenue in Chesterfield Township. Theodore and his wife, Maria Margarethe Fahs (1831–1896), raised three children—Ernest, Josephine, and Alvina—and worked this farm, where three succeeding Gundlach Granzow generations lived. Their daughter Alvina Marie (1869–1942) married Charles August Granzow (1869–1952), her second cousin, on April 19, 1894, and lived on the family farm on 25 Mile Road, where they raised their family: son Clyde August (1897–1975) and daughter Edna. Pictured below in front of the car are Charles and Alvina Granzow. (Both, courtesy of the Donald Granzow collection.)

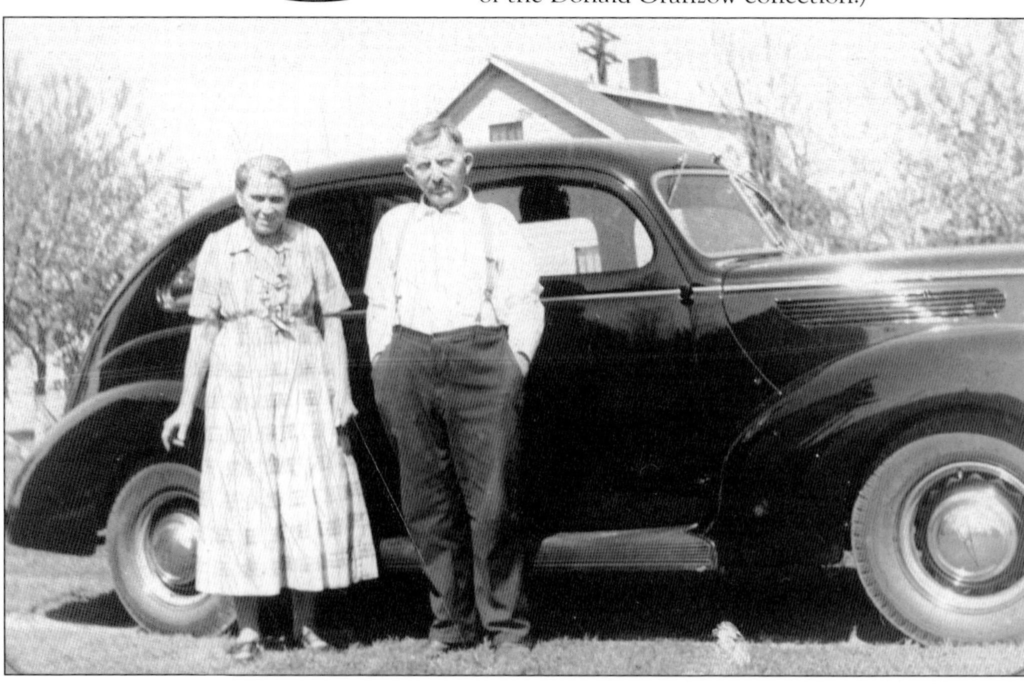

CLYDE GRANZOW AND SONS. Pictured here are Clyde and Marie Granzow on the farm, where they raised three children: sons Donald and Lyle and daughter Lorraine. Pictured below is a hand-drawn aerial view of the Granzow farm. The family made a trip to Detroit's Eastern Market, a distance of about 30 miles, with cases of chicken eggs in the trunk of the car and then rented a booth, along with other farmers, and waited for customers to buy their produce. The sign that read "Clyde Granzow and Sons" always made the younger generation very proud. The 80-acre farm's main source of income was from the sale of milk. All the milking was done by hand, and it was very much a family project. On the farm, the family raised wheat, alfalfa, oats, and corn. The farm became a Centennial Farm in 1960 for having been in the same family for over 100 years, according to *Life on a Michigan Farm*, by Donald E. Granzow. (Both, courtesy of the Donald Granzow collection.)

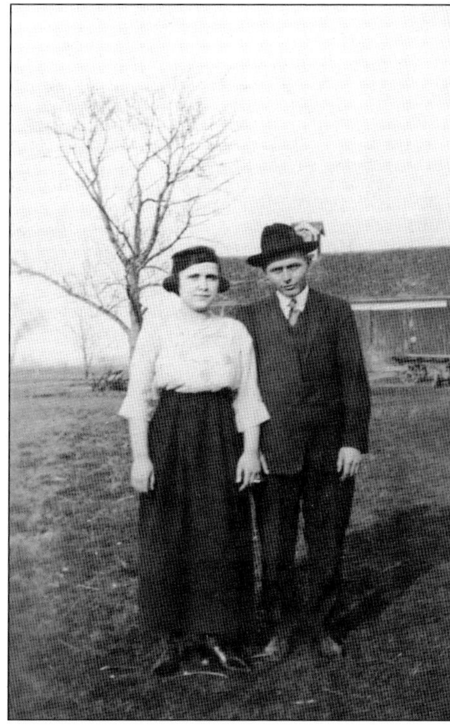

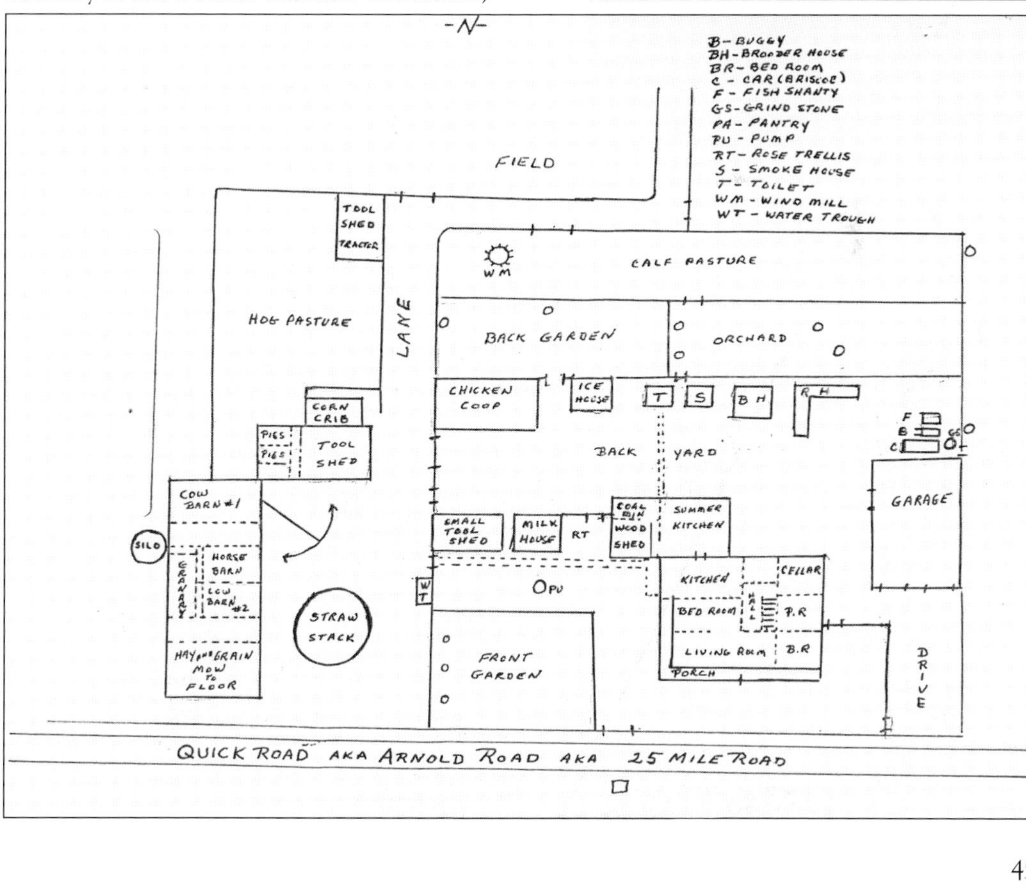

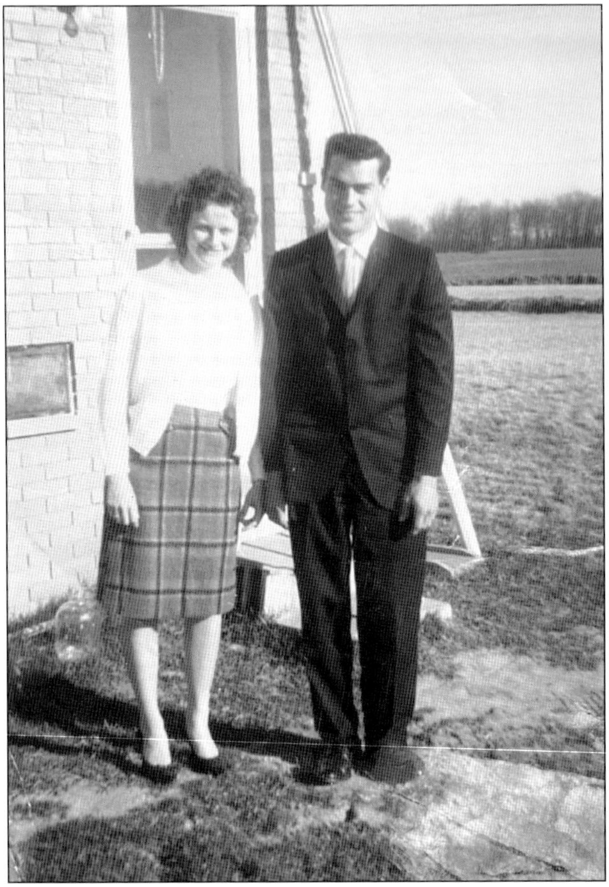

Van Thomme Farm. In 1963, Blase and Eleanore Van Thomme had the opportunity to rent a 40-acre farm they called Van Thomme Produce, as the plan was to grow vegetables and sell them at their roadside stand on 23 Mile Road. Part of the acreage was used to grow pansies to sell at Detroit's Eastern Market. In the spring of 1964, with about half the pansies selling at the farm, a small greenhouse was built to start vegetable plants to add to what they sold at the stand. Another greenhouse was built in 1965, when almost all the plants were sold at the farm stand. (Both, courtesy of the Van Thomme family collection.)

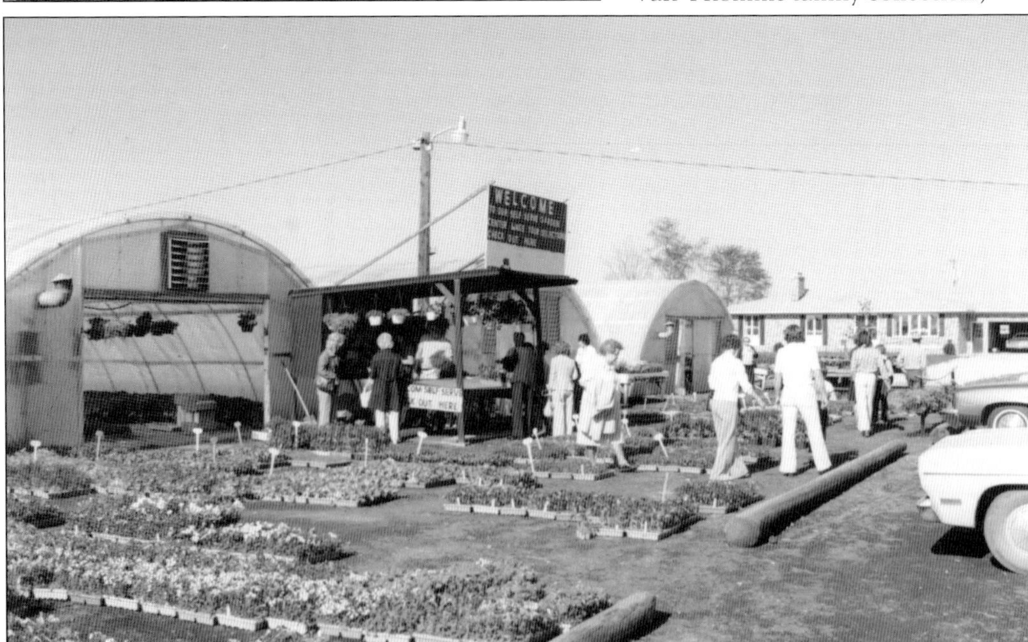

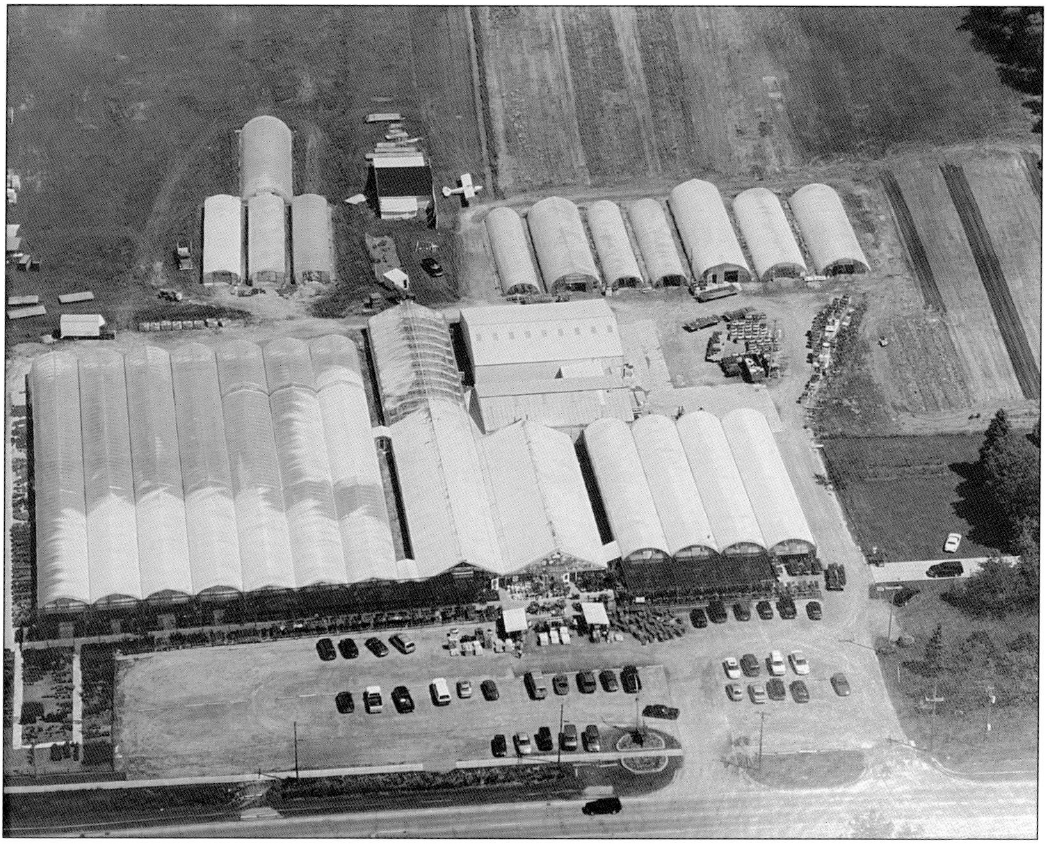

Expanding the Greenhouses. In 1967, the Van Thommes purchased the farm. They continued growing the produce and flowers until 1977. During that time, they were so involved in flowers that they discontinued growing field vegetables, and the name was changed to Van Thomme Greenhouse. They expanded into year-round flower production, with spring bedding plants, fall hardy mums, and potted plants for the various holidays. Blase and Eleanore raised three children—Debra, Don, and Carol—on the farm, and with their help, it was a family experience where their children pretty much run the business. They now have 25 greenhouses taking up 100,000 square feet of growing space and continue to fill the needs of the community around them. (Both, courtesy of the Van Thomme family collection.)

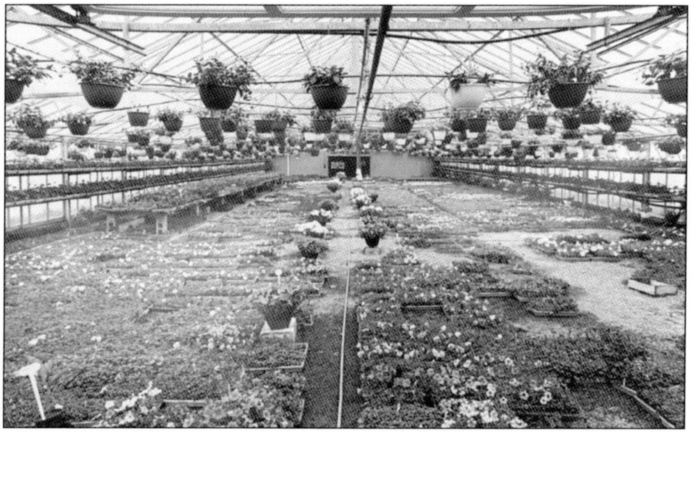

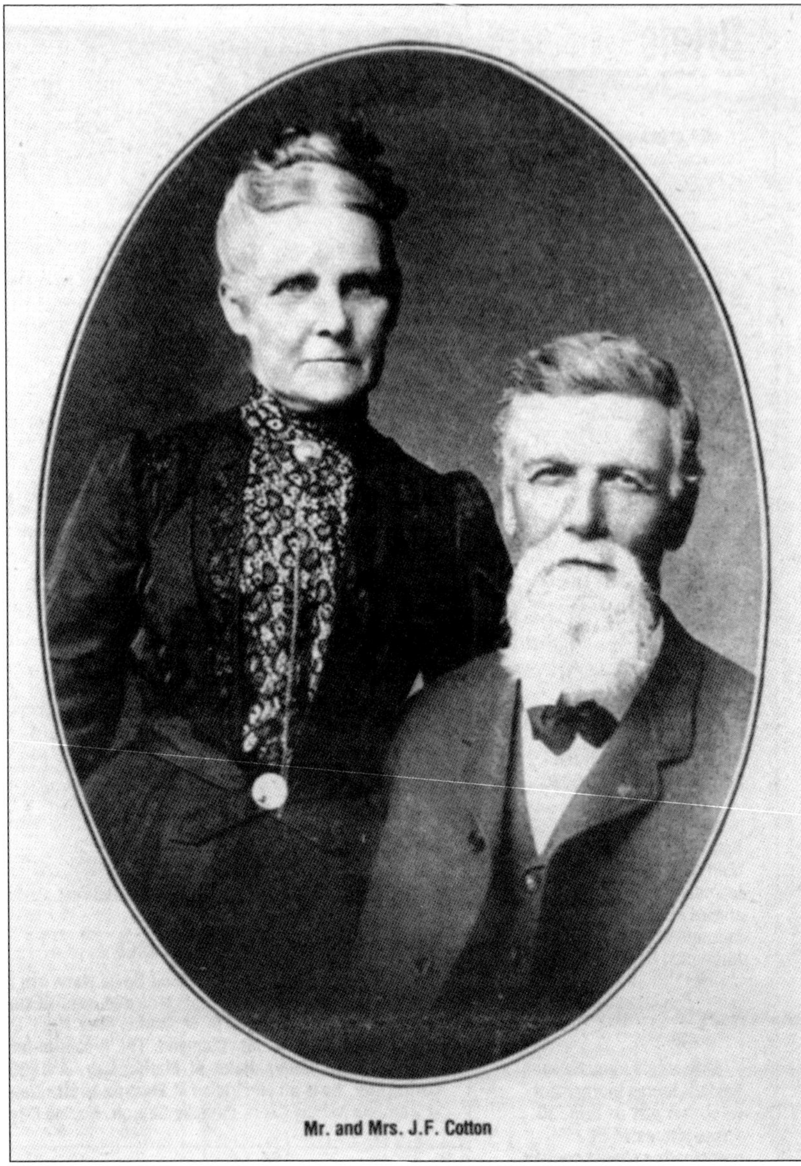

COTTON FARM. Otis W. Cotton arrived in Chesterfield in 1832–1833, when Michigan was still a territory. Cotton purchased 128 acres on the new road about where Cotton Road touches Gratiot Road. One of his neighbors was Martha Fairchild, the daughter of early Chesterfield pioneers, and though clearing the land was arduous work, there was still time for romance. In August 1833, Otis and Martha were married. Because of the harsh times, even the loss of a cow was a heavy burden, and wolves brought additional hardships. At one point, the Cottons lost their entire flock of sheep to a pack. When depending on the wool for clothing and bedding, this was a serious loss. This first generation of Cottons passed away with Otis in 1884 and Martha in 1887. One of their nine children, Jay, spent time in the Civil War and at a farm out in Nebraska for some years. After the death of his first wife, Jennie Ensminger, he returned to Michigan and purchased the old family homestead. Jay married a second time to Maria Tucker. Although the Cotton farm is only a memory now, the family name does live on in the street that bears their name. (Courtesy of the Michael Sullivan collection.)

Four

Washington Township

The meeting to organize the township of Washington was held at the house of Alvin Nye in April 1827. Daniel Thurston was called upon to preside, and Otis Lamb was chosen as clerk. They decided after much thought that the town should be called in honor of the father of the country, and the name was accepted enthusiastically and confirmed by the act of organization. At that point in time, there were less than 40 families in the area. The land was rich for farming and the orchards it would soon become known for.

The greater portion of the families that came to the area arrived from New York during the years 1822–1824; each would purchase 80 to 160 acres at $1.25 per acre. The principal roads at the time were Native American trails.

By 1838, the first building raised in the township without the use of whiskey was the residence of Elias Wilcox. The architect and builder at the time was Chauncey Church, and he was very interested in the temperance cause, so he would have no spirituous liquors at any of his raisings. After all the work was done, he climbed on the topmost height he could get to and gave the following toast:

This frame is of oak, it stands upon rocks,
Twas framed upon honor for Elias Wilcox,
And since it is raised and things are all right,
Tis Elias' home and Nancy's delight.
We've had no whiskey, we don't care for that,
We'll have something better than rum or wild cat.
So let us be merry, both Democrat and Whig,
And we'll go home to the house and get some baked pig.

Clifton Mills and Mount Vernon are both unincorporated communities in the township of Washington. Mount Vernon was considered a small post office village, and in the immediate vicinity were both Baptist and Methodist churches, a general store, a buggy shop, and a district school along 28 Mile Road and Mount Vernon Road. Clifton Mills was located near the intersection of 31 Mile and Dequindre Roads. There was a church, a mill, and a graveyard. The village of Romeo sits in Washington, and its neighbor to the north is Bruce Township.

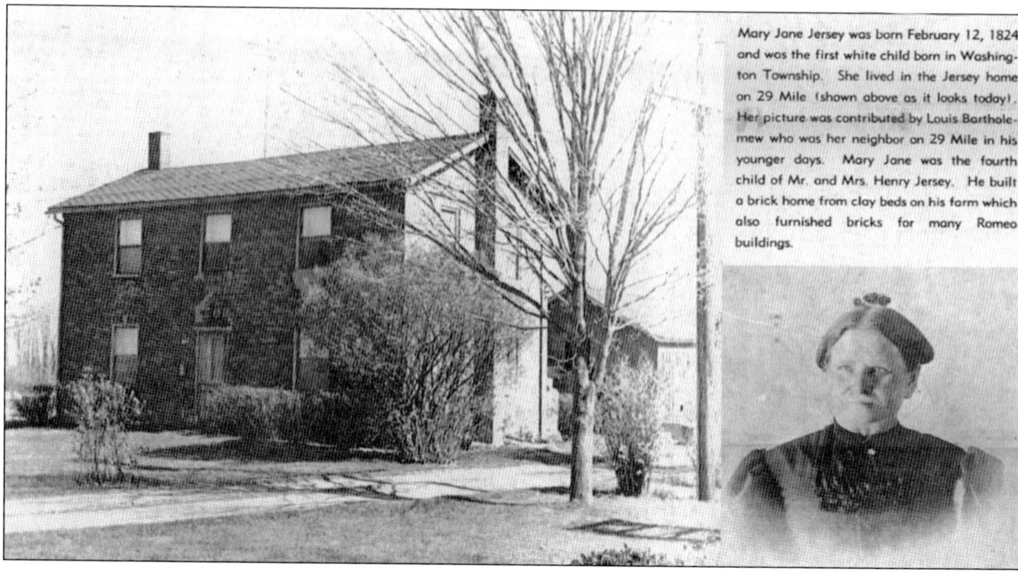

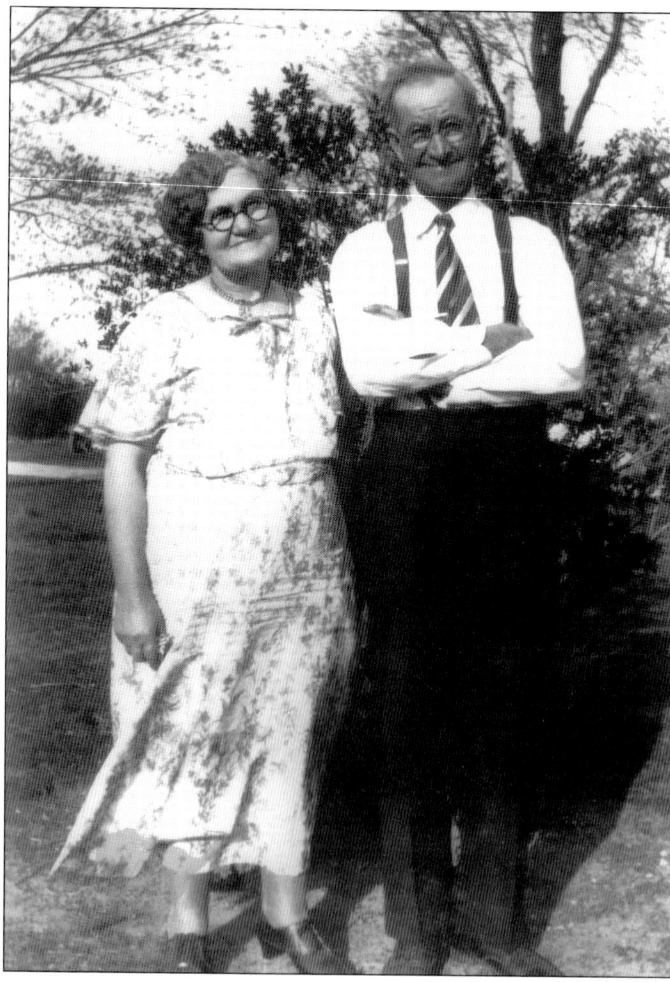

LeFever Farm. Mary Jane Jersey was born on February 12, 1824; she was the fourth child of Mr. and Mrs. Henry Jersey. She was considered the first white child born in Washington Township at the time when American Indians were their neighbors. The home was built with bricks made from the clay beds on his farm; those beds also furnished bricks for many of the Romeo buildings. Mary Jersey passed away in 1904 and is buried in the Washington Center Cemetery on 29 Mile Road. William Charles LeFever (1874–1946) and Mary Jane Smith (1879–1939) married in 1899. Both of them were from Blissfield, Michigan. The Jersey farm on 29 Mile Road was purchased between 1911 and 1912 by the LeFevers. (Above, courtesy of the Community Archives at the Romeo Kezar Library collection; left, courtesy of the Steven LeFever collection.)

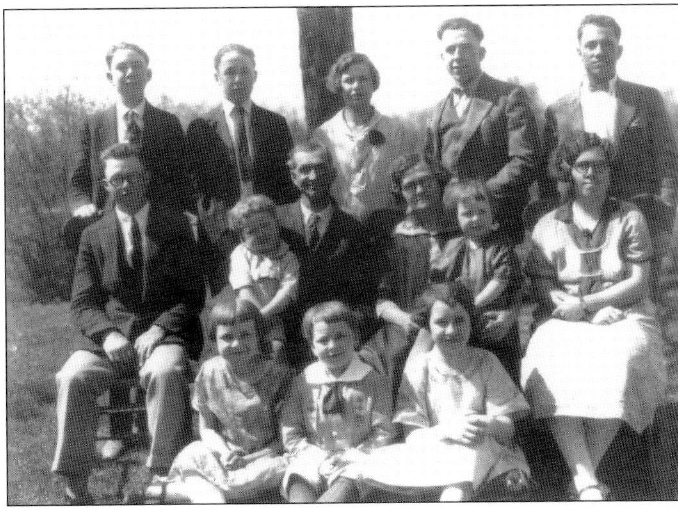

Family Patriarchs. William and Mary raised 12 children, all shown in this image. In this family photograph are, from left to right, (first row) Marian, Milton, and Beulah; (second row) Clifford, Donald, William, Mary, Vora, and Ada; (third row) Homer, Elmer, Ina, Lloyd, and Howard. Their son Elmer passed away while just a teen, so this is believed to be the only grouping of all the family members. (Courtesy of the Steven LeFever collection.)

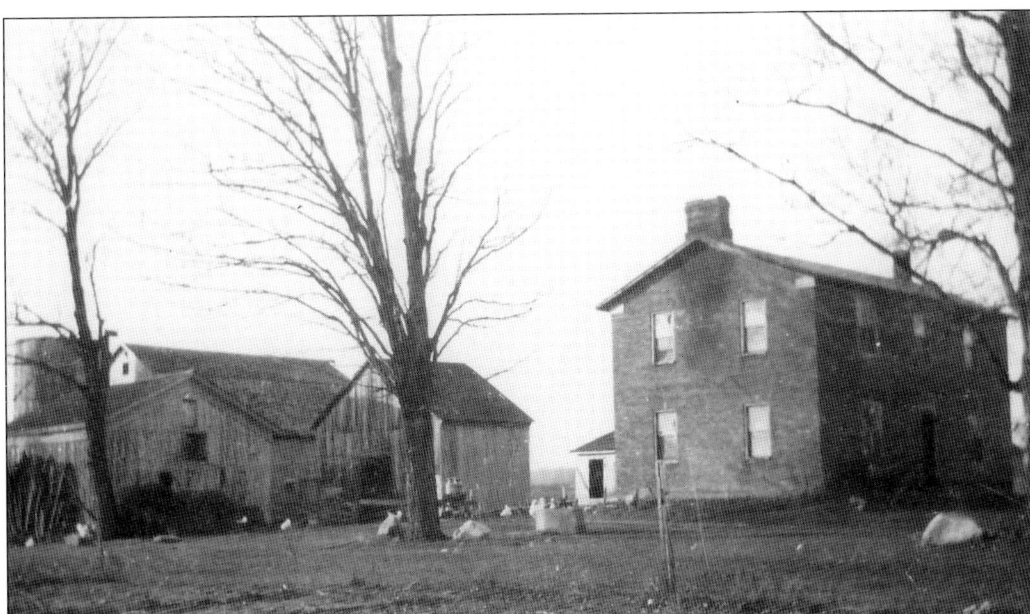

The 29 Mile Road Stagecoach Stop. The LeFever farm was said to be one of the stagecoach stops on the route from Port Huron to Pontiac, Michigan. There was a large cement-lined pond used for watering the teams of horses from the stagecoach behind the house and a large oval stone at the end of the house by a large tree where the stage would pull up and let passengers on and off. Many of the LeFever children, when grown, built houses up and down both the north and south sides of 29 Mile Road. The home and farm were eventually sold and turned into a subdivision of homes. (Courtesy of the Steven LeFever collection.)

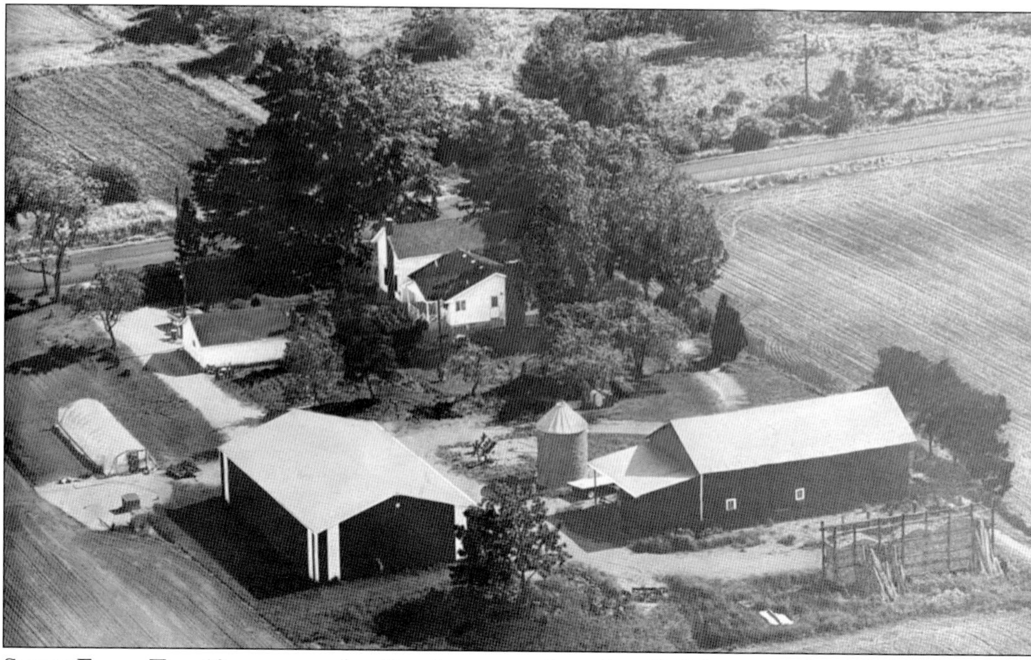

SMITH FARM. Two 40-acre parcels of land were purchased in 1833 by Samuel Barnes, and by 1839, Tim Smith's ancestor Richard Carlton Jr. owned the property, located on 27 Mile Road between Schoenherr and Hayes Roads. The sesquicentennial farm is still run and managed by the Smith family today. The family is at work in this image: Leon Smith, Tim's father, is driving; Karen Smith is on a transplanter with her mother-in-law Doris (not visible but sitting next to Karen). They are planting kale in late April 1983 on Leon and Doris's farm on 27 Mile Road. (Both, courtesy of the Tim Smith collection.)

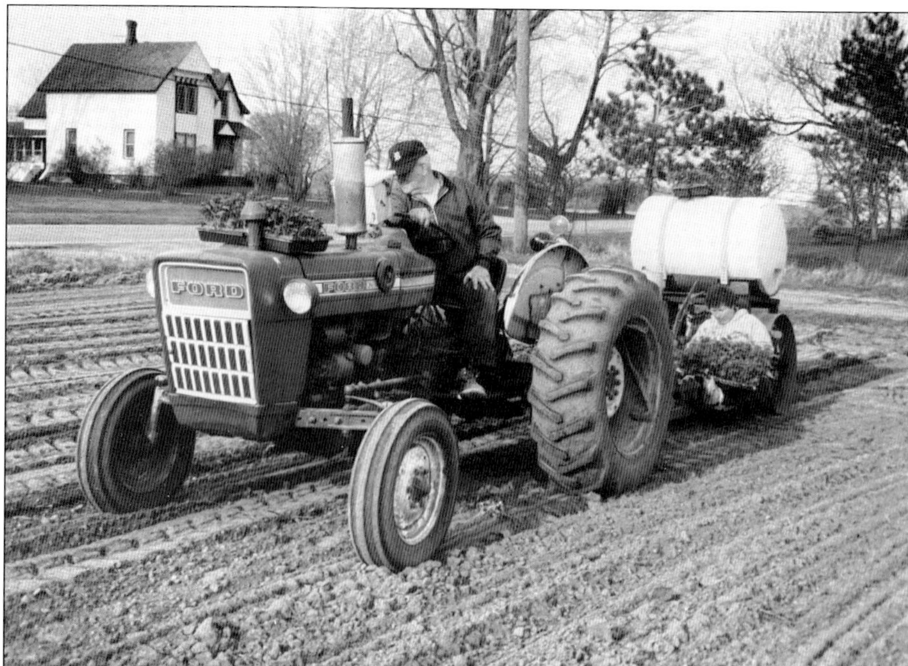

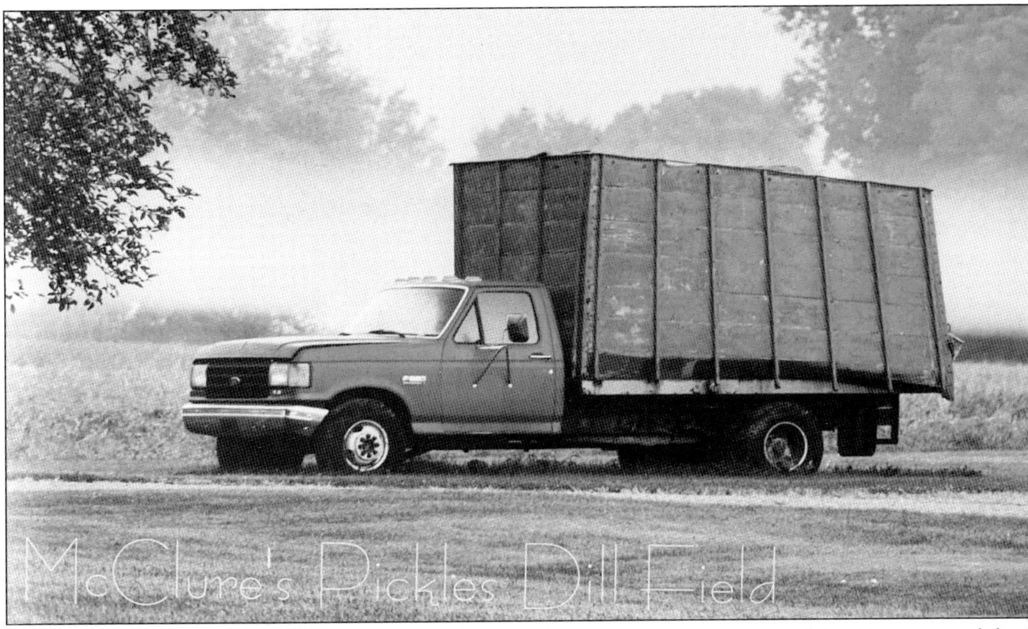

GROWING DILL WEED. This 1987 Ford truck with a homemade box was used for 20 years to deliver produce, mainly to the Eastern Market in Detroit. Tim Smith's 1950 Allis Chambers G tractor is mainly used on the vegetable farm due to its rear-engine design. It seeds three rows at a time, and here, it is seeding dill in July. Tim grows tall dill, or dill weed. It is used in the pickling of cucumbers, dilly beans, and other vegetables. Most of this dill was grown for local roadside stands and commercial picklers. This tractor belonged to Tim's father, Leon, and has been in the family for better than 70 years. (Both, courtesy of the Tim Smith collection.)

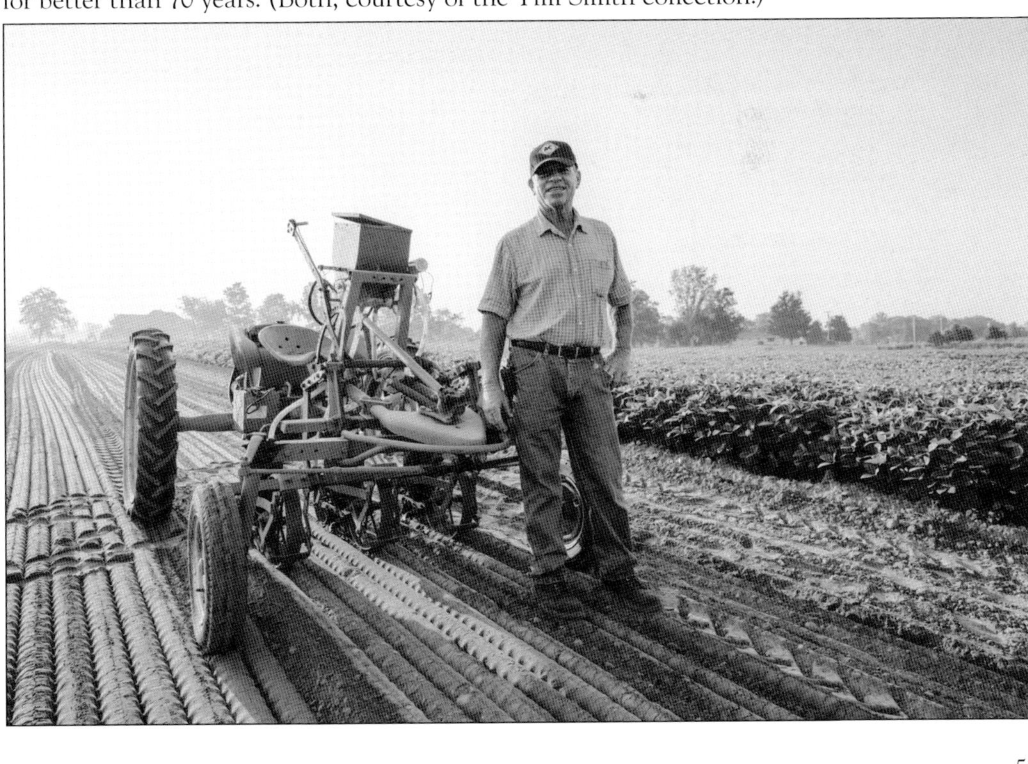

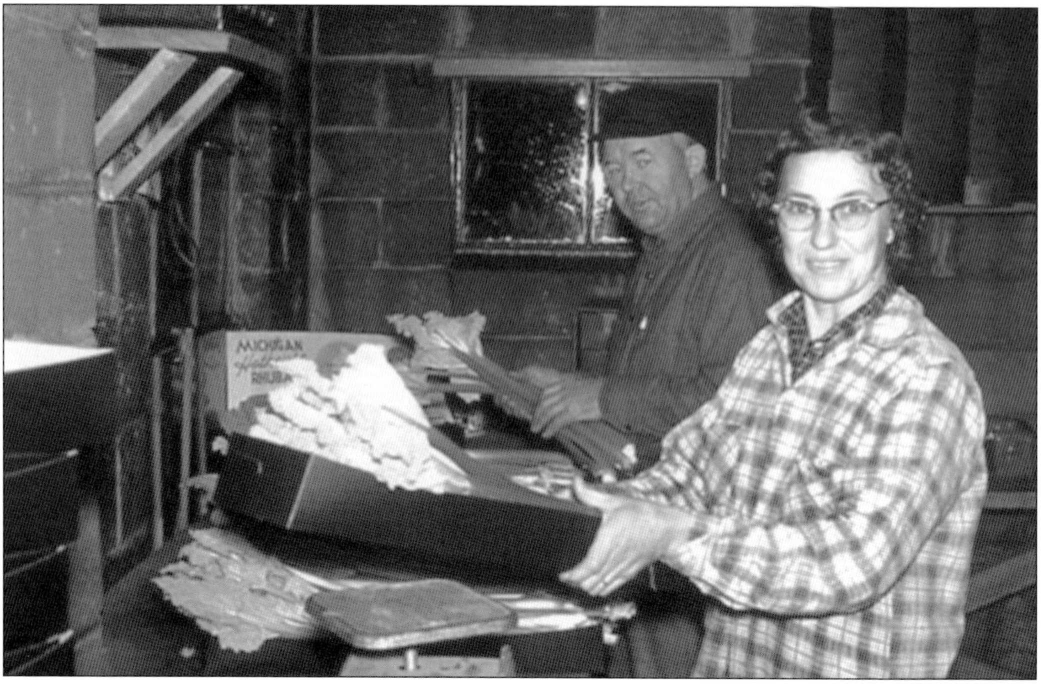

Kutchey Farm. Marvin (1913–1968) and Florence Kutchey (1913–1998) came from Warren to the northeast corner of 26 Mile and Jewel Roads in Washington in 1939. At the time, they were involved with general farming and dairy cows. In 1951, a portion of the property was sold to Detroit Edison. Pictured here, Marvin and Florence box rhubarb for shipping. Below, from left to right, are Jack Strause, Marvin Kutchey, and son Robert pulling rhubarb. By 1961, Bob Kutchey's sod farm was established, and the property became a sod farm both in Washington and on the Armada property. Robert took over the sod farm after his father's death in 1968. (Both, courtesy of the Teri Nickles collection.)

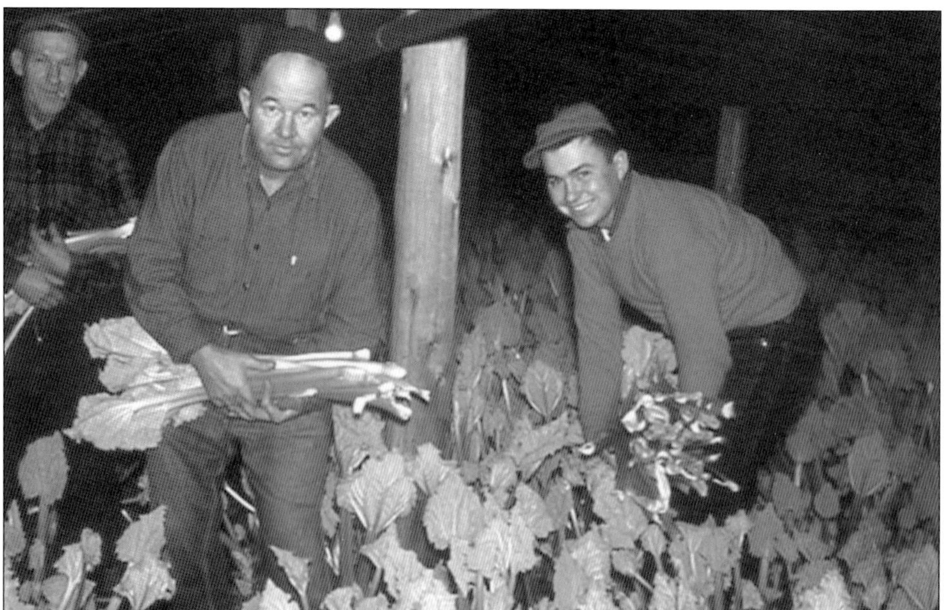

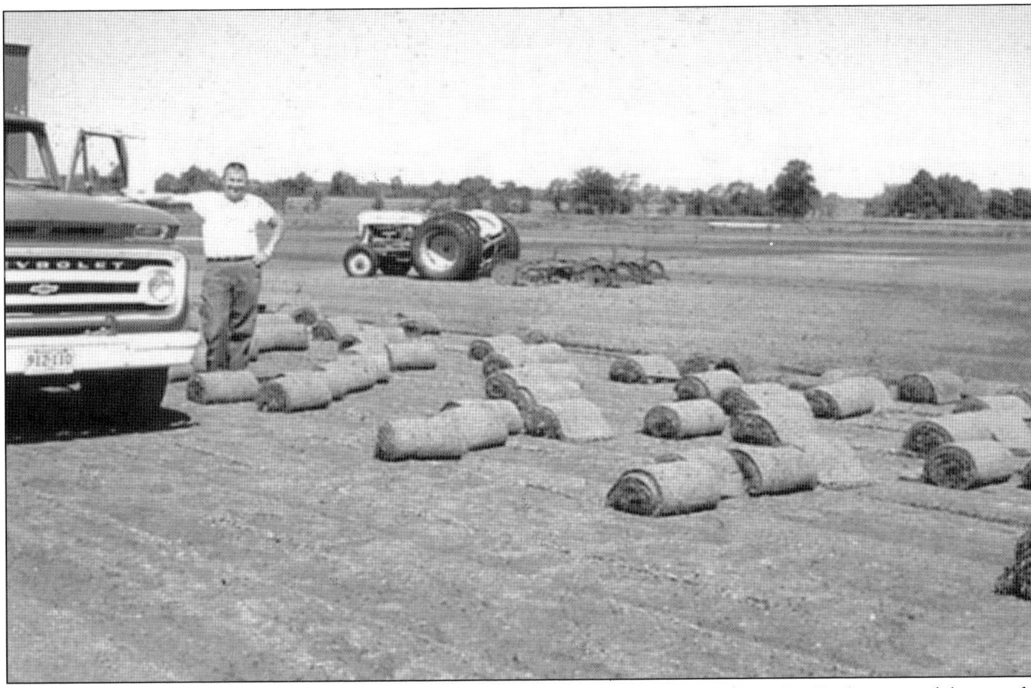

Working the Sod Farm. Robert works on the sod farm around 1962. Robert and his wife, Carol, raised four children, three daughters and a son, in the farming life. By 1973, the property was returned to growing produce, which was sold at the produce stand on 26 Mile Road. By the mid-1980s, the family leased a portion of the property and also sold a portion to developers. By mid-1998, Mary and Dave Rudish purchased the remainder of the property, and the structure was used by the Kutcheys to sell their produce. It is still used today in the form of Mary's Garden. (Both, courtesy of the Teri Nickles collection.)

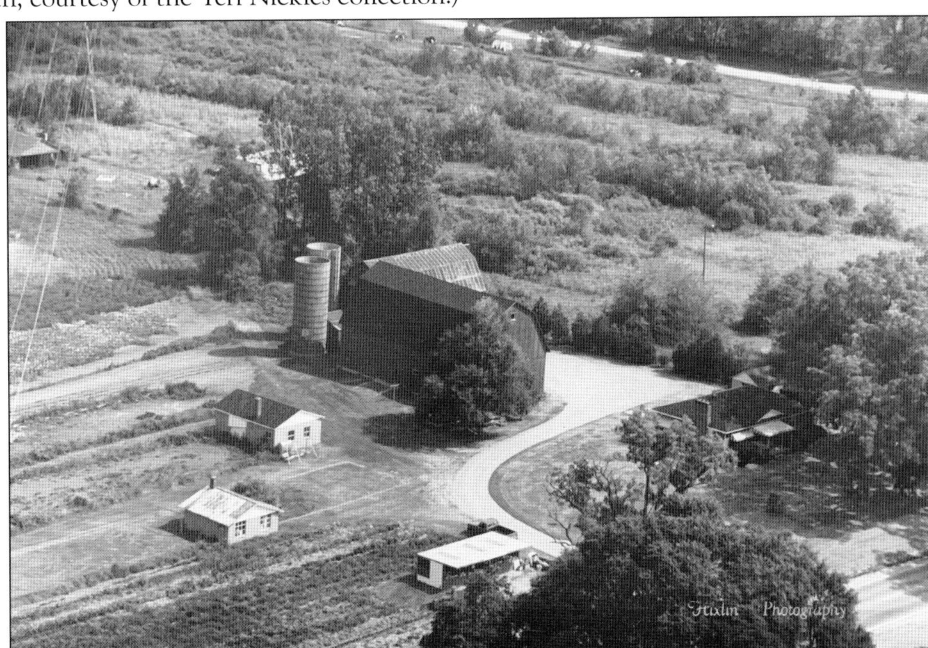

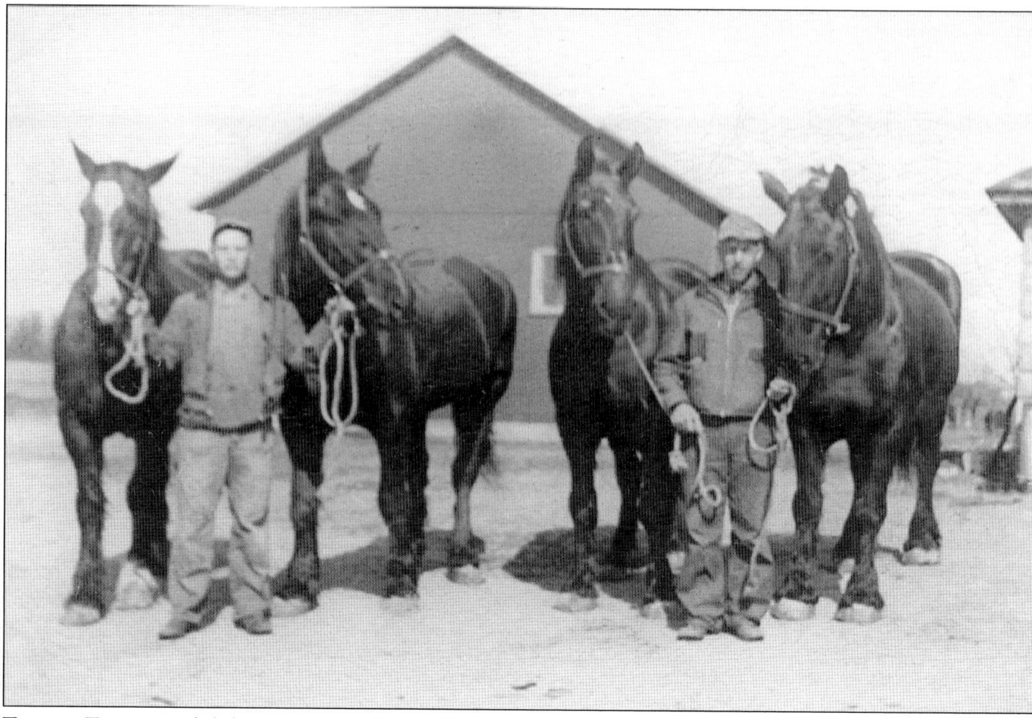

Falker Farm. Rudolph and Elizabeth Falker purchased 160 acres on February 2, 1918. The property is located on Mound Road between 30 Mile and 31 Mile Roads in Washington Township. The couple had four children born on the farm: Lydia, Louise, Martin, and Howard. While Rudolph farmed the property, raising potatoes and crops to feed his dairy cow herd, the children all helped with the farm work and had their own responsibilities. In 1968, Martin and his wife, Betty, purchased the farm from Rudolph, and along with their two children, Richard and Diane, they continued farming the property. With the dairy herd, they sold the milk to a local dairy company and also farmed cash crops, wheat, corn, and oats, along with the hay needed to feed the cattle. (Both, courtesy of the Falker family collection and Larry Sobczak and the *Record*.)

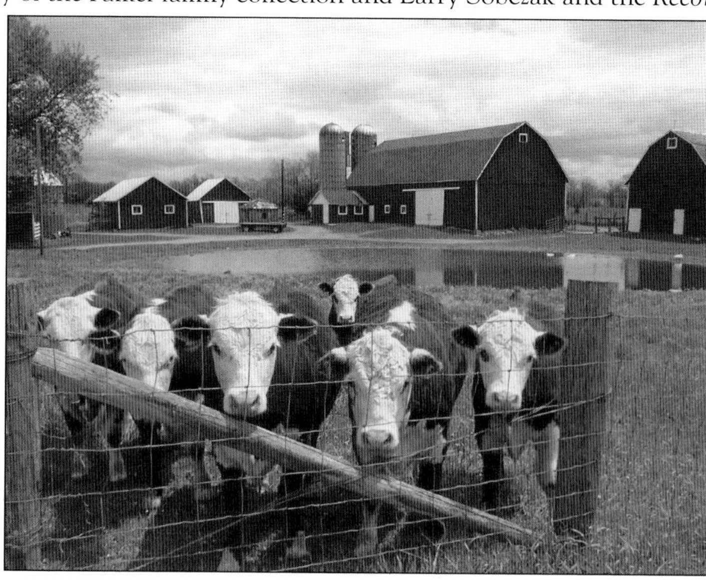

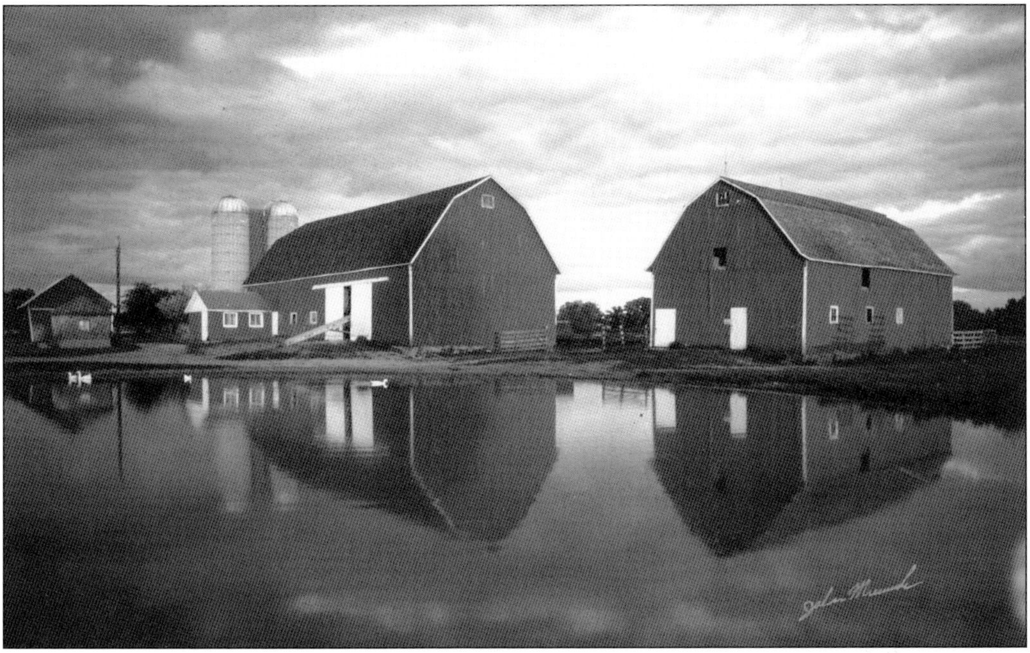

Passing the Farm On. By 1985, Martin was nearing 70 years of age and felt it was time to sell the dairy herd. He continued to work the farm until he passed away in 2012 at just over 90 years of age. His son, Richard, had continued to help with the farming while living nearby, and after his father's passing, Richard and his wife, Dianne, and their two daughters, Michelle and Lauren, moved onto the property and continued working the farm. The cash crops were still raised, but pumpkins and cut flowers were added, along with fresh eggs year-round. The property has been featured in many publications, including barn books and local calendars, and was part of the Romeo Historical Society's Barn Tour in 2012. The buildings themselves have been relatively unchanged over the 100 years that the farm has been in the family, with occasional improvements that benefit the farm. (Both, courtesy of the Falker family collection.)

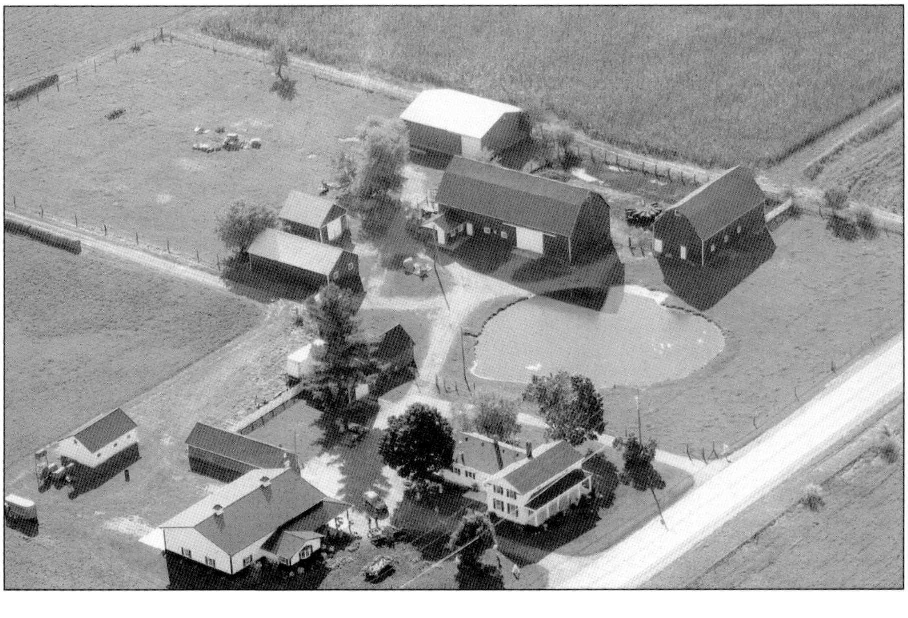

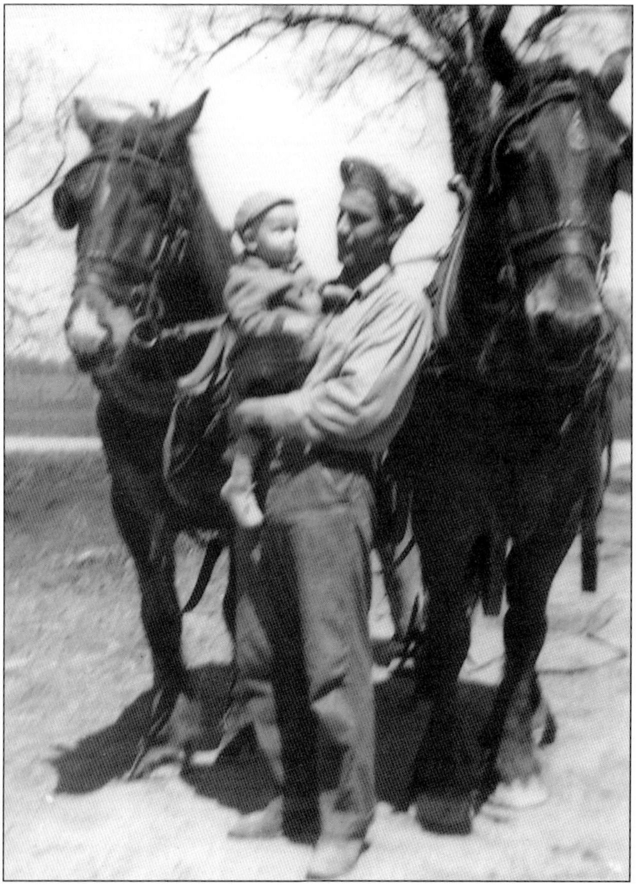

Kirsh Farm. George (1921–1980) and Arlene Kirsh (1922–1987) purchased the 102-acre farm at 14960 27 Mile Road in Washington Township in the spring of 1946. While raising their sons, Gary (1947–) and David (1952–2011), they worked the farm, raising vegetables, grain, chickens, hogs, and cattle. An egg route in Pontiac and a booth at the Royal Oak Market were part of their weekly routine. George holds his son Gary as he stands with the family's team of horses named Tom and Jerry around 1948. (Both, courtesy of the Kirsh family collection.)

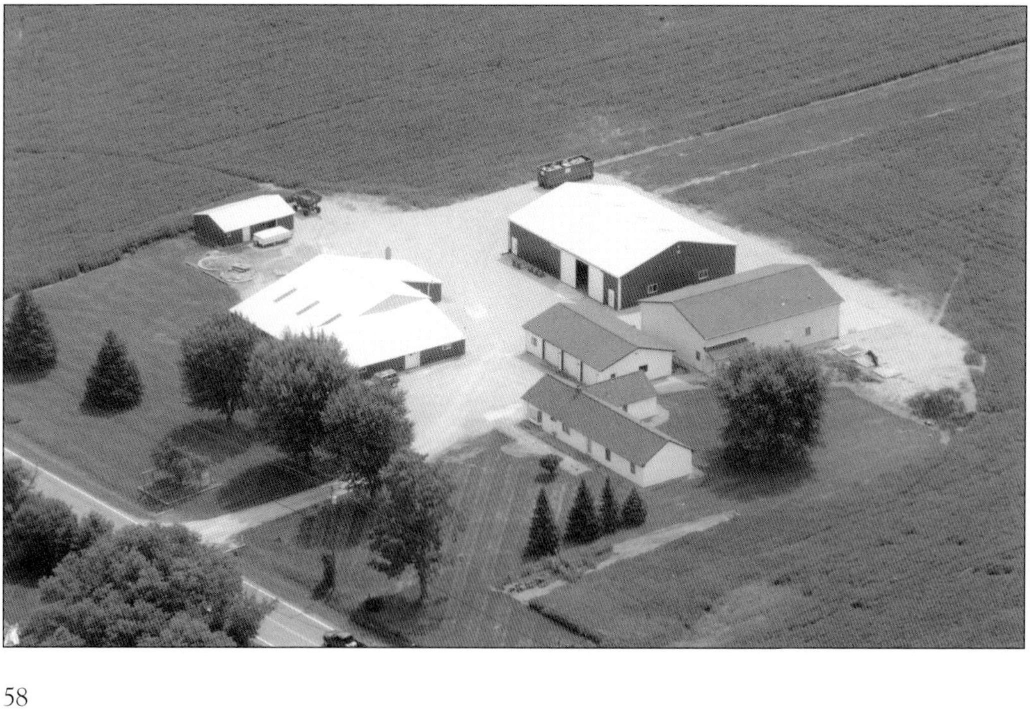

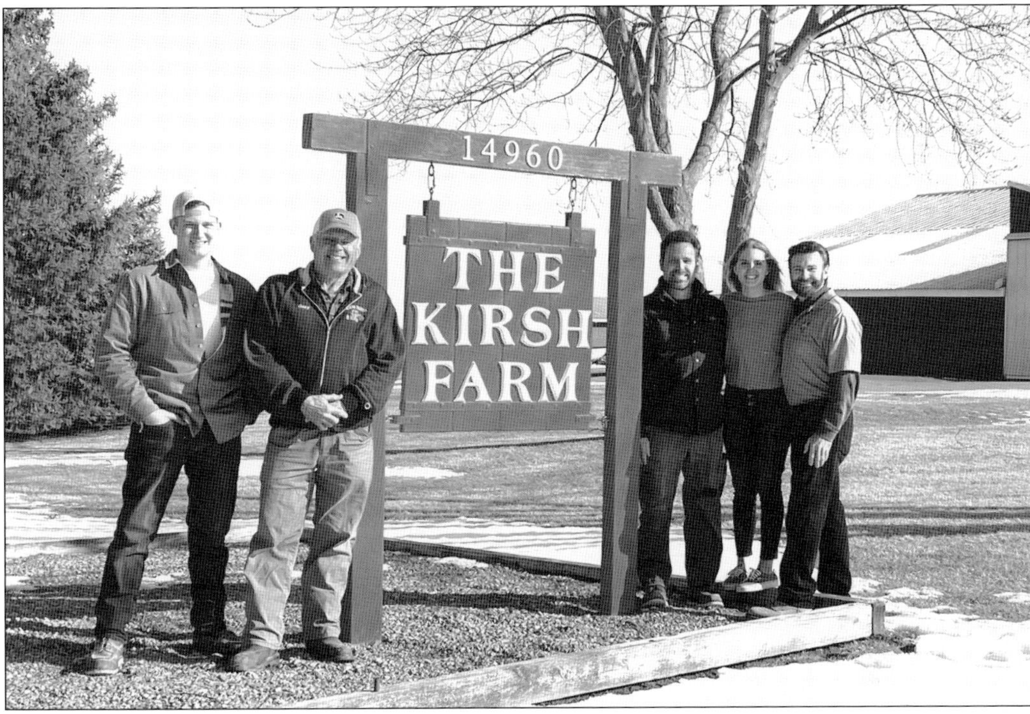

A Family's Pride. As time progressed, Gary and David continued the farming operation as partners until David's death in 2011. Today, Gary Sr. and his wife, Candace, enjoy raising corn, wheat, and soybeans on the family farm with help from their son, Gary Jr.; his wife, Margie, and son, Brian; and their three grandchildren, Josh, Gavan, and Gabriella. Pictured here, from left to right, Gavan, Gary Sr., Brian, Gabriella, and Gary Kirsh Jr. stand in front of their Washington Township farm in 2021. (Both, courtesy of the Kirsh family collection.)

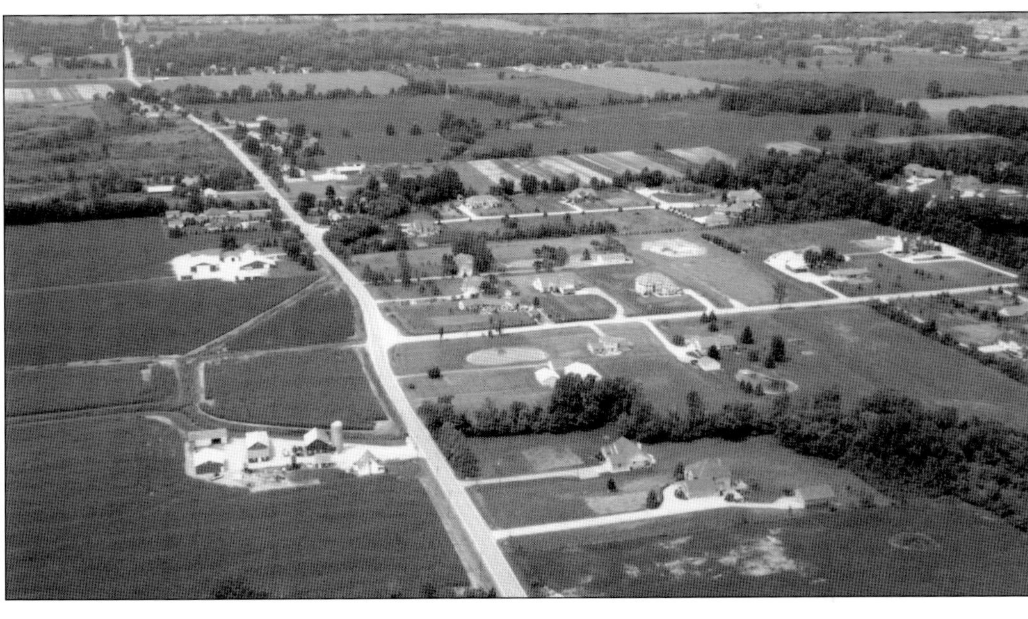

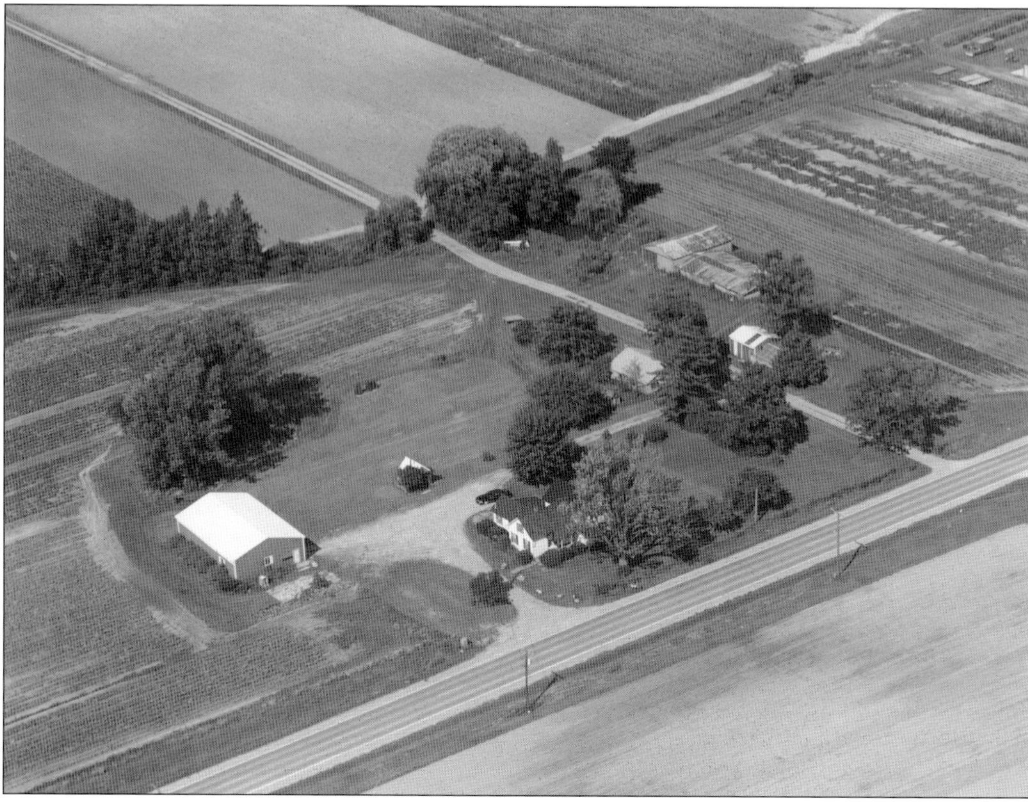

August Goike Farm. August John Goike (1914–2005) and Sybil Elzerman Goike (1918–1993) purchased 85 acres of property on 26 Mile Road in Washington Township. Gus and his brother Ed managed a herd of Holstein dairy cattle. When the cattle were sold, Gus and Sybil continued to raise chickens and work with their hothouse rhubarb. Their main income came from the vegetables they raised, such as sweet corn, potatoes, tomatoes, peppers, cantaloupes, and watermelons. Their produce was sold to local roadside produce stands or at their 26 Mile Road farm in front of the house. Below, Gus and Sybil plant cabbage seedlings in late June on their transplanter. (Both, courtesy of the Barb Goike Colpaert collection.)

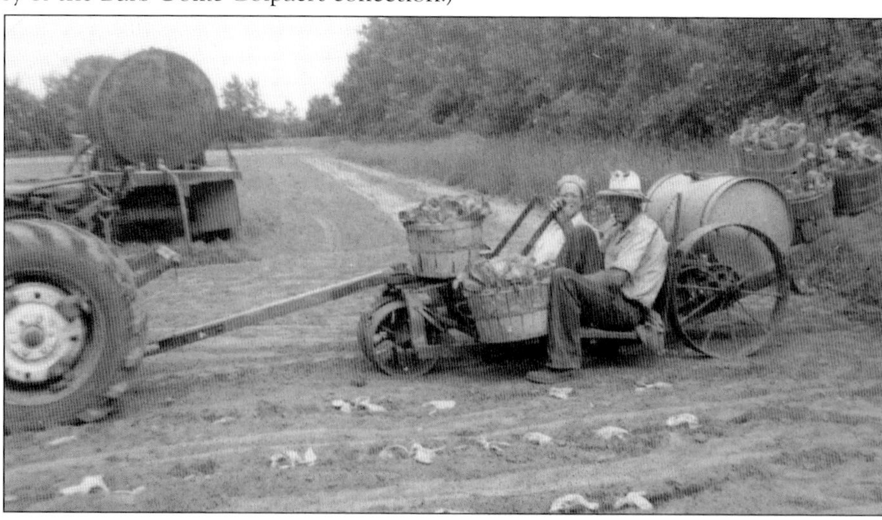

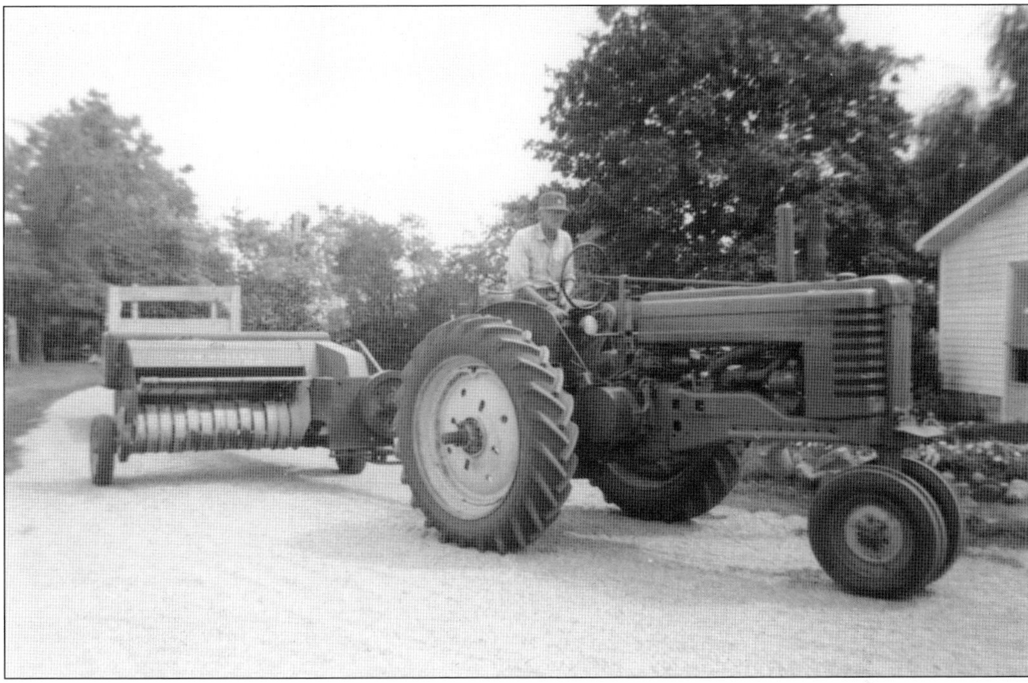

MODERN FARMING. Gus was always proud that he was the first farmer on 26 Mile to switch to rubber tractor tires from the steel lugs that compacted the soil and were unsafe. Here, Gus employs his tractor to pull the drag used to smooth out the ground. Below are August and Syble Goike on their 25th wedding anniversary in February 1967 at St. Isidore's Catholic Church in Macomb Township. (Both, courtesy of the Barb Goike Colpaert collection.)

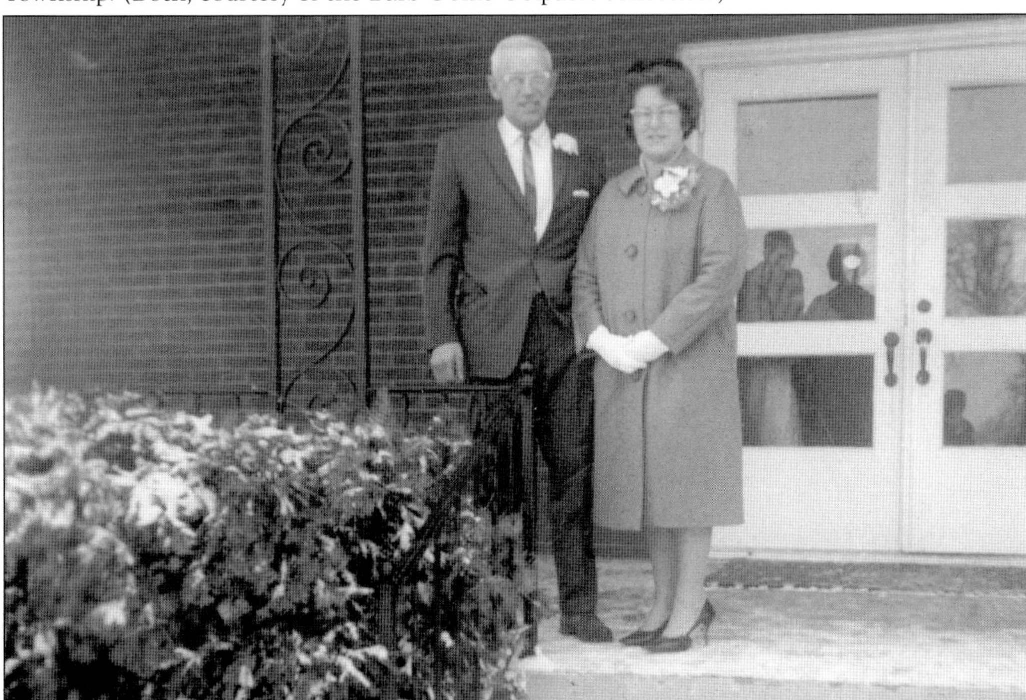

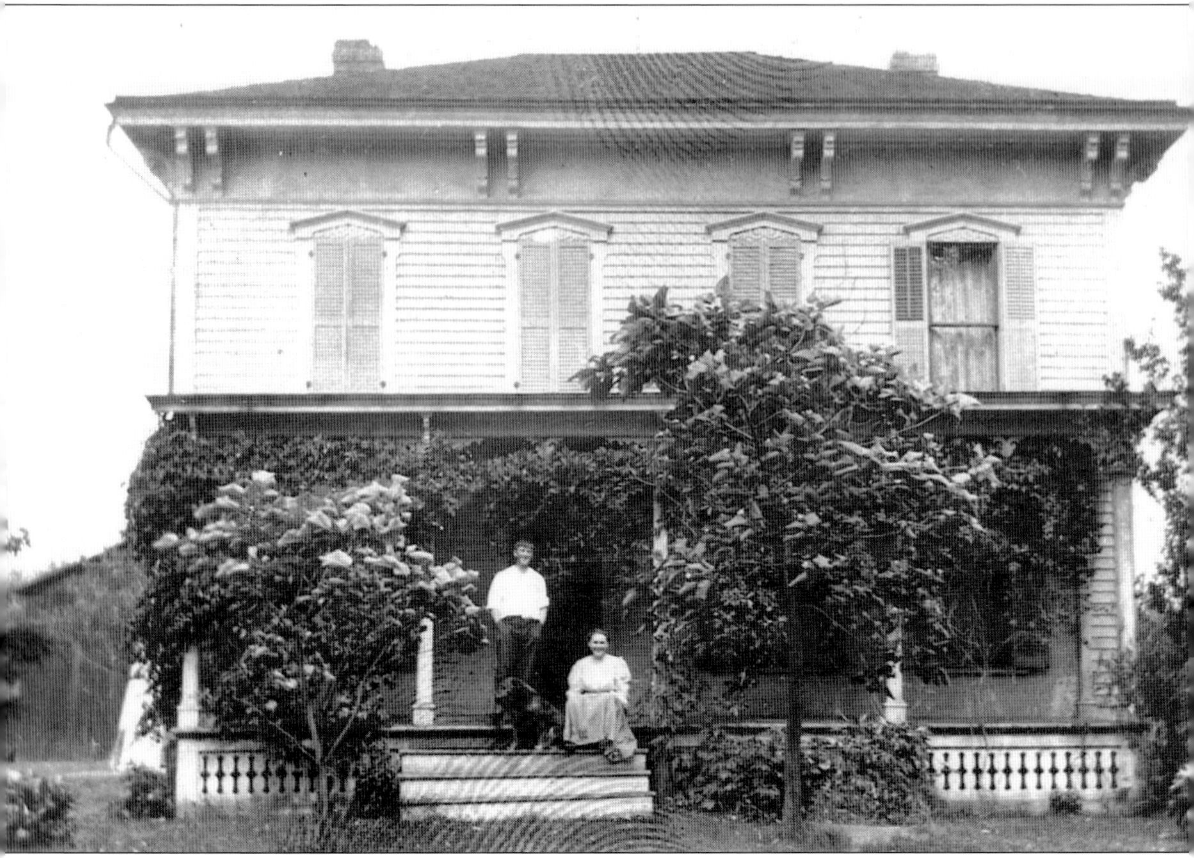

MOYERS FARM. David Thurston Jr. purchased 320 acres of land running from 29 Mile Road to 28 Mile Road on Mound Road in 1824. By 1850, Daniel and Eliza Thurston owned the property, and the decision was made to sell to their neighbors Henry and Adam Moyers for $4,000. The house the Moyers built on the land was considered to be the second oldest in the township. Located on the east side of Mound Road, south of 29 Mile Road, the front half of the home is believed to have been built between 1851 and 1857. The back half was constructed in the 1860s or 1870s. In 1891, the Henry Moyers estate sold the home to Joseph and Fredericka Slating for $4,500. In the years after that, the house has had a number of new owners and many restoration efforts through the present day. (Courtesy of the *Record*, Washington Township, and author.)

Five

Ray Township

The government survey of Ray Township was made in February 1817 by William Preston, deputy US surveyor. It was found to be level and densely timbered, and no lakes or hills were found, along with no marshes or wasteland; many small streams flowing southward gave a plentiful supply of water, and everything was there to make this a desirable place for a settlement. The first parcel of land sold in the township went to Reuben R. Smith on January 7, 1824. Only three others purchased land that year: Nathaniel Thompson, Josiah Lee, and Joseph Chubb, who purchased the entire 640 acres of section 22 between Broughton and Ray Center Roads and 28 and 29 Mile Roads. The buyers were mostly young men, and their intent was to build homes and work farms. At the time of its organization, the township included Armada and Lenox in its boundaries.

Many small, rapidly running streams in the town provided waterpower for saw- and gristmills, and in the earliest days, they were very successful. Dr. Neil Gray, of the firm Gray Bros., also ran mills in Washington, Bruce, and Oakland County. Another mill, owned and operated by Fred B. Wolcott, was located at Wolcott Road and Indian Trail. Wolcott was one of a number of unincorporated communities within Ray Township. Today, the Wolcott Mill Metropark, a 2,624-acre park, is located entirely within the township.

Davis, another community located at 27 Mile Road and Romeo Plank Road, found it difficult to choose between two prominent settlers of the area—John Gass and Jonathan E. Davis—to find its name. A general store, a hardware store, a saw- and feed mill owned by East Gass, and a Methodist church were located here. Ray Center was located at Hartway Road and 29 Mile Road, where the first school in the township was built from logs in 1834. Meade is located in the southeast portion of the township and is shared with its neighbor to the south, Macomb Township, at 26 Mile Road and North Avenue.

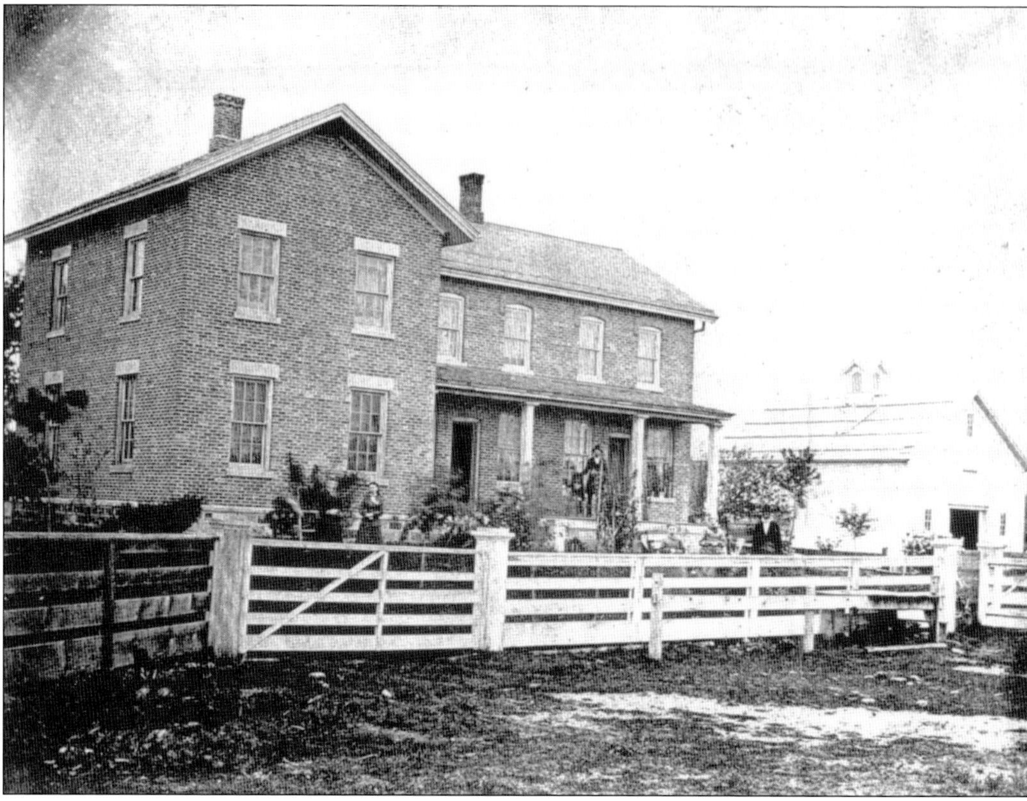

Gass Farm. George W. Gass (1813–1901) was the 9th of 14 children for parents John Gass and Rebecca McGregor. Born in New York, George came to Ray Township in 1836 and purchased 291 acres of land. In 1842, he married Rachel Johnson (1819–1903). They settled down on the farm and raised 10 children. Built in 1864 on their property at 19601 27 Mile Road, also known as Big Stone Road, in Ray Township, this home was demolished in October 2005. (Courtesy of the Friends of the Ray Township Library and the Judy Gass Lopus collection.)

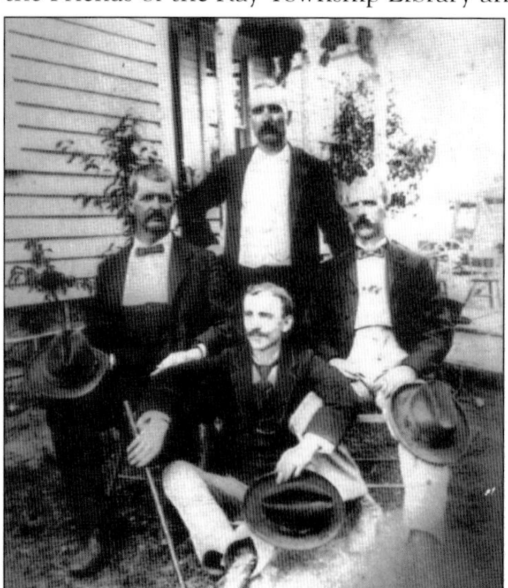

A Ripley's Story. Brothers South, East, and North, sons of James and Velora Dudley Gass, pose with their older first cousin West at a family reunion held just outside the village. This c. 1905 photograph shows the men who continued the family work as farmers in and around Ray Township. These unusual names got the relatives into a *Ripley's Believe It or Not* comic strip in the newspapers. Keeping with the tradition, East named his son South West Gass. (Courtesy of the Friends of the Ray Township Library collection and the Judy Gass Lopus collection.)

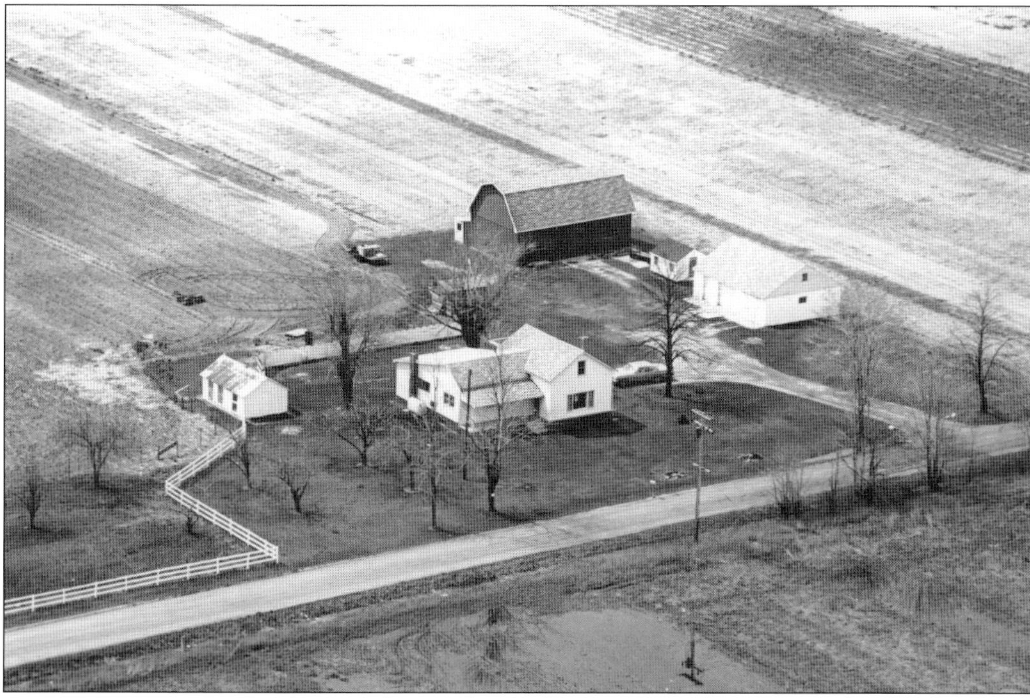

Corrion Farm. Julian Corrion (1908–2001) emigrated from Houthuist, Belgium, while his wife, Mary Duhan (1920–), emigrated from Winten, Austria, at 17 years old in 1937. They met in America, married in 1946, and raised one daughter. Their first farm was on Mulvey Road in Fraser. That property was sold to purchase the property on 31 Mile Road between North Avenue and Omo Road in Ray Township in 1957. While Julian worked at the General Motors Tech Center for a while, his love was always farming. They grew tomatoes, peppers, radishes, broccoli, and pumpkins and then made the trip down to Detroit's Eastern Market and Ferry Market to sell the produce. Well into his 80s, Julian sold his produce at the Armada Flea Market. (Both, courtesy of the Linda Corrion collection.)

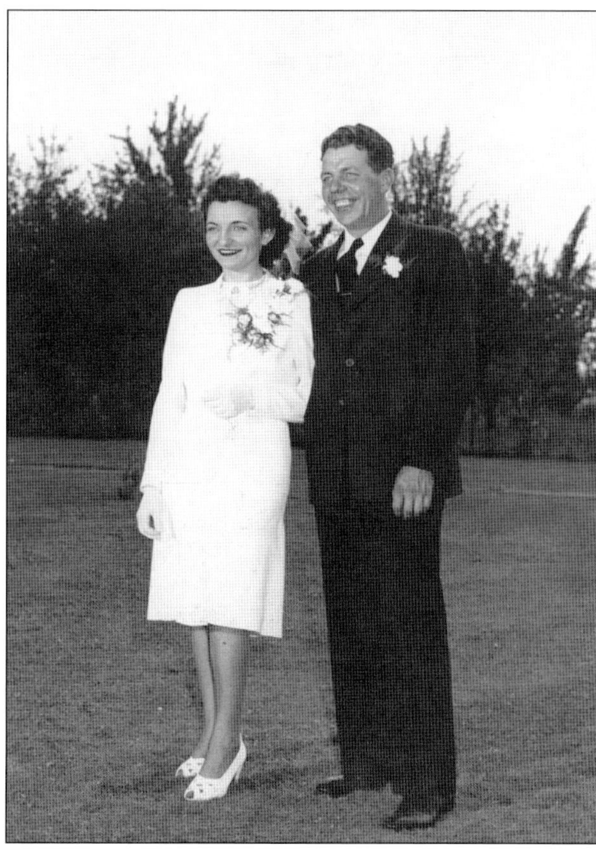

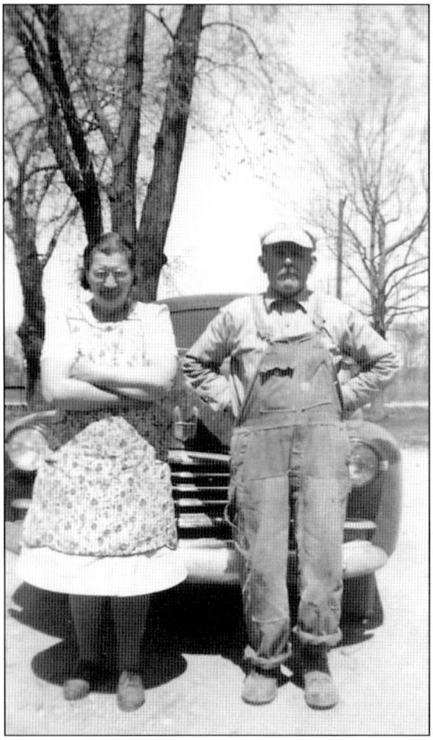

Kirsh Farm. In 1925, Carl (1885–1958) and Emma Kirsh (1896–1980) purchased the farm at 15390 27 Mile Road in Ray Township. They moved from Detroit to the farm in January 1926 with their three sons, Albert (1917–1966), George (1921–1980), and William (1925–2002). The farm consisted of dairy cows, chickens, grain crops, and vegetables. Pictured here around 1948 are Emma and Carl Kirsh on the farm. (Both, courtesy of the Kirsh family collection.)

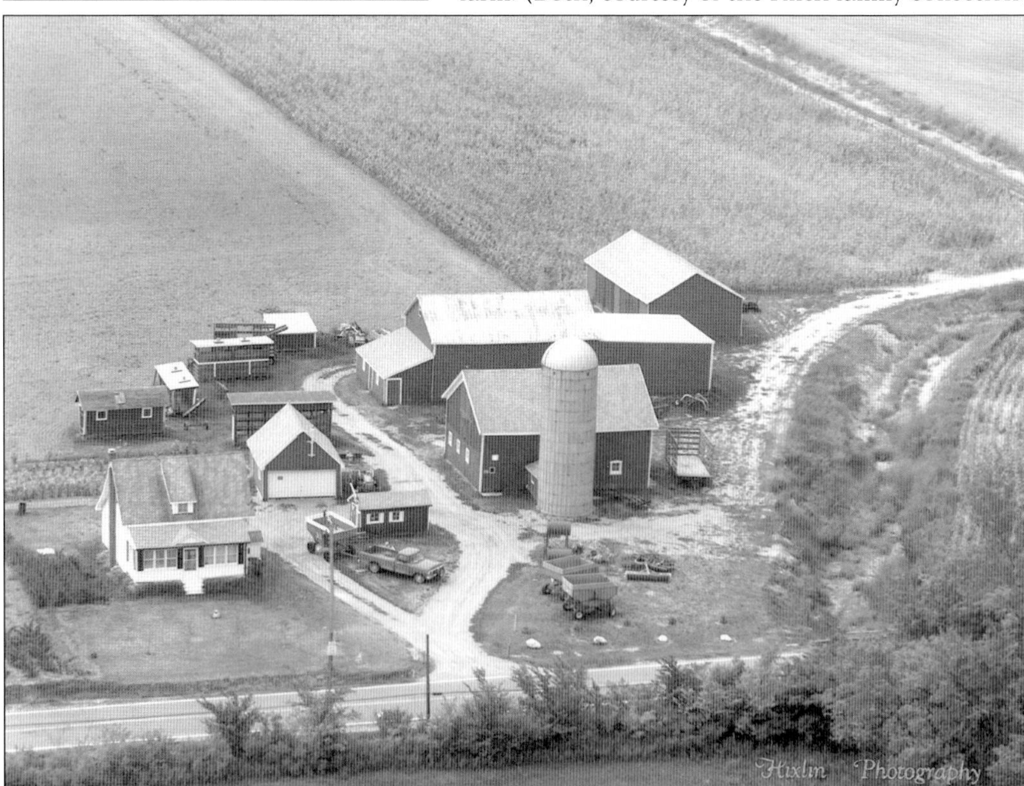

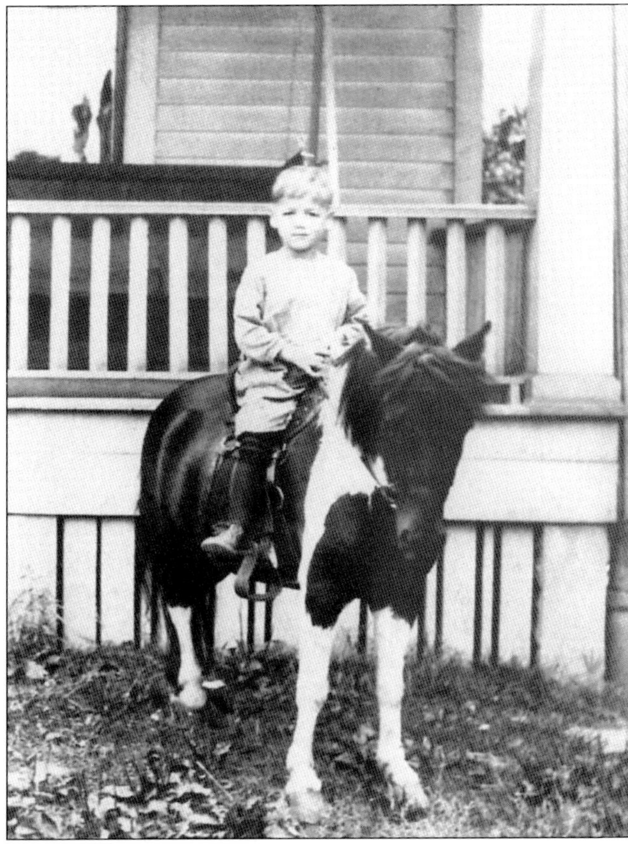

THE PATRIARCH LEARNS TO RIDE. George Kirsh is pictured on his horse at the Ray Township farm around 1928. His brother Albert moved to Mount Clemens after serving in World War II; George purchased the 102-acre property immediately west of father Carl's in neighboring Washington Township and started his own family. Brother William, after their father's death in 1958, took over the farm and lived with his mother until her death in 1980. William remained on the farm until his death in 2002. Today, Gary, George's son and farming partner, owns the 70-acre Ray Township farm with his two sons, Gary and Brian. Below, from left to right, Gavan, Gary Sr., Gabriella, Brian, and Gary Kirsh Jr. stand in front of their Morton barn on the Ray Township farm. (Both, courtesy of the Kirsh family collection.)

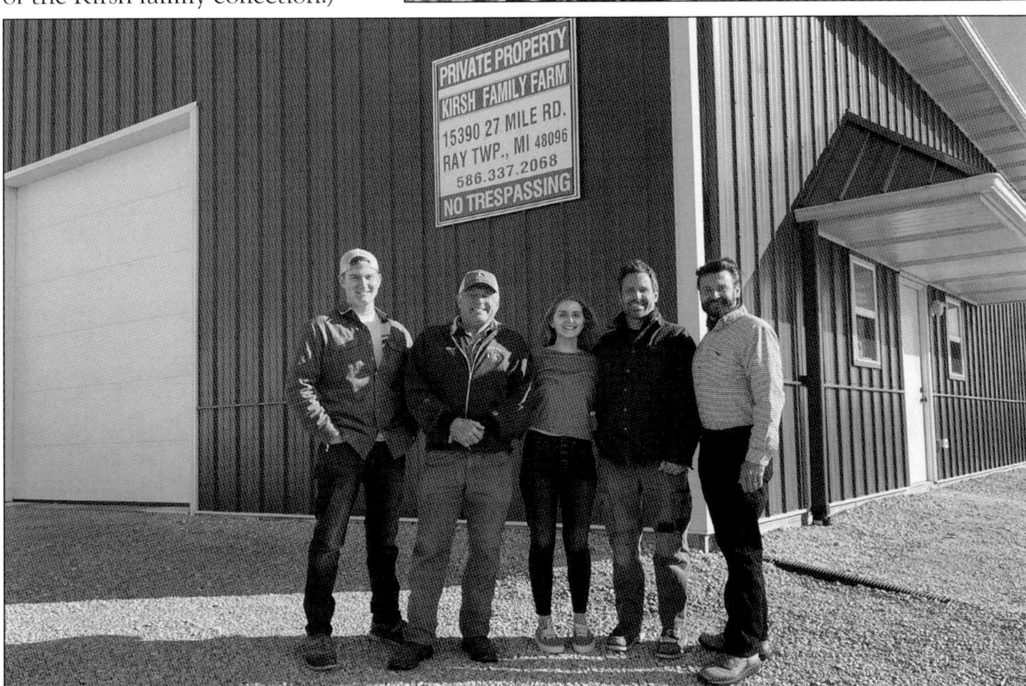

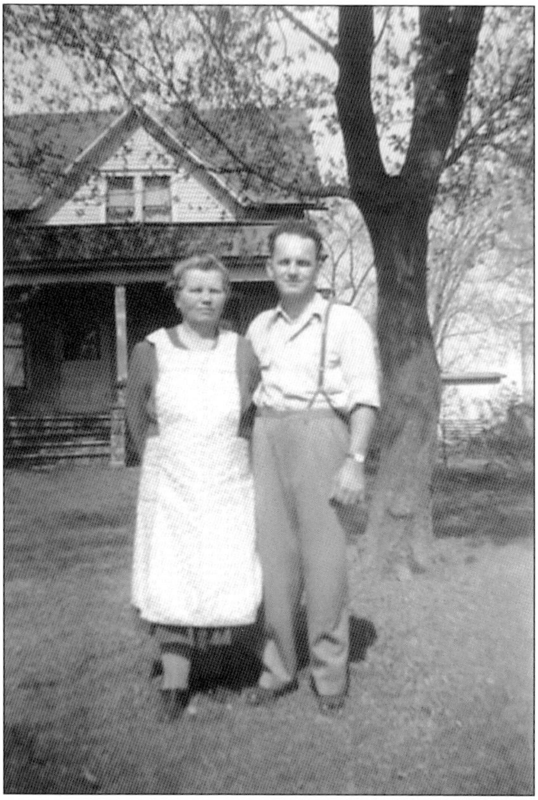

Anna Deman Farm. From the mid-1920s until the farm was auctioned off in mid-1959, Anna Chabada Deman and her six sons and two daughters worked the 125-acre farm at 62580 Indian Trail in Ray Township. With the house on 75 acres and 50 acres of pasture approximately a half-mile from the house, the family was kept busy. While living in Detroit, Anna purchased the farm because of the stream that ran behind the property. She was made aware that the water treatment might help one of her sons recover from his polio. Pictured here are Anna and her son Paul at the farm. Family members remembered the many trees that surrounded a couple of the sides of the farmhouse. (Both, courtesy of the Barbara Clark and Charles Olmstead family collections.)

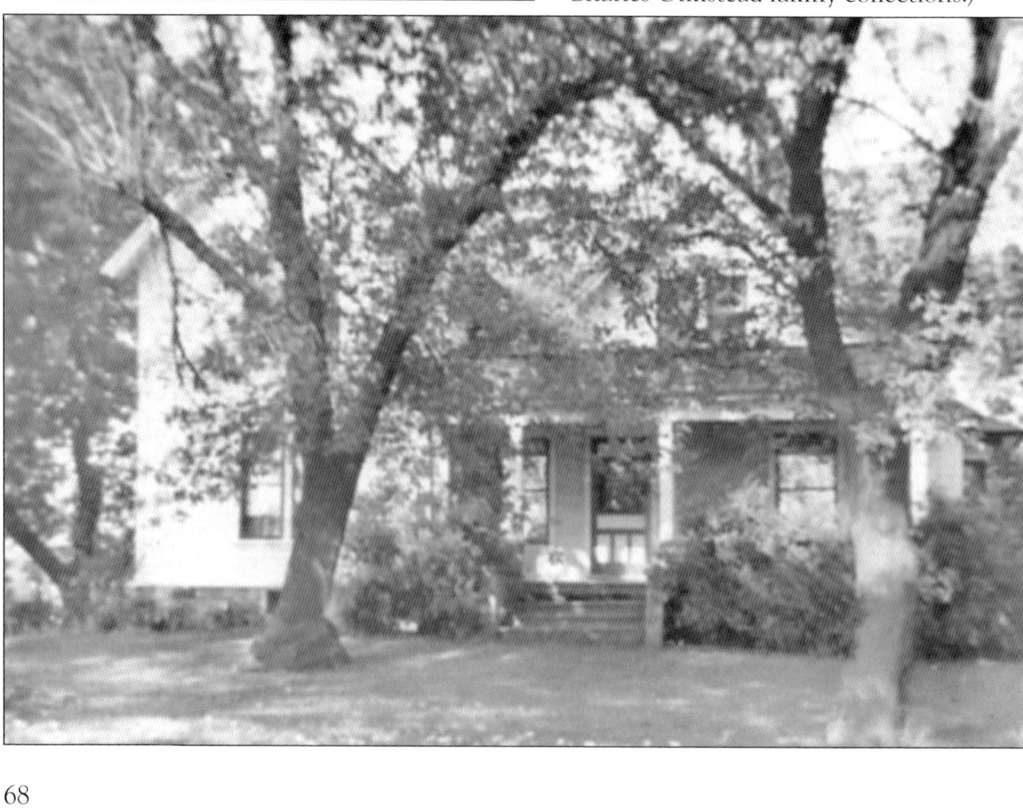

Detroit's Eastern Market. Every Saturday morning, the Demans were at the Eastern Market selling their produce of vegetables, sweet corn, and potatoes. The property was used to grow wheat, oats, hay, and feed corn. To the right, Daniel Deman stands next to the corn crop. Below are Anna and her children, from left to right, (sitting) Paul, Yvonne, Anna Deman, Anne, and John; (standing) Harold, Henry, James, and Don. Anna lost two of her children as infants during the flu epidemic after World War I. (Both, courtesy of the Barbara Clark and Charles Olmstead family collections.)

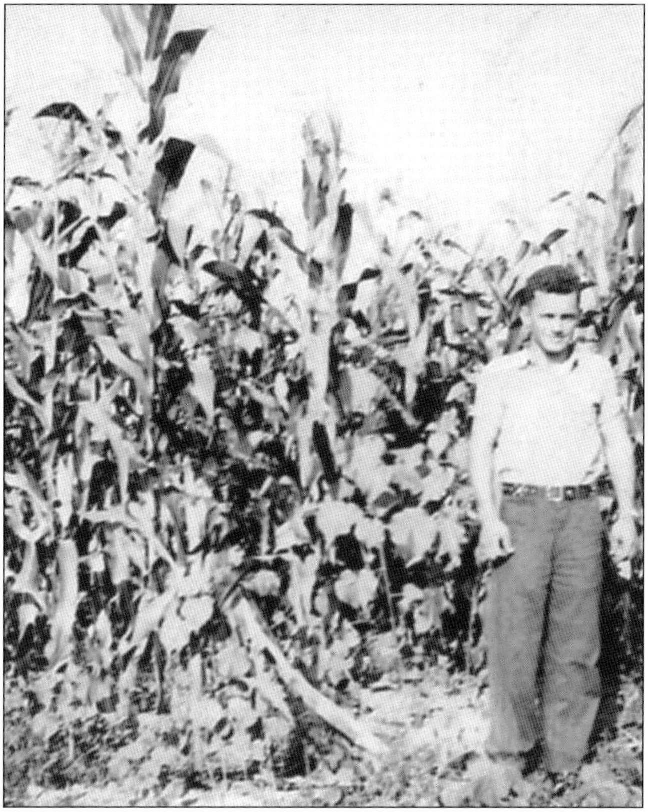

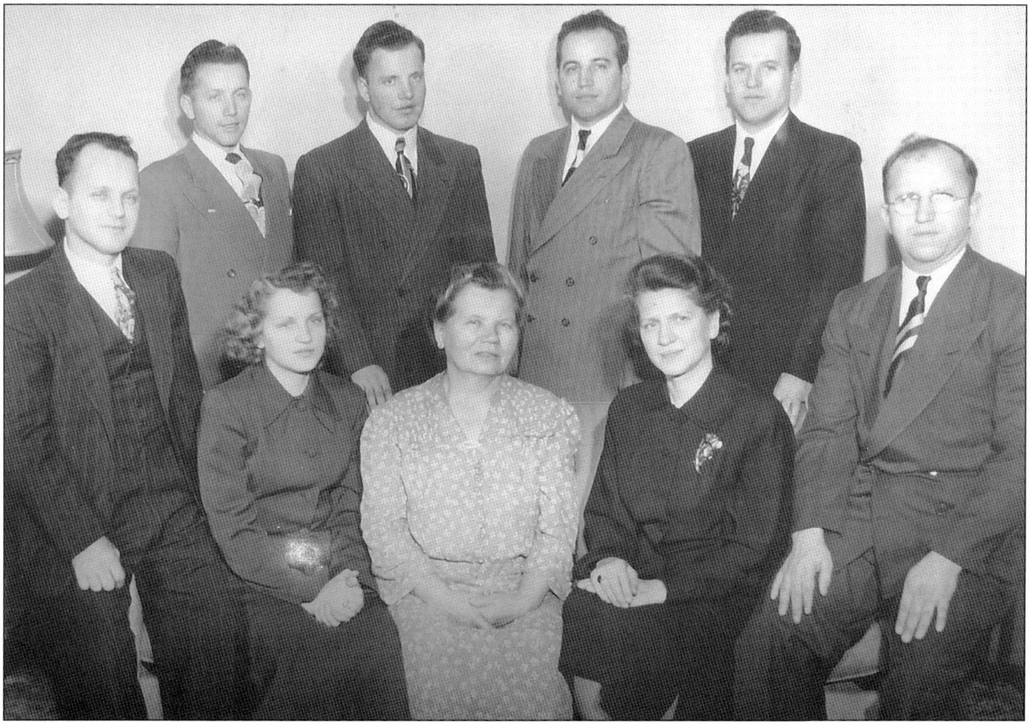

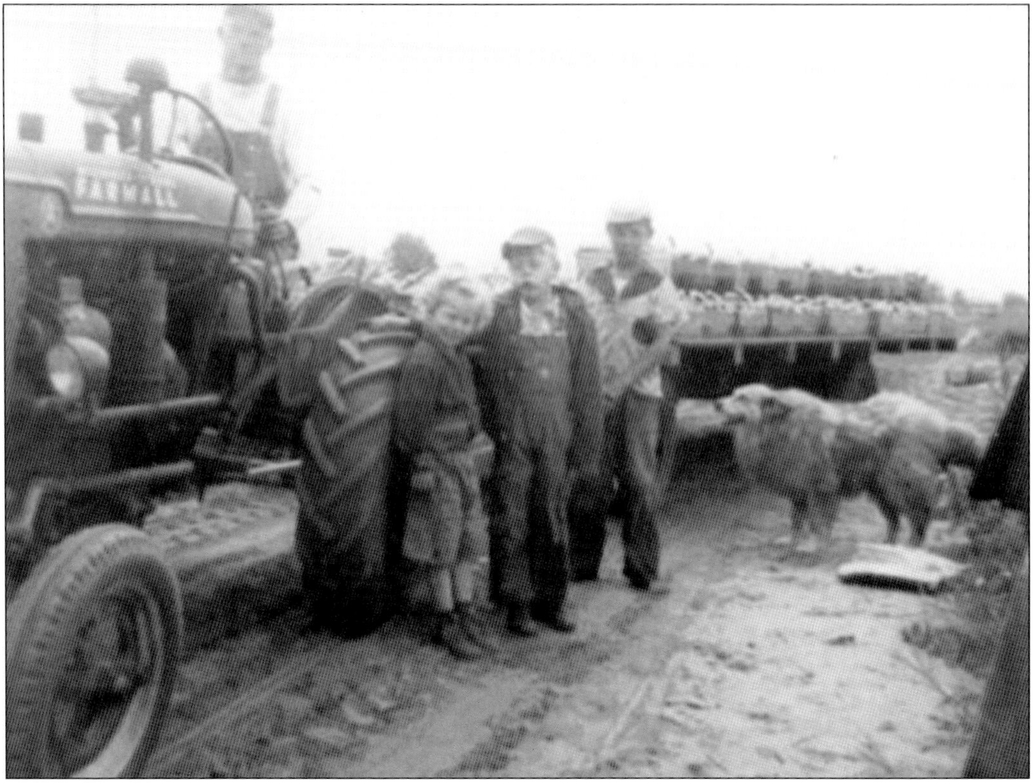

SCHOENHERR FARM. Schoenherr Farms was established in 1976 when Cecil took over his father Louis Schoenherr's farm on 24 Mile Road in Macomb Township after his father's death. He moved everything to Ray Township on 29 Mile Road, where they worked 1,500 acres in various areas but predominately in Ray Township. Pictured here around 1950 are William "Willie" Colpaert (on tractor); (standing, from left to right) Mary Ann Colpaert Schoenherr (the future wife of Cecil); Lawrence Colpaert, an unidentified boy, and Sandy the dog. The image below gives a glimpse of daily life on the farm. (Above, courtesy of the Schoenherr family collection; below, courtesy of the Barbara Colpaert collection.)

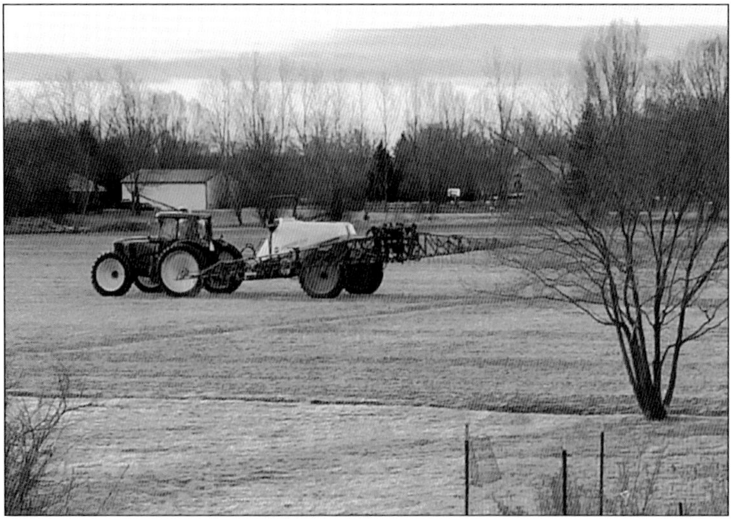

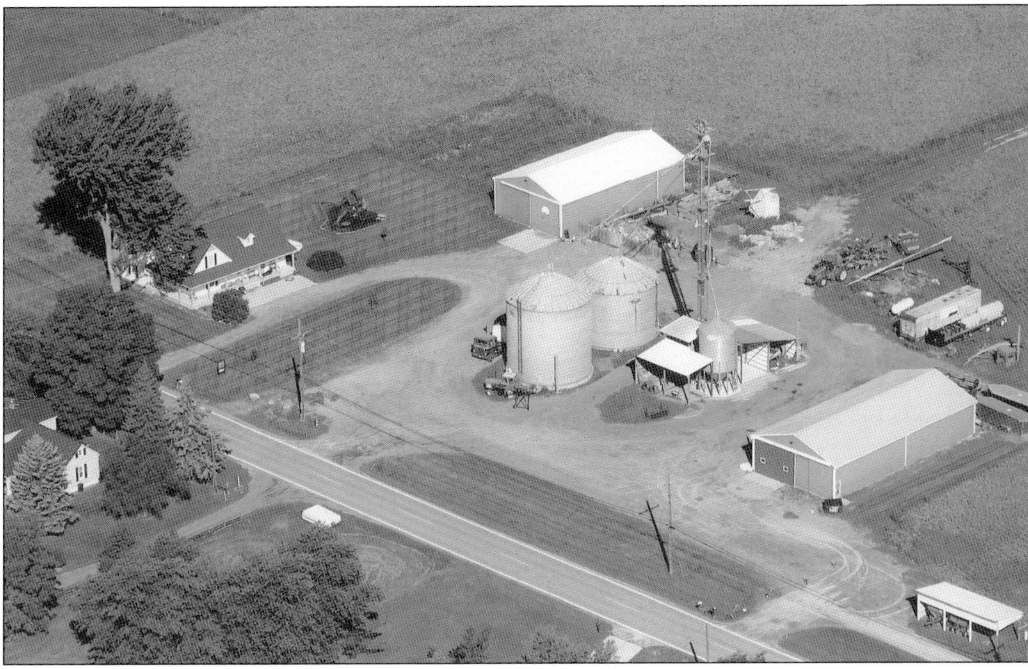

FIFTH GENERATION. Cecil's son Steve is a partner in the farming business and the fourth generation of Schoenherrs to learn and live the farming business. Over the years, the farm has transitioned from dairy farming to vegetables and grain crops, currently producing nearly 100,000 bushels of various grains, wheat, soybeans, oats, and corn. Below are Reed Schoenherr (left, 8 years old)and his sister Violet (right, 10 years old), the fifth generation to be involved in Schoenherr Farms. (Both, courtesy of the Schoenherr family collection.)

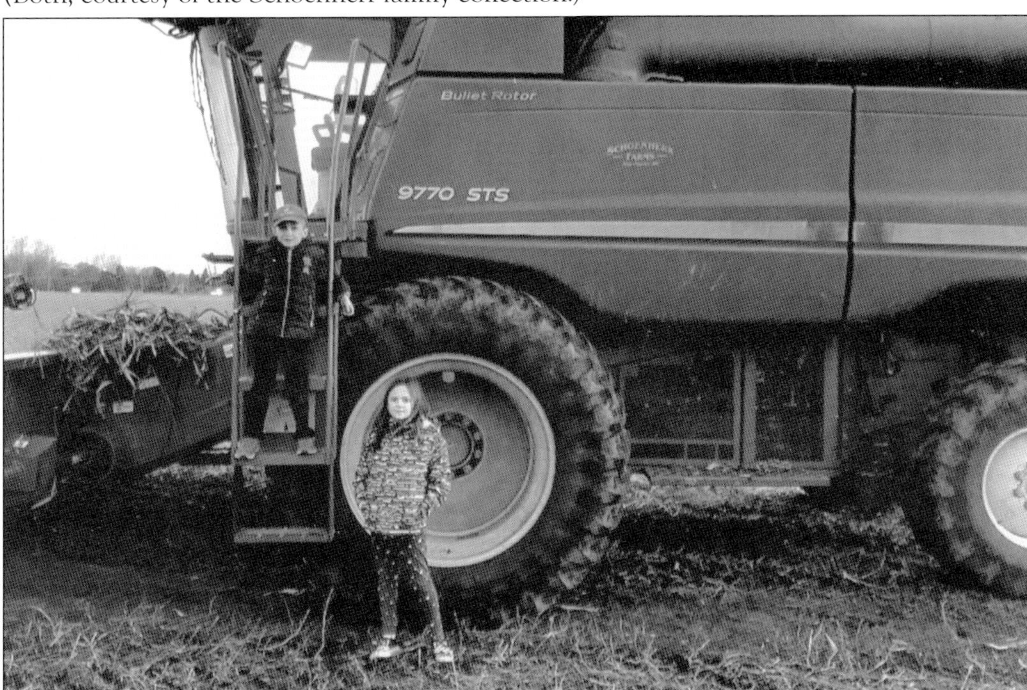

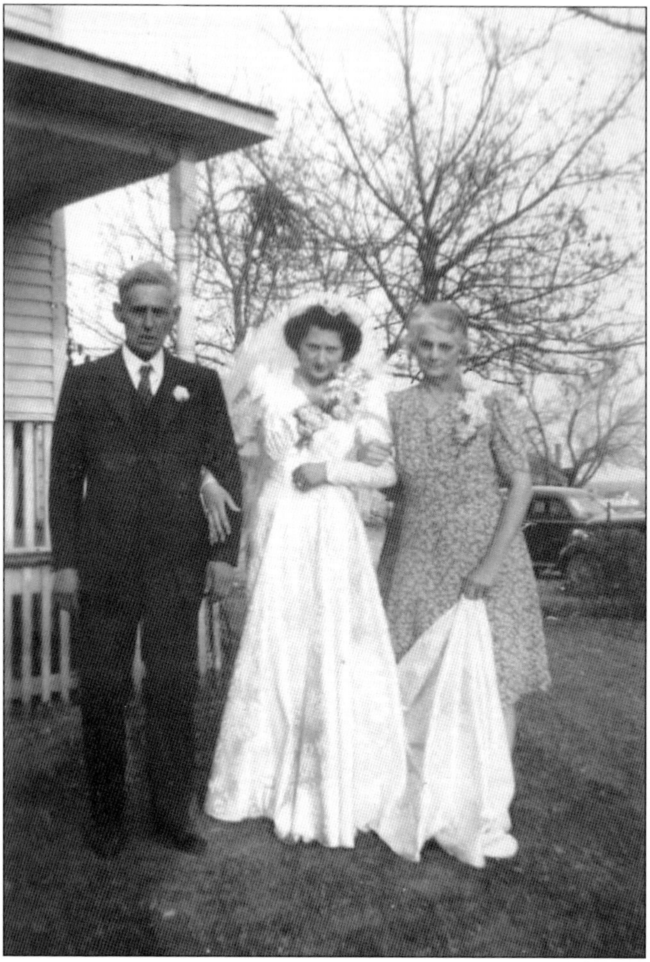

BALLOR ACRES. Frederick Ballor (1883–1966) married Anna Mouilleseaux (1887–1973) at Sacred Heart Church in Roseville in 1910. They raised 12 children on the 80-acre farm called Ballor Acres in Ray Township. Pictured here are Fred and Anna with their daughter Margaret on her wedding day in 1943, with the farmhouse in the background. Hay, wheat, and thrashing for other local farms was their usual source of income. (Both, courtesy of the Julie Dosenberger collection.)

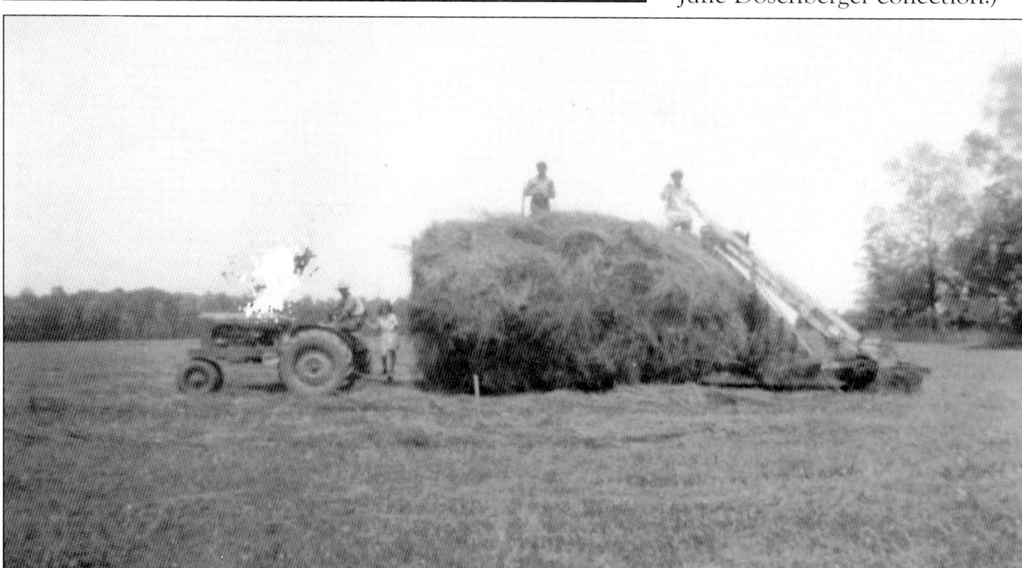

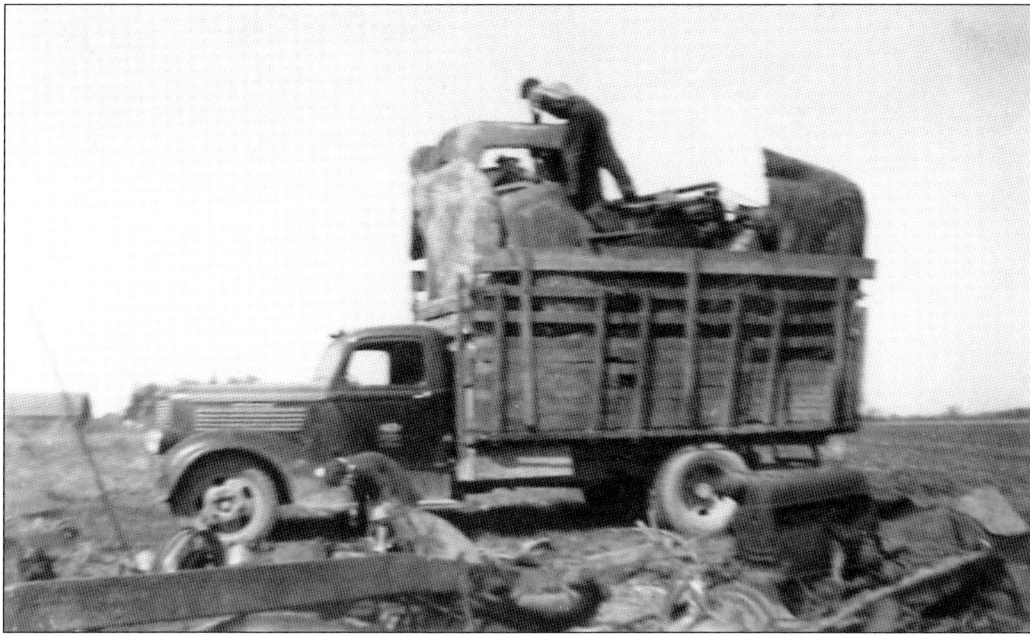

Helping the War Effort. Pictured here are Fred and his sons loading up a truck with scrap car parts. Scrap metal became very important to the war effort during World War II. Fred's son Joe, when done with scrapping in the area, went on to start repairing cars and started Joe Ballor Towing in New Haven. Pictured below is the family home on the Ray Township farm. (Both, courtesy of the Julie Dosenberger collection.)

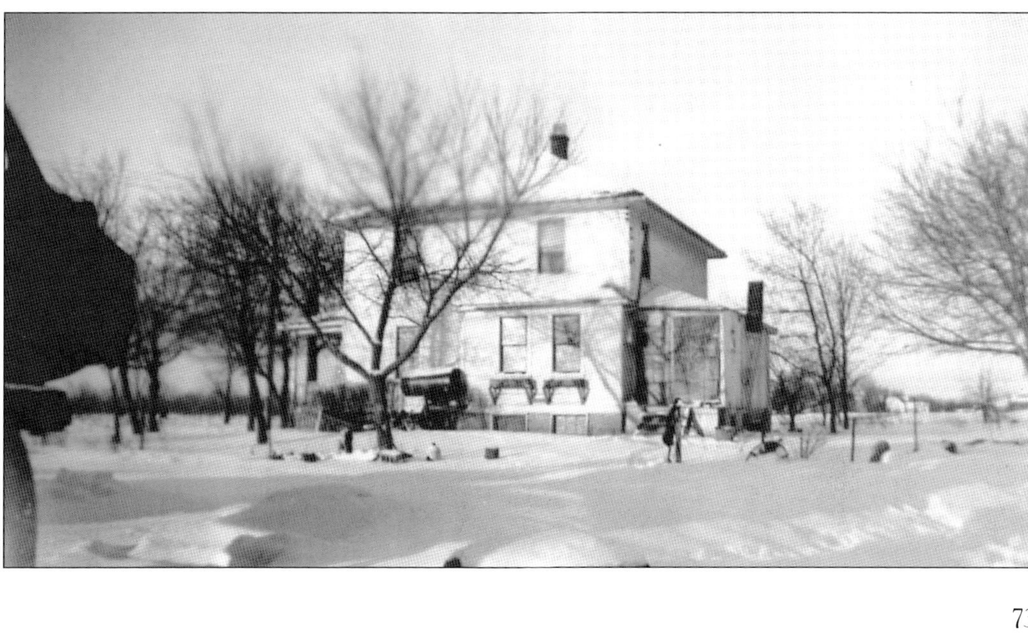

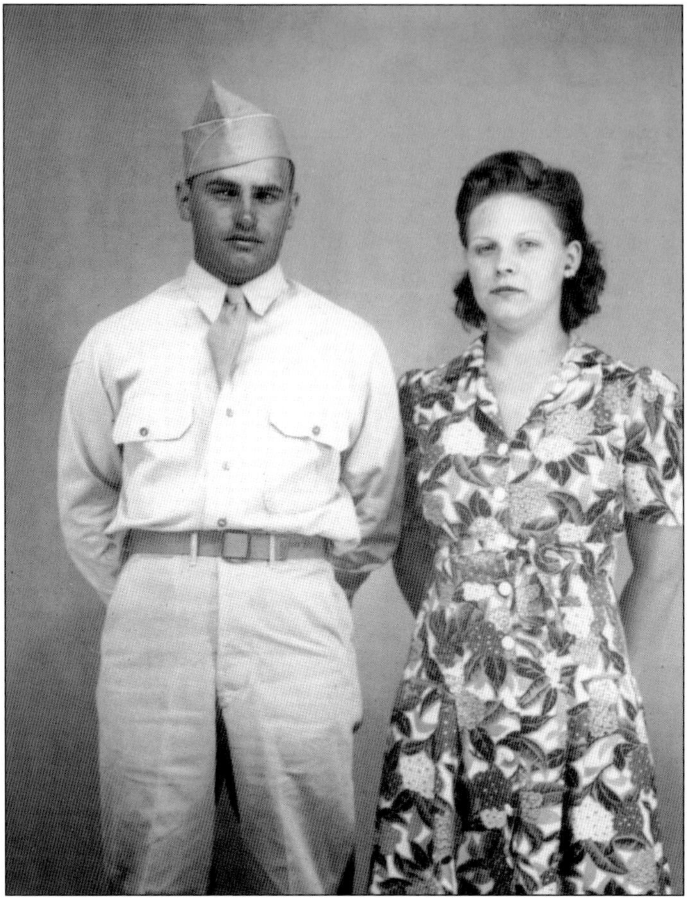

Sherman Youngblood Farm. Carrell T. Sherman (1919–1995) married his wife, Helen (1920–2003), in 1940. Carrell worked for the Ford Motor Company, where he was featured in the *Detroit News* photograph and article "These Are the Arms that Count." He was soon serving in Italy during his time in the US Army in World War II. When Carrell returned home, he and Helen purchased a 50-acre property in Ray Township. Carrell added cattle and raised many calves that became part of their dairy herd. The couple's daughter, Betty, was born in 1945. Carrell did custom bailing of hay and straw for other farmers all over Macomb County. Pictured here are Helen and Carrell during his time in the Army. Pictured below is part of the cattle herd in front of the barn. (Both, courtesy of the Betty Youngblood collection.)

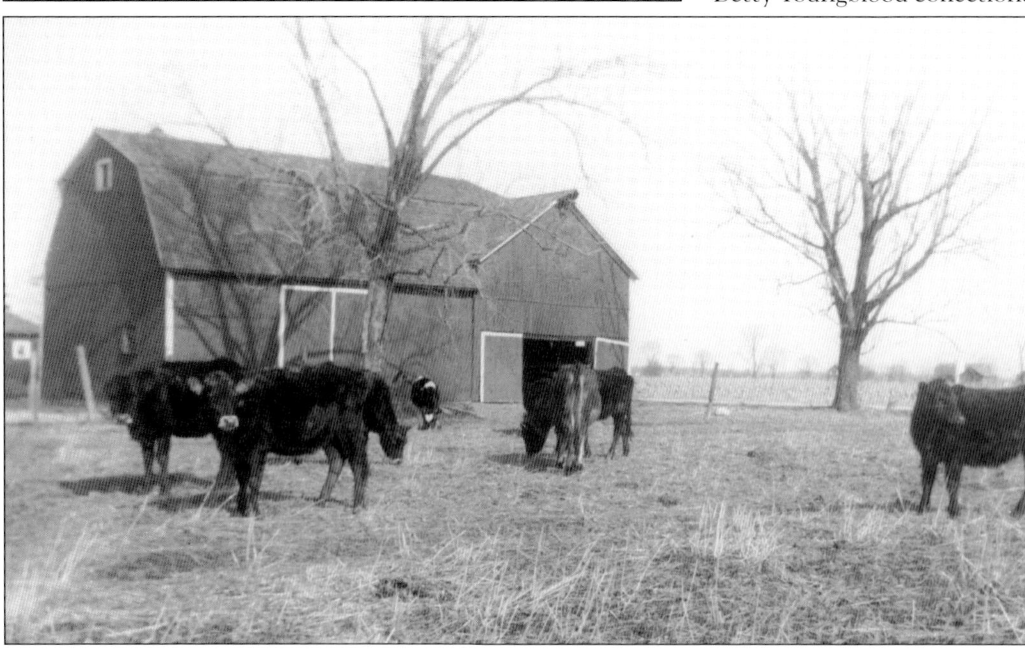

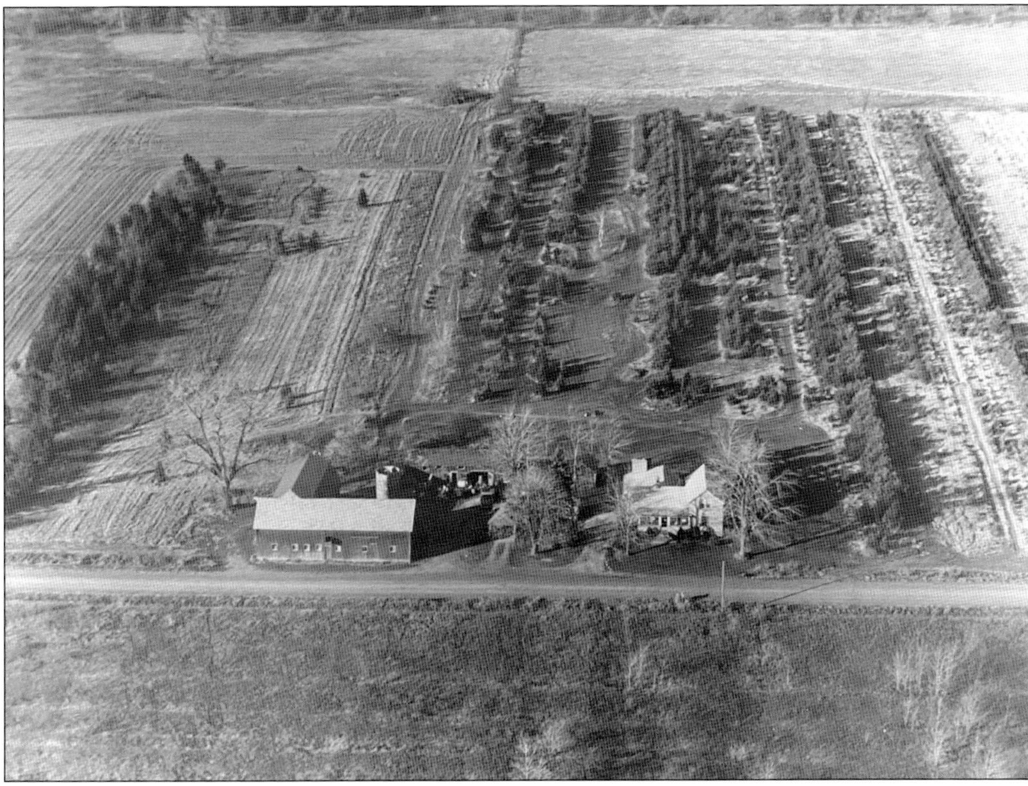

Nursery Operations. In the 1950s, Carrell Sherman started a tree nursery operation on part of the farm; it included primarily Colorado blue spruce but also Norway and Black Hills spruce. The farm also cultivated varieties of other trees and shrubs on the property. For many years, Carrell sold these trees to area residents, digging and moving the trees to numerous locations. Many trees were sold live or cut and as Christmas trees, and branches were used to make grave blankets and wreaths. In 1965, Carrell joined the Juvenile Division of the Macomb County Probate Court, working in what was called the "Youth Home." He started a program teaching young people about farming and selling their produce. In 1976, he was named Child Care Worker of the Year, and he was to receive many awards over the years until his retirement. Pictured below is Carrell Sherman with his grandson David. (Both, courtesy of the Betty Youngblood collection.)

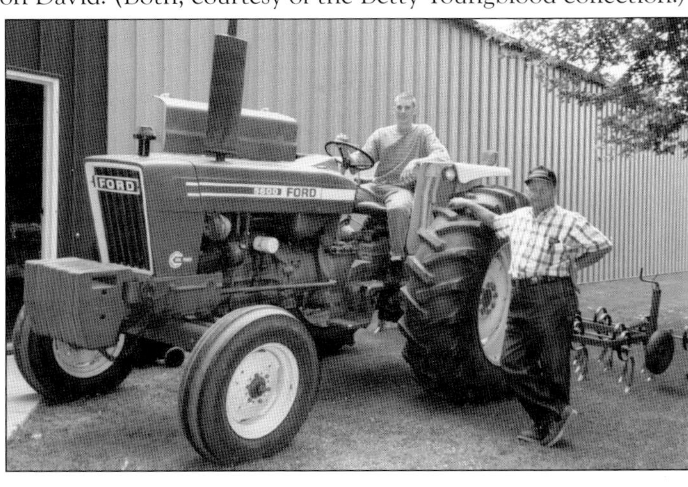

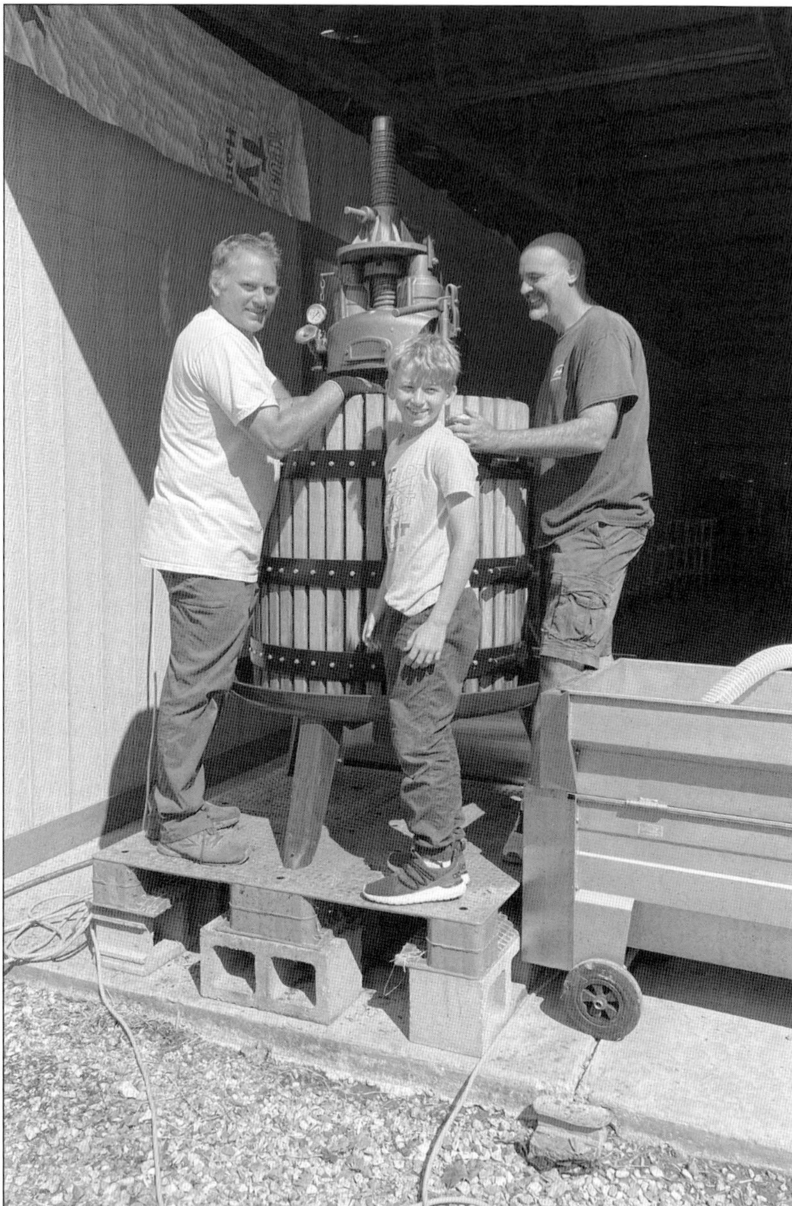

The Start of the Vineyard. The Sherman farm in Ray Township has now become the home of Youngblood Vineyard, metro Detroit's only commercial vineyard. The Youngblood name came when Carrell Sherman's daughter, Betty, married Ralph Youngblood. Betty had grown up as an only child, working alongside her father, cultivating the trees, working with the cattle, and doing any farming chore that was needed. Betty's husband, Ralph, passed away in 2006. Their son Dave and his wife, Jessica, are the owners of this vineyard. In 2016, the Youngbloods traded in their fields of soybeans, corn, and Christmas trees and planted wine grapes on the family farm. Betty, who continues to live in one of the two homes at the vineyard, still helps where she can, and Dave, Jessica, and their three children live in the other home and continue with the farm's transformation. Pictured here from left to right are Dave, son Wyatt, and unidentified. (Courtesy of the Betty Youngblood collection.)

Six

Lenox Township

The organization of the township in 1837 took place in the home of Sterling Case. At the time, it was proposed that a name be selected and that the three oldest men in the township should be the ones to select the name. Benjamin Haight, Mason Harris, and Israel Dryer each selected a name. But as the choices made by Haight and Harris had already been used in other townships in the state, Dryer's name of Lenox was chosen.

The governmental land was all purchased between 1836 and 1838, with the exception of Phineas D. Pelton from New York, who made the earliest selection on June 4, 1831. The principal stream in Lenox is the Salt River, which runs due south through the eastern part of the township, giving motive power for several mills along its path. There is also Deer Creek, which helped for agricultural purposes. The original settlers of the township were hardworking and inventive people with names such as Abner Stevens, Richard D. Bailey, Lance Flowers, Ebenezer Brooks, John Church, Apolas A. Fublar, and Owen Sheridan. The early settlers had a flourishing town library that was well read for many years. The first schoolhouse, built by David Burt in 1851, was 16 by 17 feet in size and cost $67. It burned down in 1860, and a new framed building was erected in 1861, but this time, it cost $650.

The village of Lenox Station went on to become a part of the neighboring township of Richmond. The other village in the township is New Haven. It was situated on the Grand Trunk Railroad, and for a while, it was known as New Baltimore Station when it was built in 1865. The village was organized in 1869, and the name of the depot changed to New Haven Depot. New Haven had an electric light plant, a bank, grain elevator, creamery, roller mill, and numerous denominations of churches, as well as a hotel mainly known as the Graustark Hotel. New Haven was the shipping point for Meade and Ray Center in Ray Township and Omo, a settlement in Lenox.

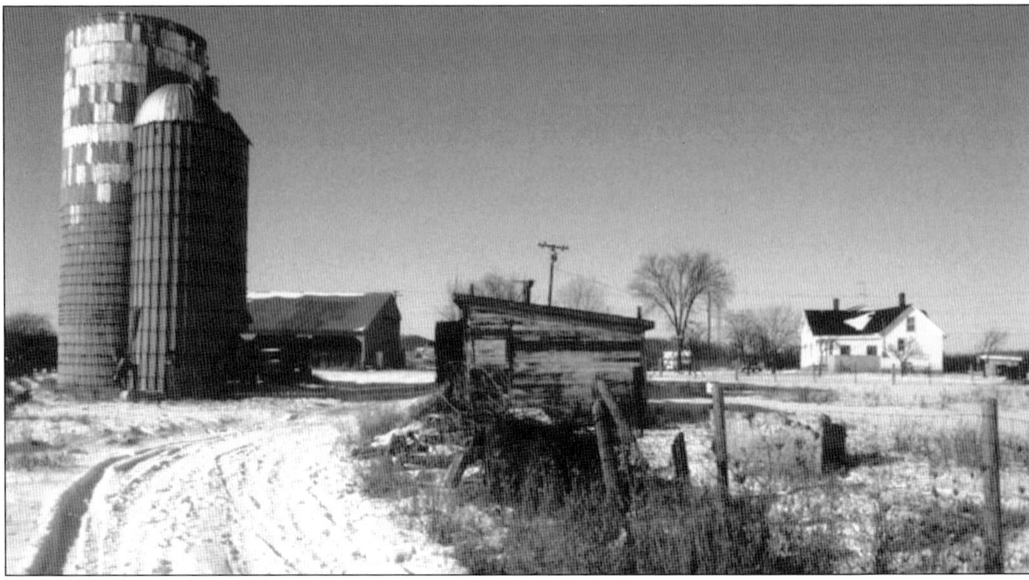

Battestilli Farm. In 1953, Ray and Fran Battestilli purchased 124 acres of property at 60114 Gratiot Avenue in New Haven, where they raised five children. There was no basement and no upstairs, but with three bedrooms and a small added family room, this was their family home by the 1970s. This c. 1969 image shows the property where the farm produced beef cattle, corn, wheat, and hay. Chickens and beef and a large family garden put fresh food on the table. Below, in 1974, Ray Battestilli picks his last crop of corn on his beloved Oliver 77 tractor, which he purchased new in 1953. Ray called his tractor "my Cadillac," as it represented a major purchase for the farm. Ray passed away in 1976. (Both, courtesy of Ray Battestilli family collection.)

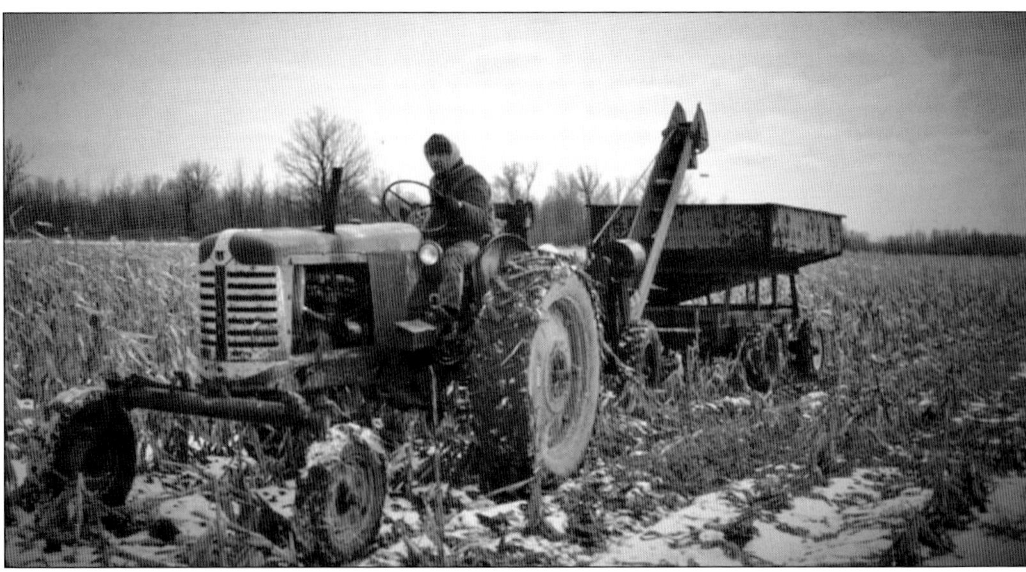

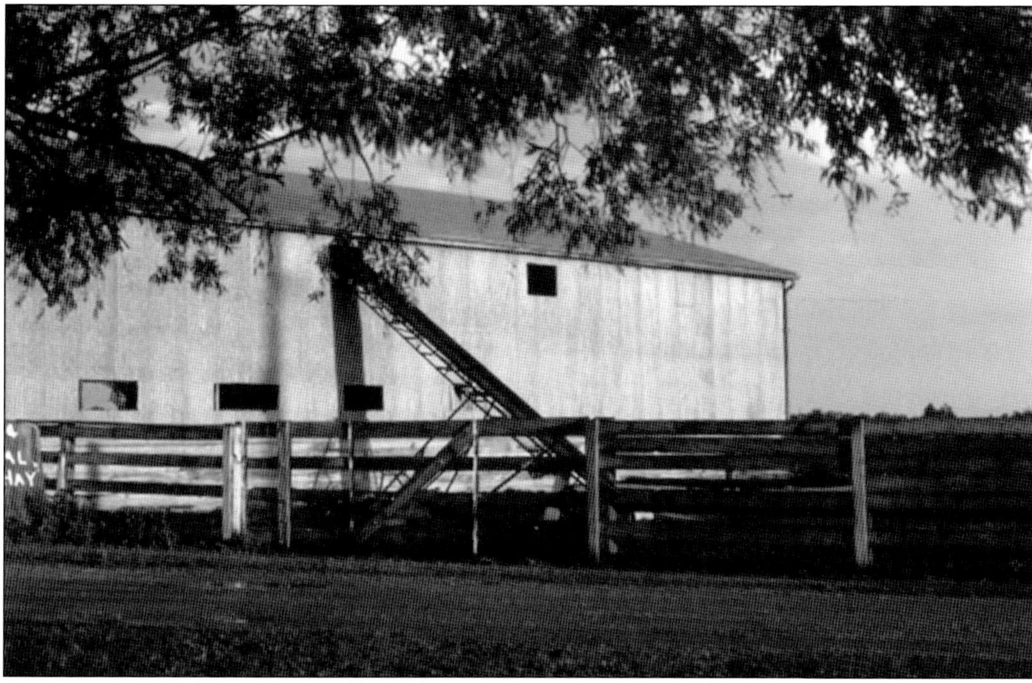

MICHIGAN STATE GRAND CHAMPION. After losing the original classic barn to a fire in the early 1960s, this new-style pole barn replaced it and was used to raise Hereford and Angus steers and occasional hogs. In 1962, the Michigan State Grand Champion Black Angus steer was raised at the Battestilli farm. Below, around 1969, Susan Battestilli proudly shows her winning 4-H steer at the Armada Fair. The Armada Fair was looked forward to with great anticipation, as it signaled an end to the summer harvest. (Both, courtesy of the Roy Battestilli family collection.)

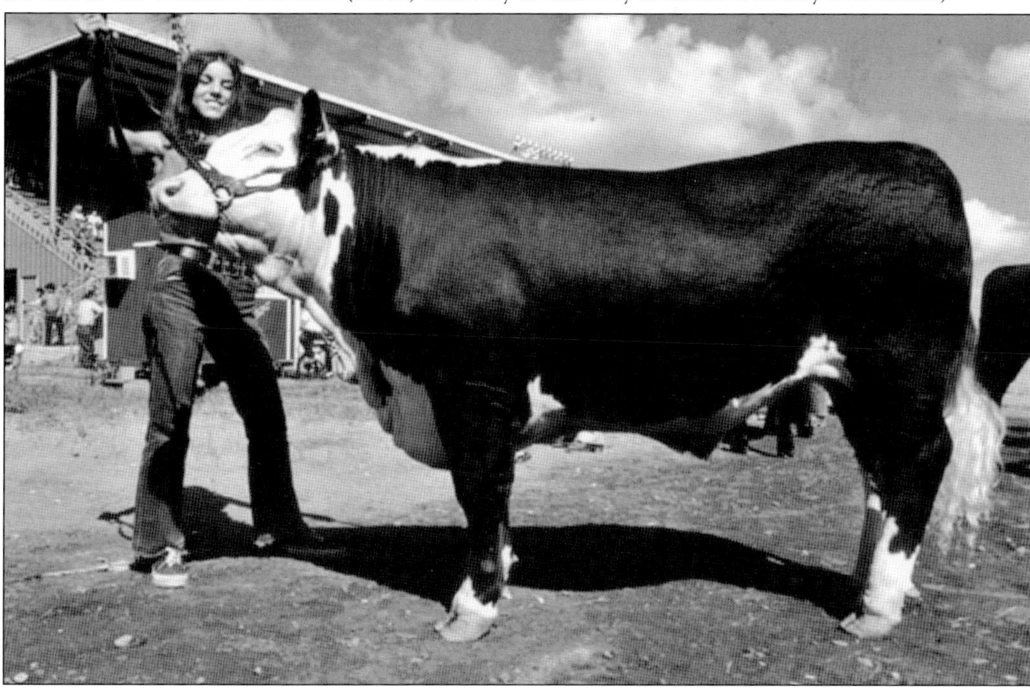

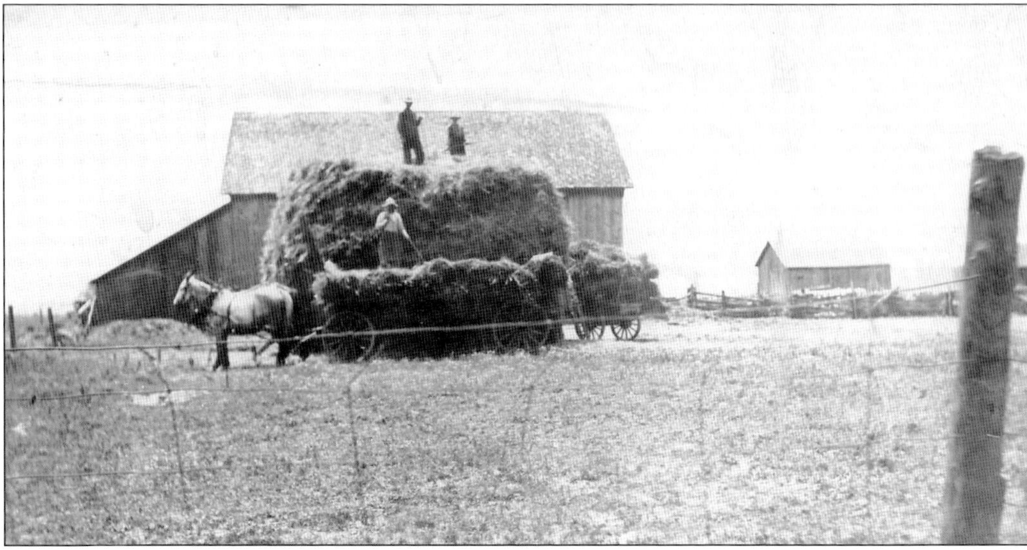

Sullivan Farm. In 1855, John Sullivan purchased 80 acres of property on 29 Mile Road in Lenox Township after his emigration from Ireland. He left the farm to his daughter Mary Sullivan; she married Daniel Sullivan around 1880, preserving the family name. As pictured here, sheep farming and growing hay, corn, wheat, and beans were the main trades of the Sullivan farm. Pictured below is the Sullivan family around 1905; from left to right are (first row) Mary Sullivan, Bridget Sullivan, Daniel Sullivan (owner of the homestead), Fred Sullivan, Thomas Sullivan, and Joe Fitzgerald; (second row) Humphrey Sullivan, Frank Sullivan, Leo Sullivan, Will Sullivan, Mary Sullivan, Hugh Donley, Ann Sullivan, and Jim Sullivan. (Both, courtesy of the Michael Sullivan family collection.)

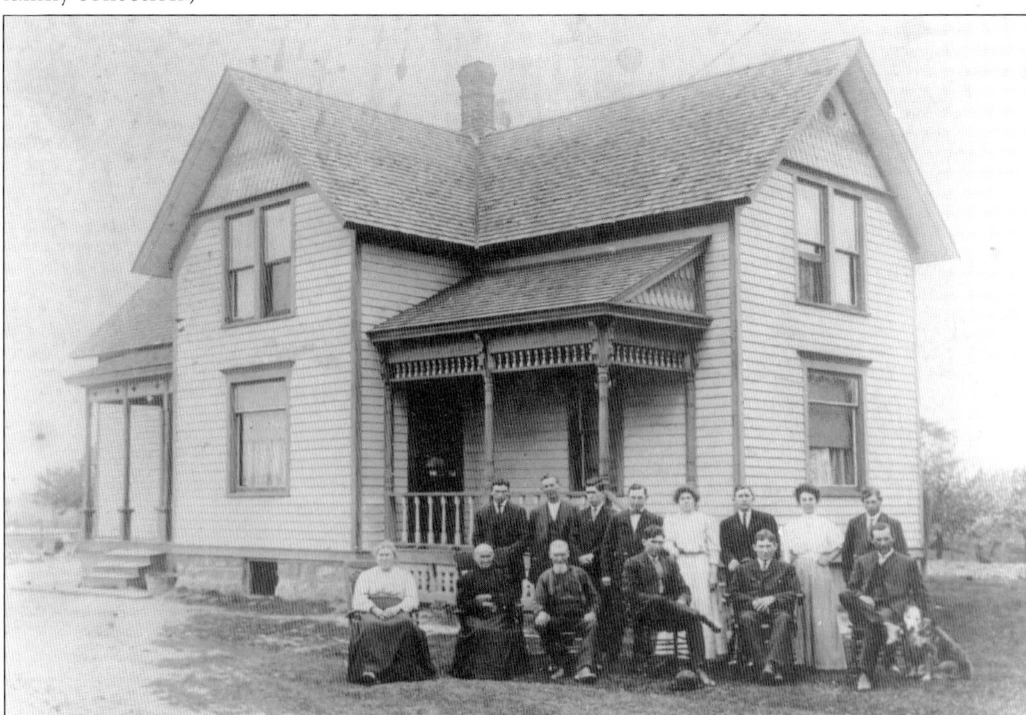

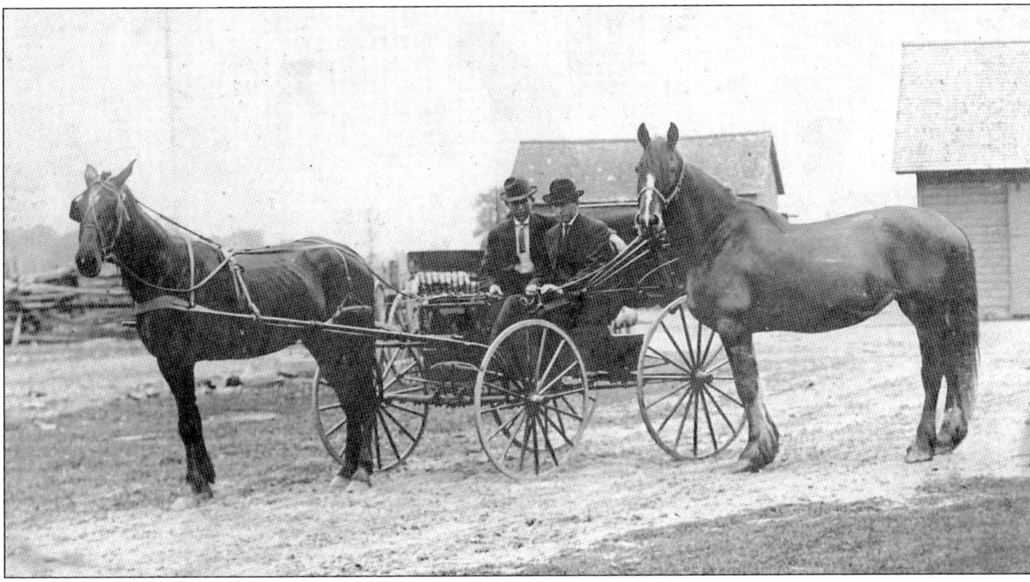

Attendees at a Party. Daniel and Mary Sullivan's sons Tom (left) and Humphrey are pictured in the buggy outside at the farm. Son Leo passed away while serving in World War I in Chateau Thierry, France, in 1918. Tom passed away after an accident while at a bar with friends due to a burning lantern. Below is a birthday party for one of the Fitzgerald girls. Among the party attendees are, from left to right, (first row) Mike Riedel, Fred Sullivan, Margaret Thelen, Mary Donley, Hugh Donley, and Ruth Fitzgerald; (second row) Irving Kelley, Elizabeth Howe, Mary Sullivan, Grace Fitzgerald, Louise Winkel, Susie Thelen, Anna Thelen, and Maude Nolan; (third row) Wilfred Thelen, Will Seiferd, Mike Gramer, Frank Sullivan, Leo Sullivan, John Thelen, John Newman, Mike Winkler, Joe Riedel, Tom Sullivan, Lou Thelen, Joe Fitzgerald, Mike Thelen, Ray Thelen, George Riedel, Leo Thelen, and Humphrey Sullivan. (Both, courtesy of the Michael Sullivan family collection.)

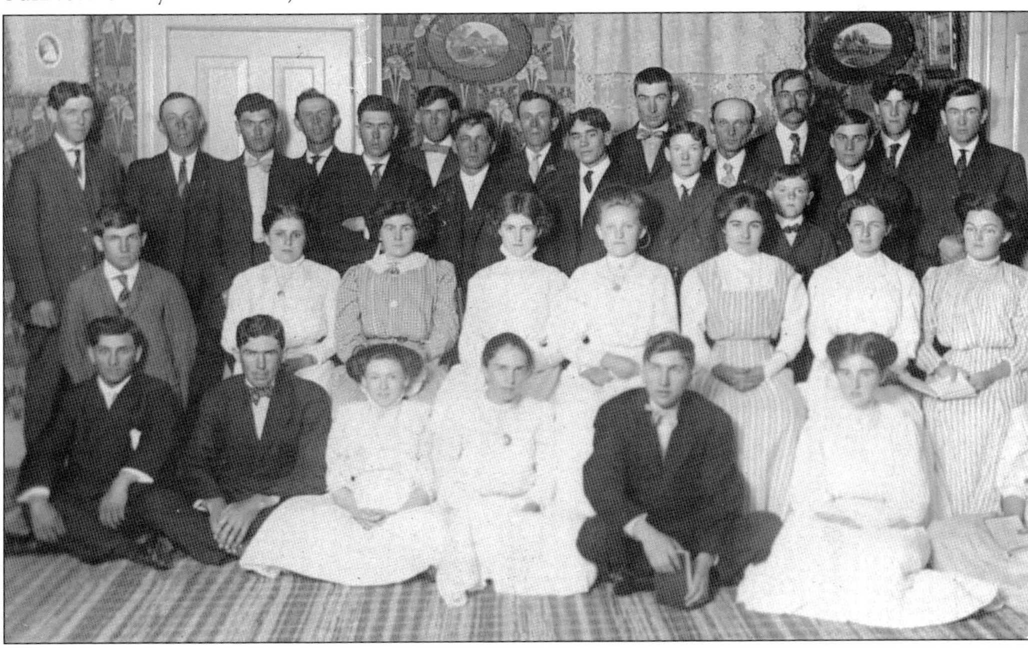

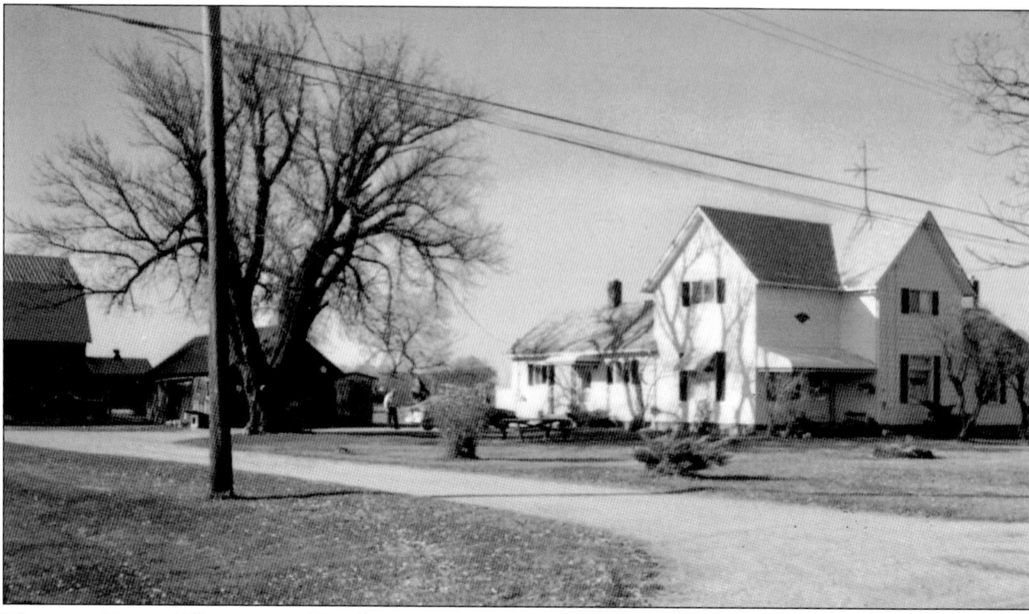

Hummel Farm. The original land grant to Thomas Dryer on April 10, 1837, was signed by Pres. Martin Van Buren for the property at 63581 Bates Road, Lenox. From Thomas Dryer, it passed to his son Nathan, who was in the Civil War and died in 1869. The farm was then sold to Frederick and Minna Bade, whose son William inherited and sold it in 1941 to the Siegers of Fraser. On April 15, 1946, it was sold to Fred and Helen Rohrbeck Hummel; the farmhouse stayed in the Hummel family until May 22, 1991. The small dark building behind the large tree was likely the first house on the farm, which at one point was turned into a sawmill. Below, the barn came from East Detroit after the original barn burned in 1938. It was dismantled, removed, and rebuilt, and signs of that process are still seen on the interior walls. (Both, courtesy of the Tina Kacanowski family collection.)

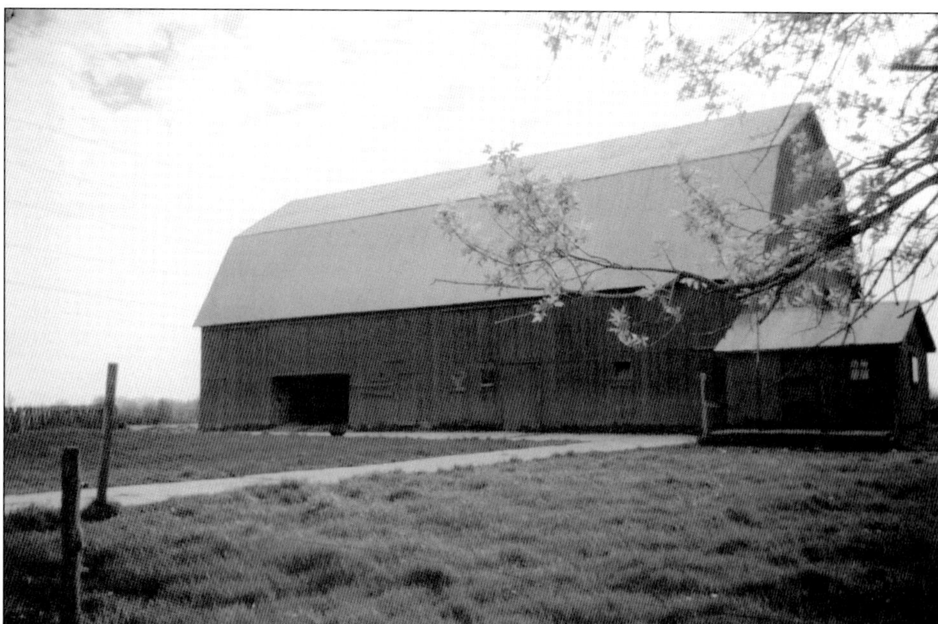

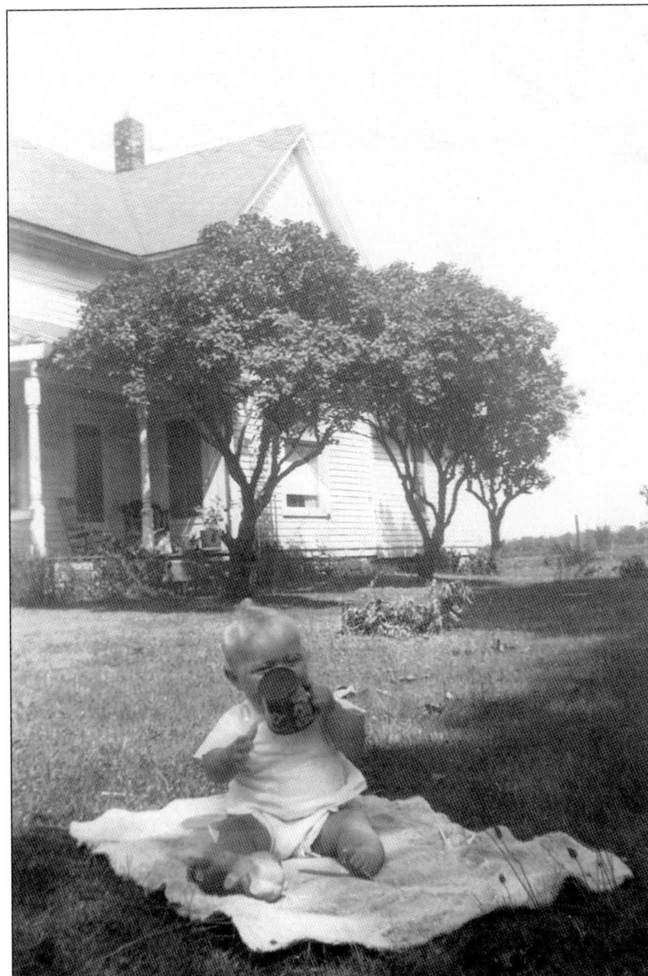

Two Farming Families. Seen here is the front of the Bates Road farm in 1954 before it was remodeled in the 1970s. The baby playing on the lawn is William Hummel, son of Adelbert and Leona Hummel. Below are two farming families from Macomb County that were long-standing friends at a confirmation party on June 8, 1952, at 30 Mile Road and Place Road. The three girls in front are, from left to right, Laura Hummel and Patricia Hummel Podolan with Linda Hummel standing behind them. The adults are, from left to right, Wilbur Knust, Harold Knust, Delores Knust Bertossi, Shirley Knust Arft, Nancy Knust Kardas, Hazel Bade Knust, Marion Knust Krakowski, Ernest Knust, Patricia Knust, and Adelbert Hummel. (Both, courtesy of the Tina Kacanowski family collection.)

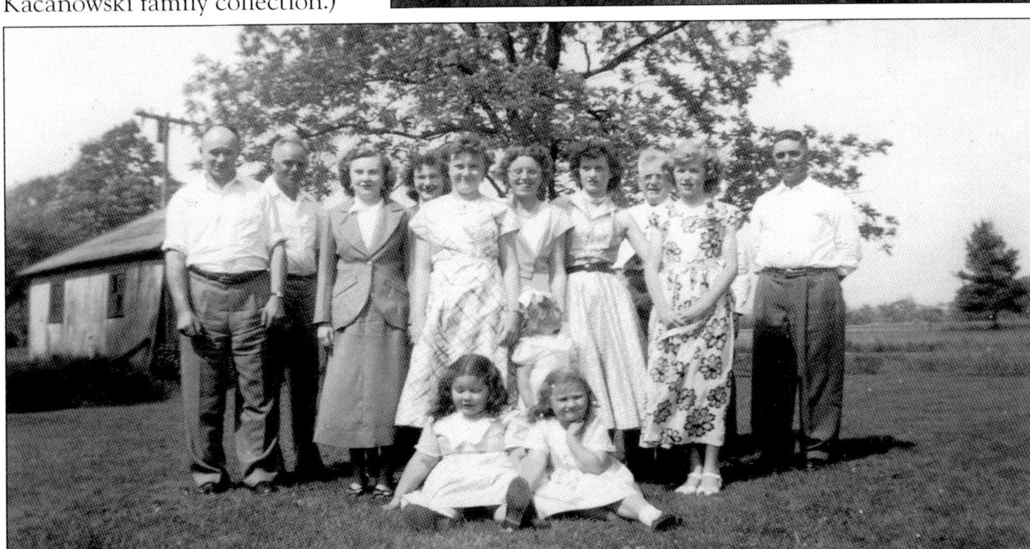

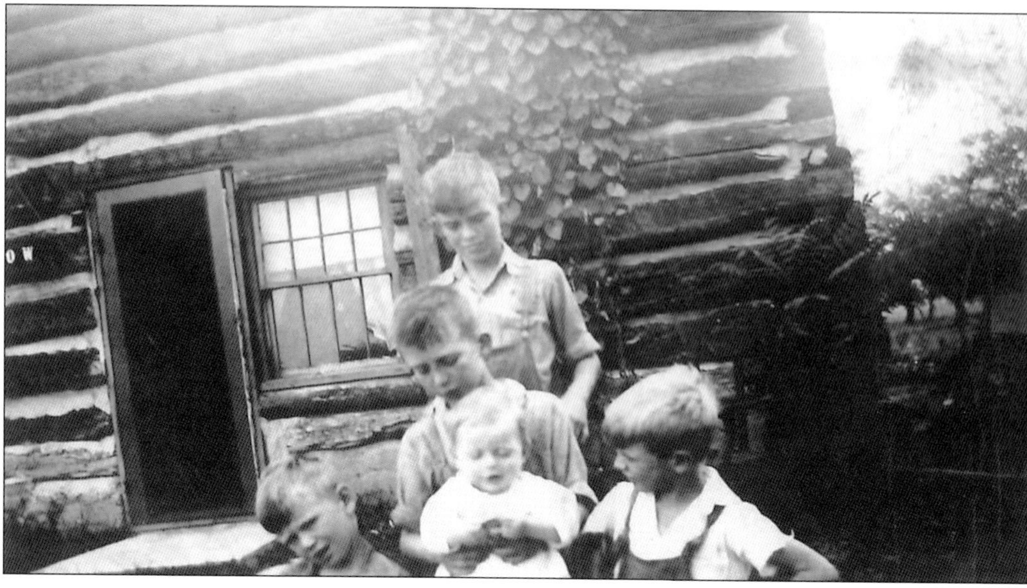

Donley Farm. John Donley (1826–1885) of Ballyporeen, County Tipperary, Ireland, came to New York in 1848. In 1850, John and Ellen Donley bought a farm on Irish Road, now known as 29 Mile Road, just east of Gratiot Avenue. No road led from Gratiot Avenue to their property, so a path was cut, clearing the land and felling the trees to build a cabin and make a home for their family. Four generations of the Donley family lived in the cabin for over 100 years. Pictured here around 1933–1934 are, from left to right, (first row) Hugh Donley, Larry Donley, and Joe Donley; (second row) Frank Donley; (third row) Ed Donley. In 1931, John's grandson Hugh Donley took on the task of preserving the cabin with a new foundation and new mortar between the logs. (Both, courtesy of the Donley family collection.)

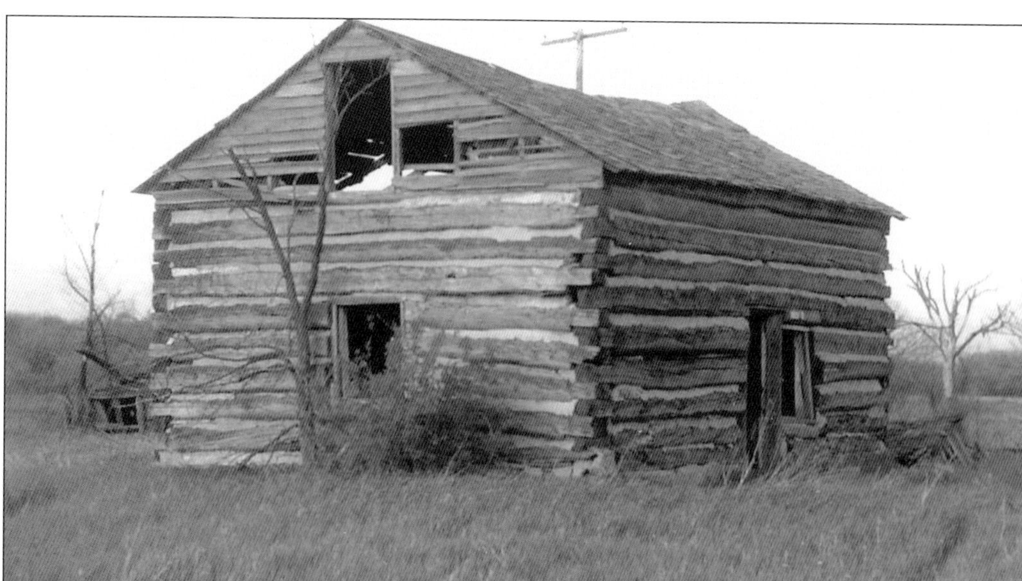

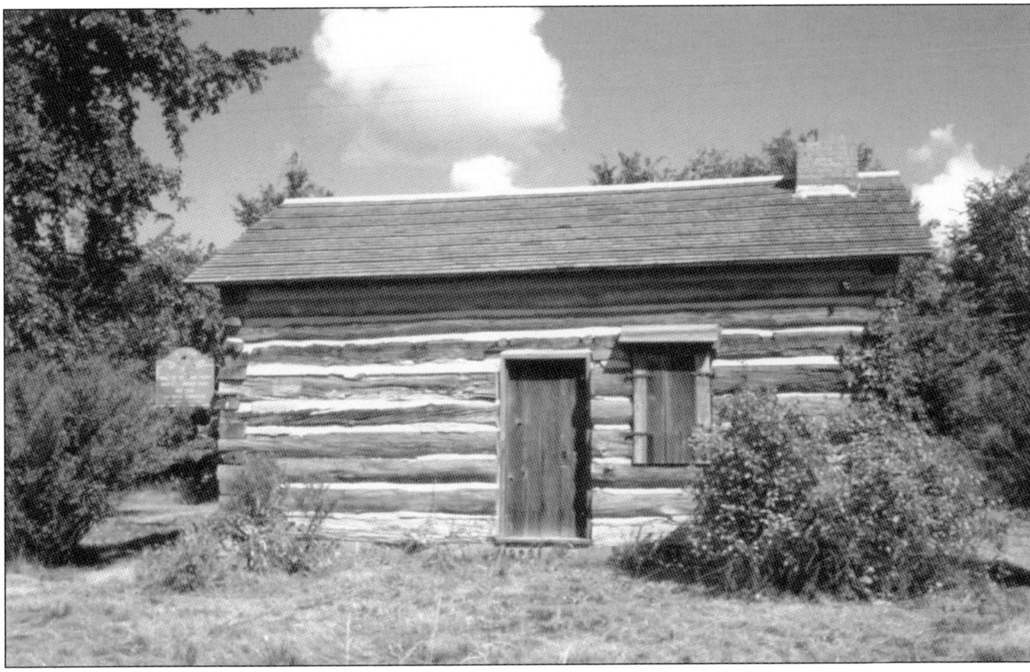

A New Home in Richmond. Pictured here is the cabin after the onsite restoration project in 1972 by the great-grandsons, overseen by Larry Donley. They took the cabin apart, numbering each log and rebuilding it using the old mortar mixed in with new. After the restoration, the realization that individuals were, and would continue, vandalizing and damaging the preserved cabin in the woods over the years came to light, so the Donley family donated it to the Richmond Area Historical and Genealogical Society for use at its Historic Village at Bailey Memorial Park in 1997. Pictured below, the cabin is being transported from the farm in Lenox to Bailey Park in Richmond around 1998. In 2019, the society restored the cabin with two new logs and new beams, roof, windows, and doors. (Both, courtesy of the Donley family collection.)

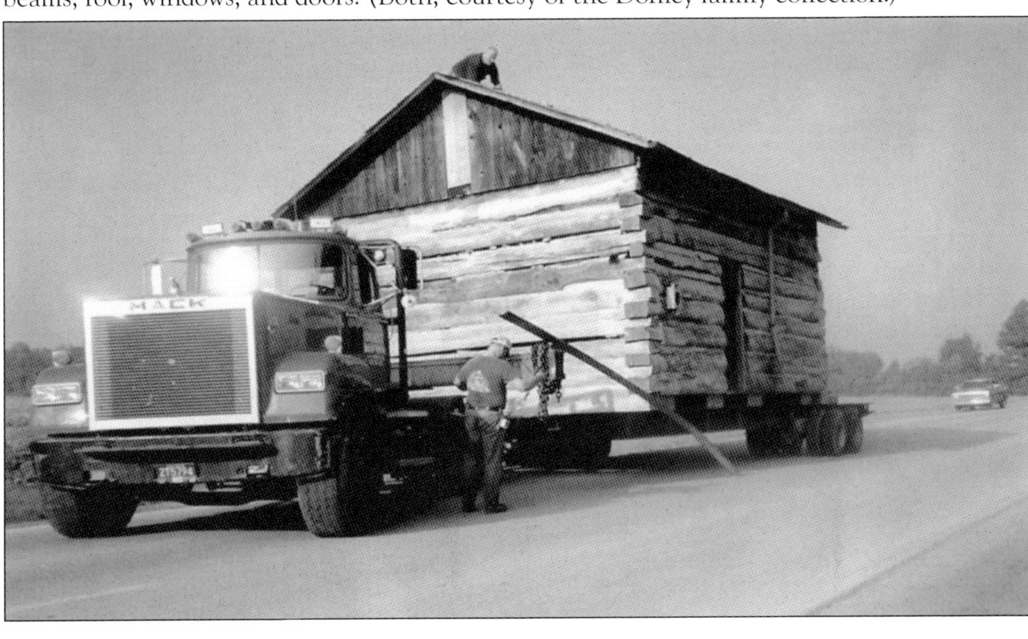

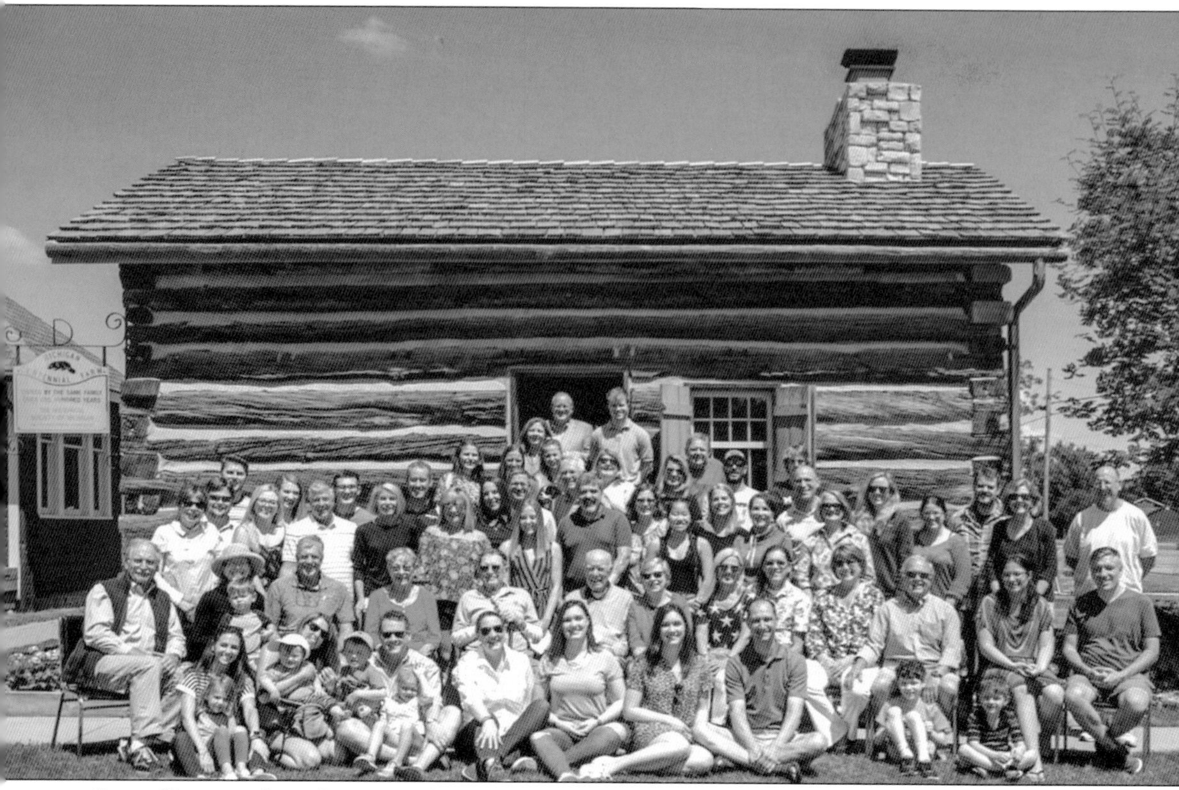

John Donley Sets Sail for America. According to family lore, the late spring of 1848 saw heavy rain, while early and midsummer experienced very hot temperatures, two conditions that spelled disaster for the autumn harvest. Realizing the severity of conditions, early in 1848, John Donley, the adventurous third son of John and Joanna, said goodbye to his parents and brothers and set out from their home in Ballyporeen, County Tipperary, on the 35-mile walk to Cork with £3 (equal to about $15 or approximately six months' wages) in his pockets. There were two ships sailing to North America that week from Cork: one bound for Halifax, Nova Scotia, and one for New York City. John asked who the president of Halifax was, and the ticket clerk informed him that Halifax was loyal to Queen Victoria. John quickly took out his £3 and placed it on the table, saying, "I'll take New York." John, the 22-year-old farm laborer, set sail from Cork, Ireland, on the bark *Christianna* for the port of New York. Pictured here, the Donley family reunion was held in Bailey Park in 2019 in recognition of the renovation project. (Courtesy of the Richmond Area Historical and Genealogical Society and the Lawrence Donley collection.)

Seven

Bruce Township

When it was originally surveyed, Forth Town was considered well-timbered with hickory, ash, elm, maple, and linden, as well as some cedar and tamarack along the marshes or streams. The governmental surveyor, Joseph Wampler, found the township contained 23,347 acres. David Hill, from St. Clair County, bought the first parcel of land on November 20, 1821, and Asahel Bailey bought in the same section on April 16, 1822. Asahel had already bought land south of Bruce on the border of Washington in 1821. Among the buyers were several women, such as Mary Gray, Leona Kittridge, Rebecca Day, Mary Ann Dyer, and Lucinda Leavenworth.

The township was speedily settled, so a move was made early in the spring of 1832 to form a separate township, as the territory had been attached and formed as part of its neighbor to the south, Washington Township. When a meeting was called to the log schoolhouse four miles north of Romeo by settlers in April 1832 for the purpose of forming a township, one of the Grays who were present proposed the name of Bruce in honor of the renowned Scotch chieftain, as many of these early settlers were of Scottish extraction; this name then seemed acceptable to all. A year later, on March 9, 1833, the township organization was put into effect.

A portion of the township known as the "Scotch Settlement" began to be settled by families with names like the Resides, Reids, Hopkinses, Muirs, Wassons, Hamiltons, Borlans, and Stephensons, with many more to follow. Throughout the 1800s, the farms maintained in the township grew at a very high rate as a testimony to the fertile soil and attractive topography that the township had to offer.

The village of Romeo sits in section 2 and the east half of section 3 in the township of Washington and the south half of section 34 in the township of Bruce. The act of incorporating the village was approved on March 9, 1838, and it would be run by a governmental board. Romeo became the centrally located area for the exceptional educational needs of both Bruce and Washington Townships.

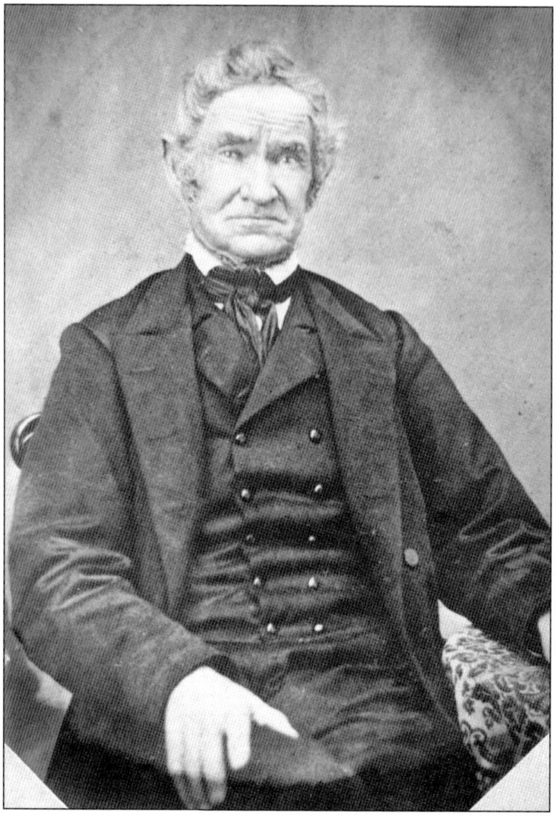

Bishop Farm. John, the eldest son of Elihu and Hester Townsend, was born in 1793. John and his wife, Ann Miller, were among the earliest settlers to Michigan and its extreme frontier. John and Hester located, improved, and spent the remainder of their lives on the 160-acre property. They bought the land from the government on July 5, 1833, on Boardman Road between 38 Mile and Fisher Roads in section 5. They raised eight children, and four of the children that survived to adulthood would all continue to live in the area. The youngest son, Arthur, married Amanda Bishop in 1874. Not long after, Arthur traveled west to purchase horses, contracted typhoid fever, and died. This left his widow, Amanda, and a young daughter, Ethel, to run the farm. (Both, courtesy of the Don and Diane Bishop collection.)

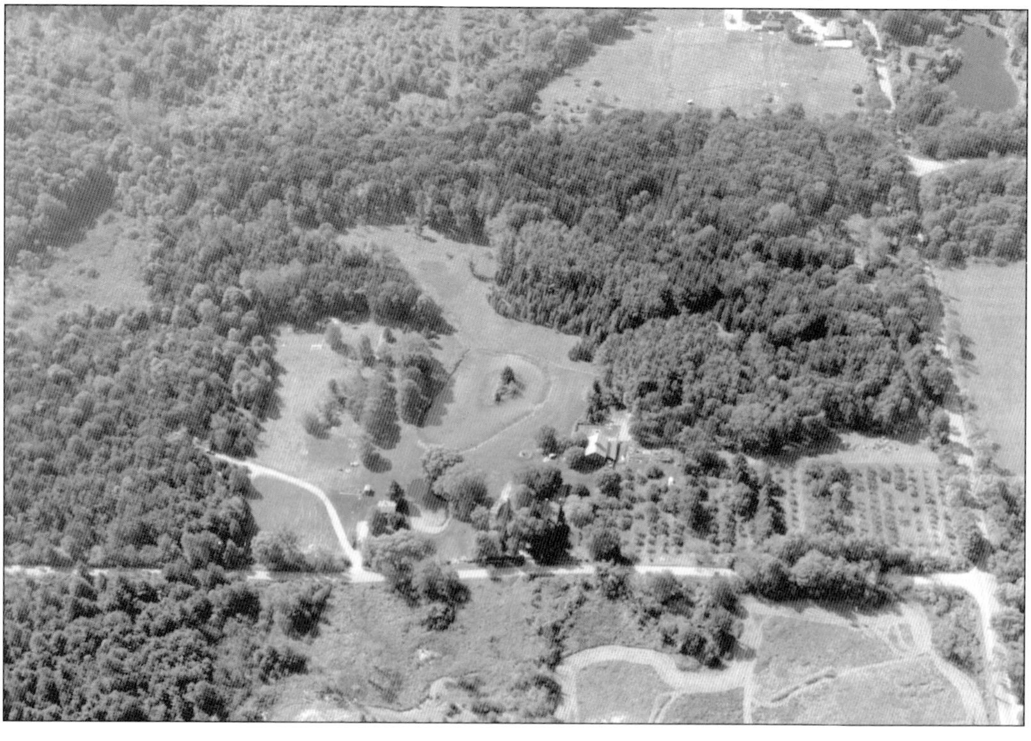

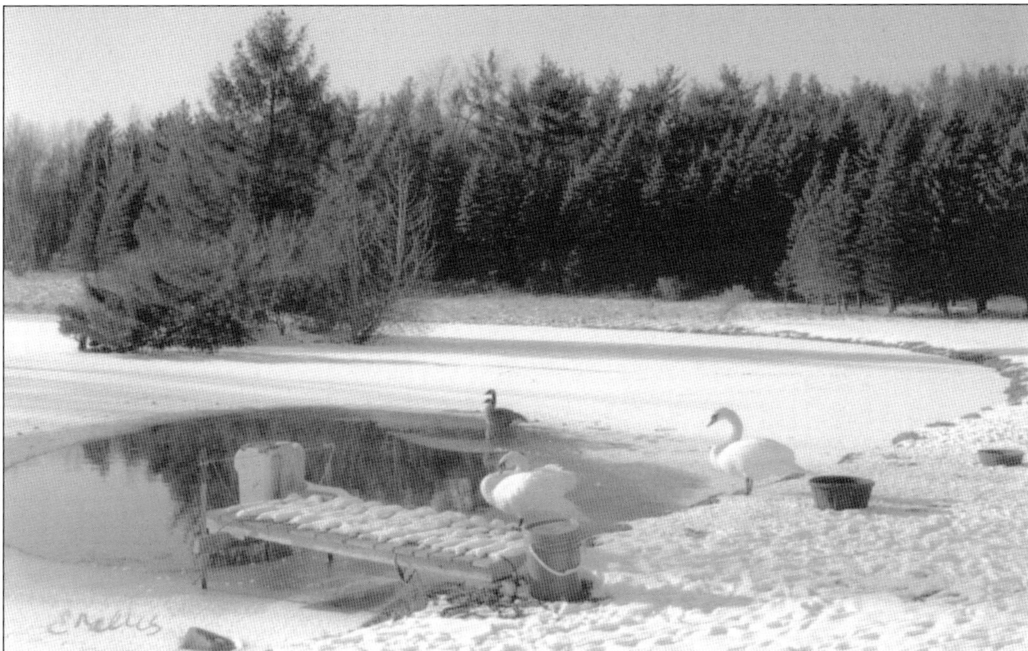

A CERTIFIED ORCHARD AND TREE FARM. Amanda Bishop died in 1933, and her daughter Ethel never married and lived on the farm alone for most of her life. Dr. G. Claire Bishop and his wife, Jane, acquired the farm in 1958, and Ethel's death occurred in 1968. The farm was used to raise livestock and grow vegetables and continues as a certified orchard and tree farm in the care of the Bishops' son Don and Diane Bishop today. On February 10, 2000, the Michigan Historical Commission certified this farm a Centennial Farm after it came into Amanda Bishop's hands back in 1885. (Both, courtesy of the Don and Diane Bishop collection.)

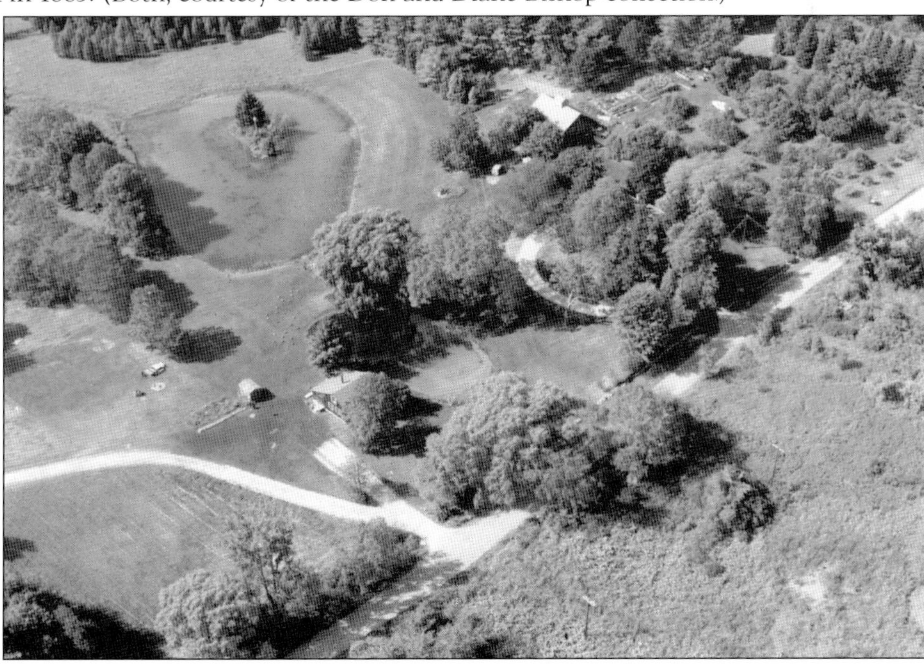

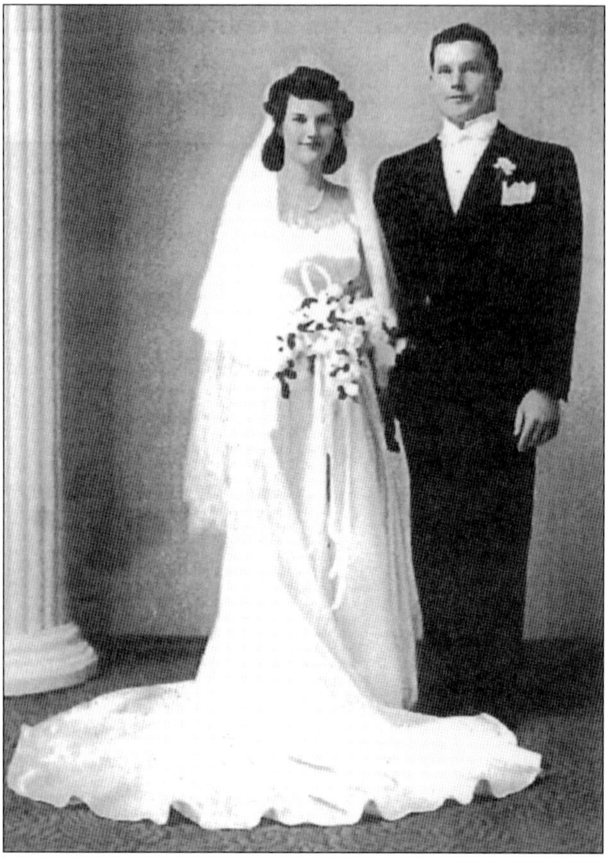

VAN HOUTTE FARM. Pictured here, Albert Van Houtte and Dorothy Govaere met and later married on November 26, 1949, at St. Mary Mystical Rose Church in Armada. The couple bought an 80-acre farm in Armada Township and raised eight children: five boys and three girls. Albert and Dorothy enjoyed garden farming, along with growing rhubarb, and then taking their produce down to Detroit's Eastern, Pontiac, and Royal Oak Markets. Below around 2000 is grandson Brian Van Houtte, son of George Van Houtte, and friend Rachel Krawchuk. (Both, courtesy of the George Van Houtte collection.)

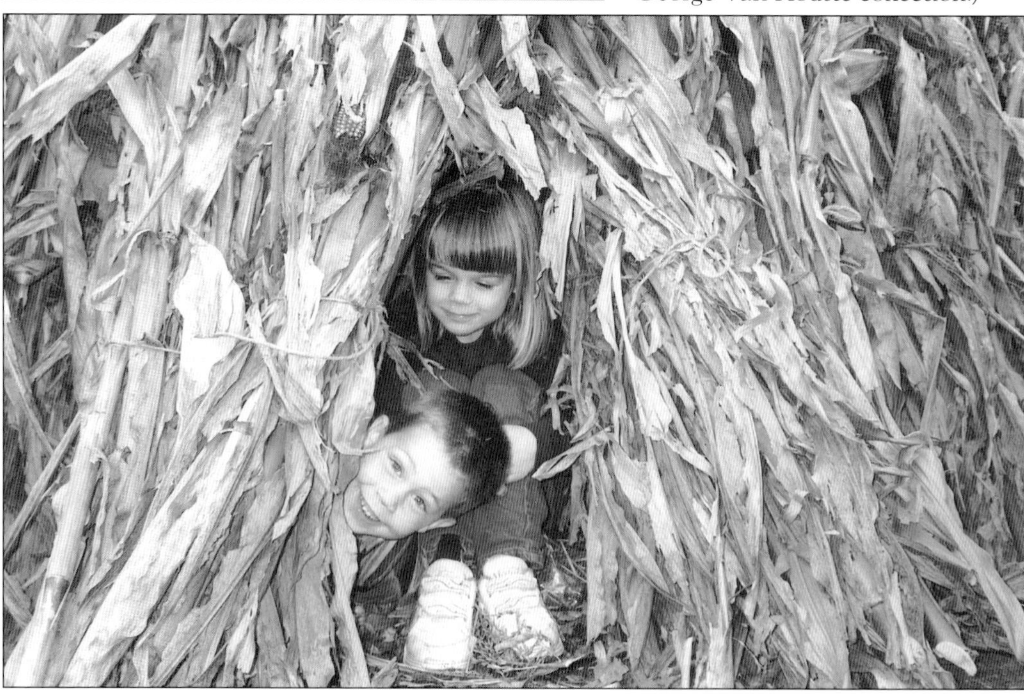

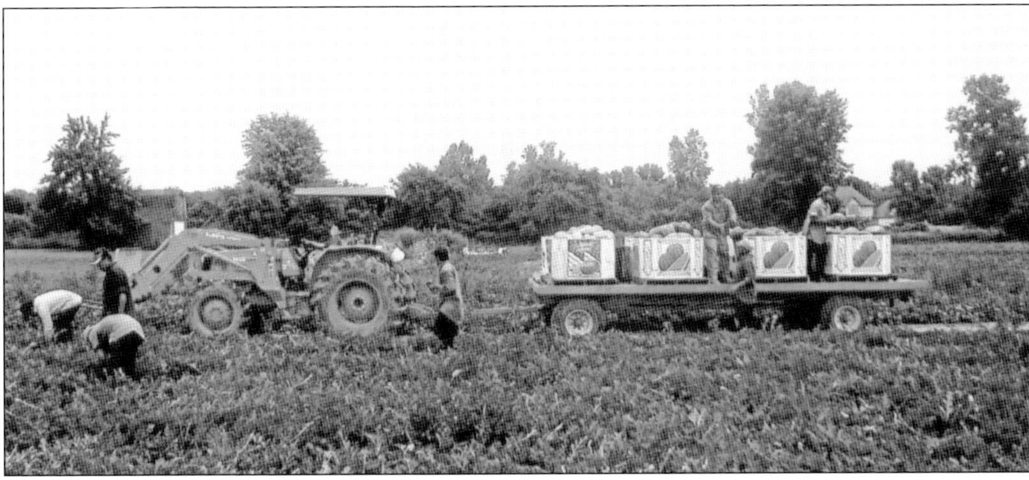

Selling the Produce. Albert and Dorothy also bought a six-acre property (six lots at $500 each) in 1963 on Van Dyke Road between 34 Mile and 35 Mile Roads. Grown on the farm, sweet corn, cold crops, cabbage, cauliflower, Brussels sprouts, kale, and watermelons were sold at the family's farm market. Son George Van Houtte farms 550 acres of 33 Mile Road. Pictured above are workers in the field, and below is the farm market on Van Dyke Road. (Both, courtesy of the George Van Houtte collection.)

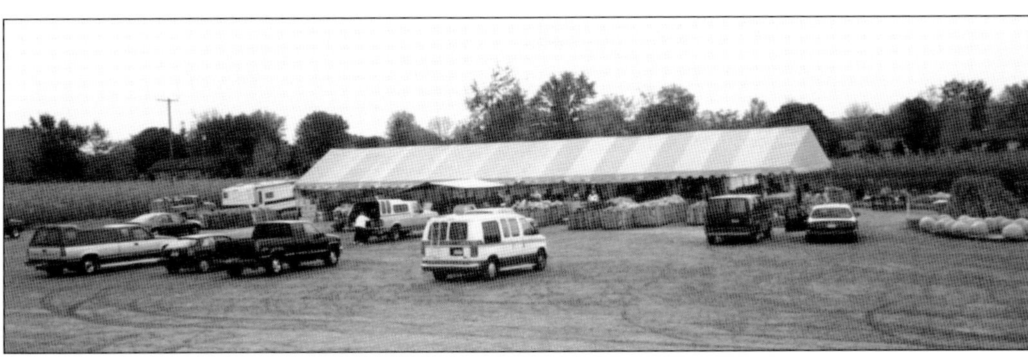

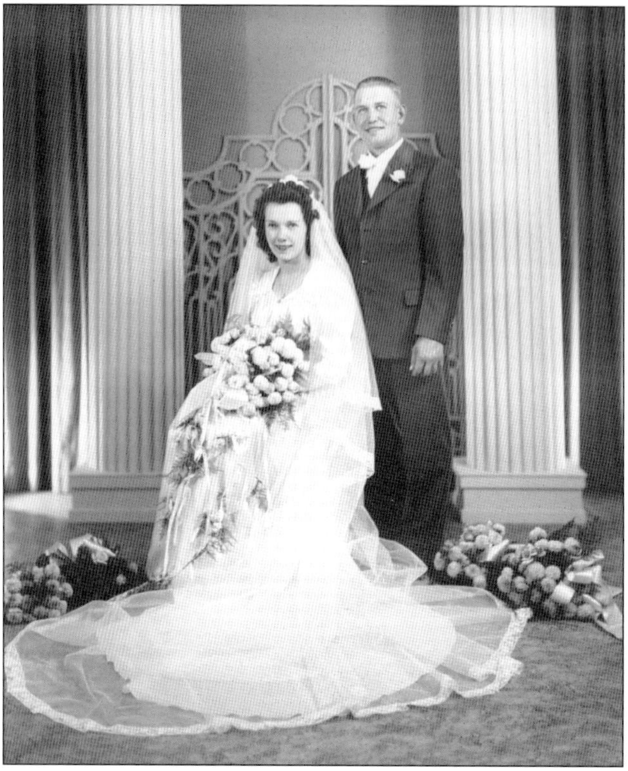

Falker Farm. Howard (1922–2018) and Marjorie (1924–1992) Falker were sharecroppers in 1948, but by 1960, they purchased property in Bruce Township on McKay Road between 33 Mile and 34 Mile Roads. They raised four children on their dairy farm, where they also grew feed for the cattle. In 1979, Howard's youngest son, Mark, and his wife, Robin, took on a partnership with his father to work the farm, and Howard continued working until his son purchased it fully in 1992. Pictured here are Howard and Marjorie on their wedding day. Pictured below is the farm in the early years. (Both, courtesy of the Falker family collection.)

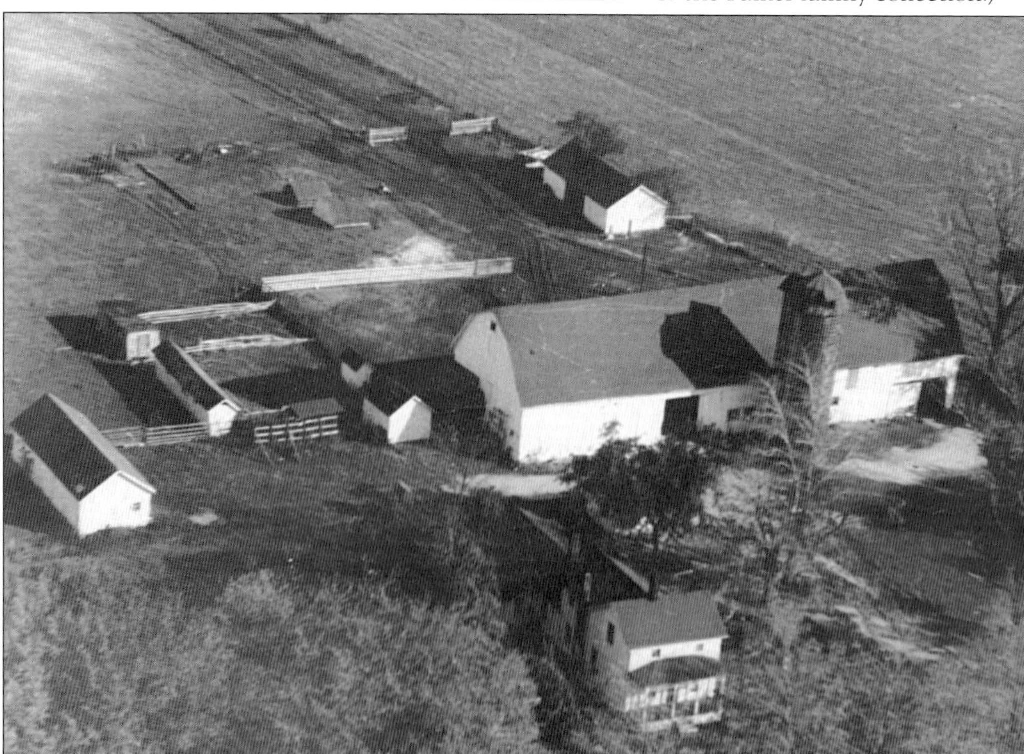

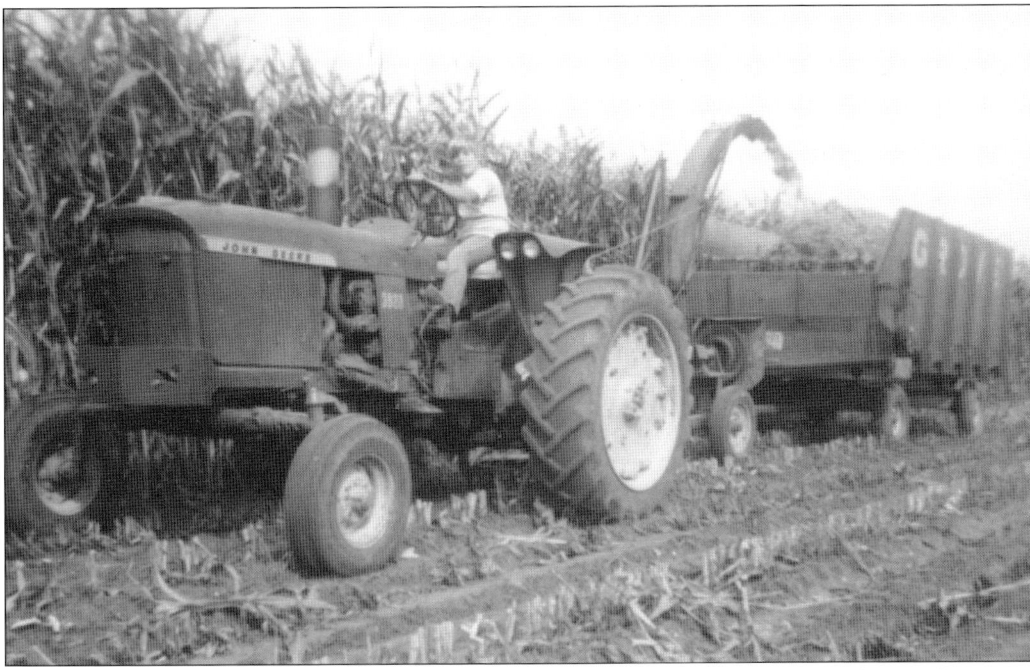

Land Preservation. Pictured here, Mark Falker, as a young boy, learns the workings of a tractor. Mark has taken on a project that is very important to him in farmland preservation. He has agreed to sell the development rights for some of his property to ensure the acres stay agricultural forever. The sale was made under a county program designed to preserve the county's farmland and agricultural industry. Under the program, farmers retain ownership of their property while selling the right to develop it in the future. The agreement also bans future use of the land for residential, commercial, or industrial projects. Today, Mark and Robin Falker raise 1,000 turkeys and chickens and sell eggs. Pictured below is the Falker farm in recent years. (Both, courtesy of the Falker family collection.)

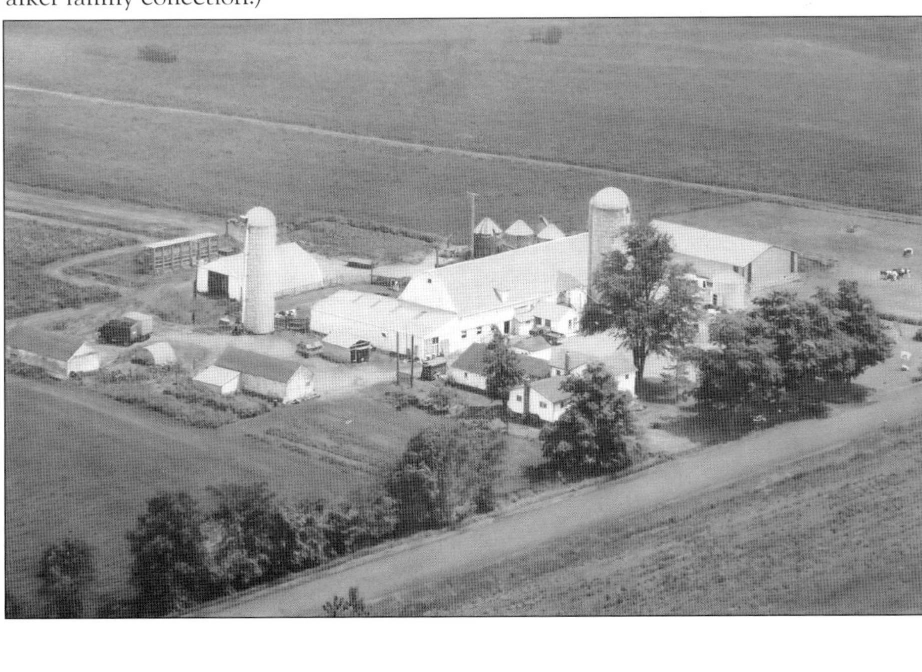

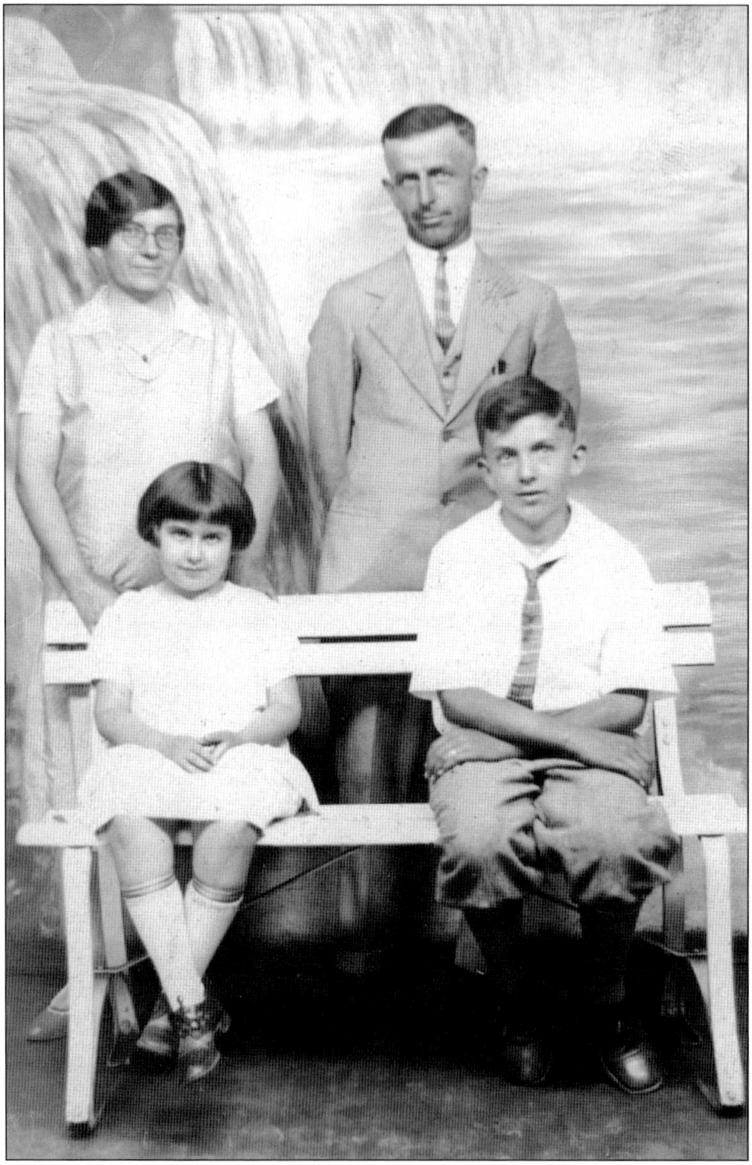

Pine Grove Farm. Christ Schoof (1867–1945) and Ada Hirsack (1871–1957) married in 1890. They purchased the farm on Dequindre Road in Bruce Township from Maria Starkweather Thorington in 1913, the same year that their son Edward (1891–1972) married Eleanor Schneider (1891–1963). In 1920, Christ and Ada turned the farm over to their son Edward and his wife, Ella. Pictured here are Edward and Ella with their son, Jerome, born in 1914, and daughter, Eleanor, born in 1918, while on a trip to Niagara Falls in 1926. While Edward ran the farm, they raised animals as well as corn, oats, wheat, and hay. His son, Jerome, did the same until the orchards matured. The orchards included apples, peaches, cherries, and pears. (Both, courtesy of the Vickie Bower collection.)

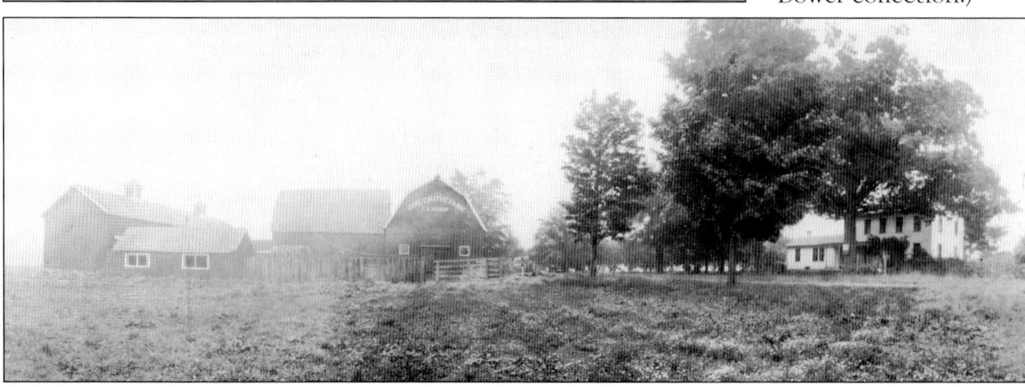

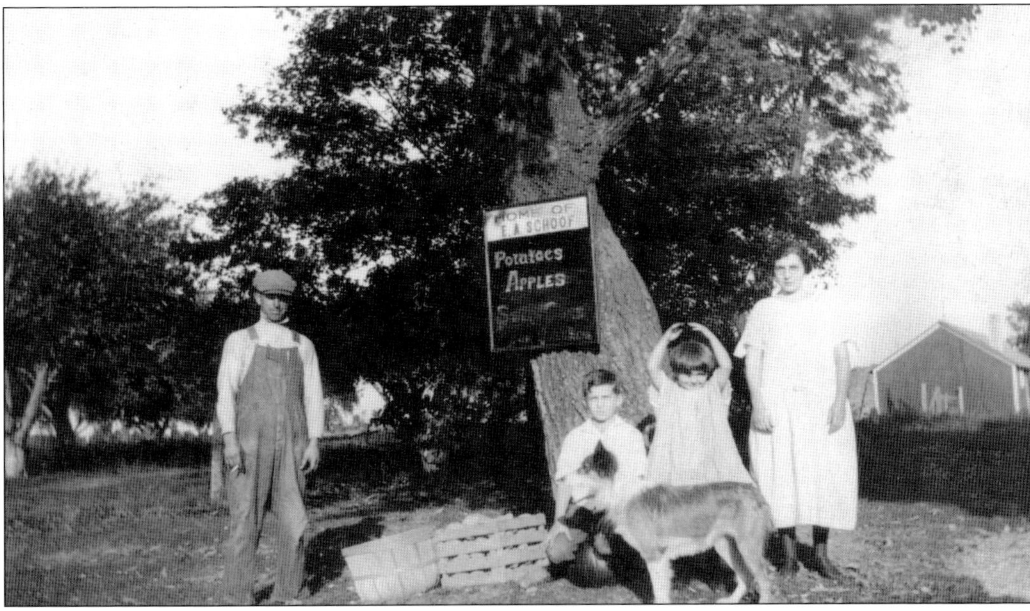

SELLING THE CASH CROPS. Pictured here are Edward and Ella Schoof and their kids selling the produce in front of the farm; they would also take their produce to the Detroit Eastern Market. Edward and Ella also had a few hundred "layers" and an egg route into Detroit. Richard Schoof, the son of Jerome and Eleanor, helped with the chores, including milking the cows and raising 4-H steers through the years. Pine Grove was a full agricultural farm where everyone did their share. In 1930, the family had to deal with a tragedy when their barn caught fire; they lost a lot of their produce that night. Jerome was active in the community and was the Bruce Township supervisor from 1963 to 1969. He was appointed a member of the Michigan Apple Committee Board in 1958 and became the chairman of the board from 1961 to 1963. A decision was made to sell the farm in 1980. Pictured to the right are Ed and Ella later in life. (Both, courtesy of the Vickie Bower collection.)

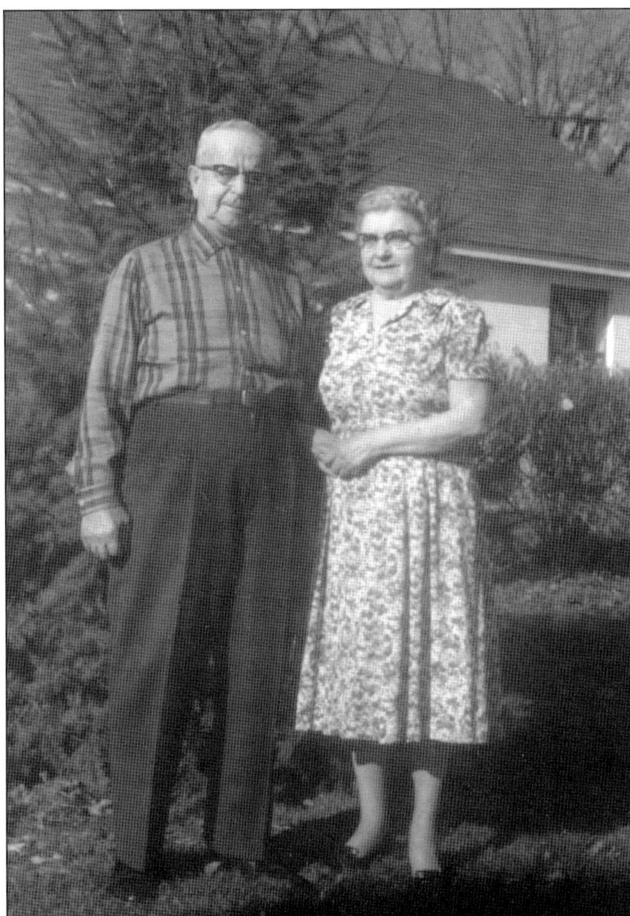

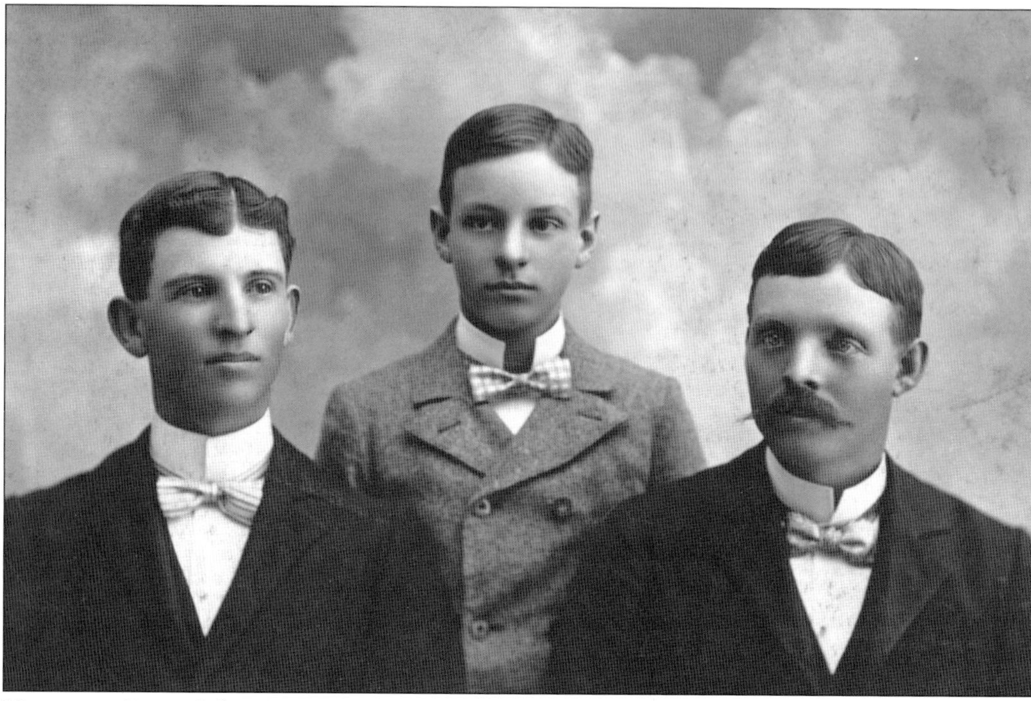

Hagaman Farm. John F. Hagaman, a native of Germany, was born in 1845 and immigrated to the United States in 1851 with his family. After suffering major family losses upon their arrival, he spent his growing-up years in Detroit. In 1865, John came to Macomb County, and he married Anna Powell in 1868. The two had three sons that lived to adulthood: A. Powell (born in 1869), J. Burt (1876), and Howard A. (1884). Anna Powell's father had purchased a farm in Bruce Township in 1835, and John and Anna Hagaman started their life together on a portion of this farm. John added to his farm until it contained 320 acres of prime farming land. Pictured here are the three surviving sons of John F. and Anna Powell Hagaman; from left to right are Burt, Howard, and Powell around 1900. Pictured below is Howard's son Robert selling the farm produce. (Both, courtesy of the Nancy Kicinski collection.)

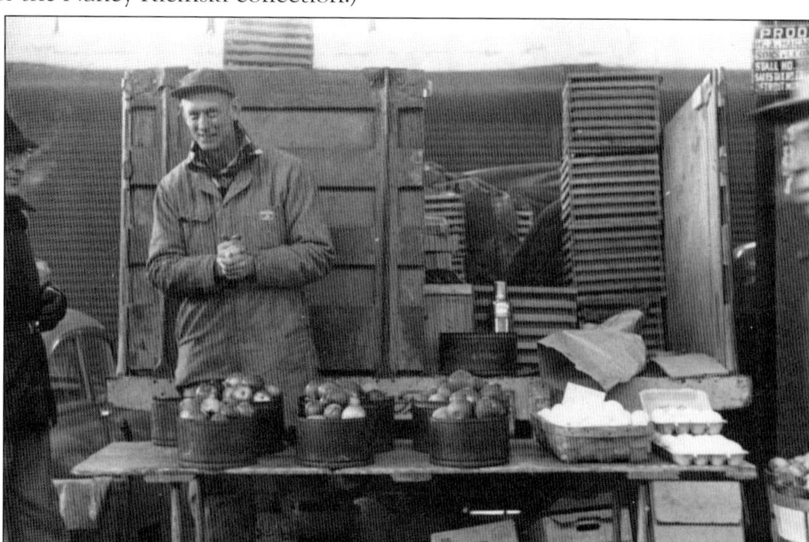

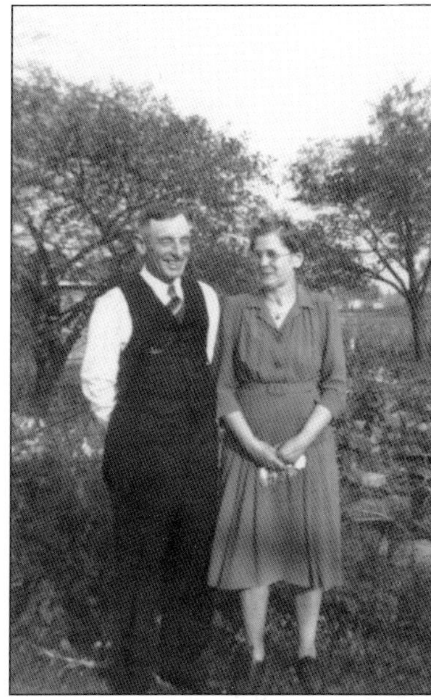

Caring for the Prized Sheep. In 1869, John started breeding shorthorn cattle, which became the chief industry of the farm. During this time, he was one of the largest breeders of this stock in eastern Michigan. He was known to win many prizes when exhibiting shorthorns at the fairs. With John's death in 1908, son Howard continued to move the farm forward. Howard married Nellie Chamberlin, and they raised two sons on this farm, Robert and Burt. Seen to the right are Howard and Nellie in later years. Pictured below are Howard (left) with his sons Robert (center) and Burt and their prized sheep. (Both, courtesy of the Nancy Kicinski collection.)

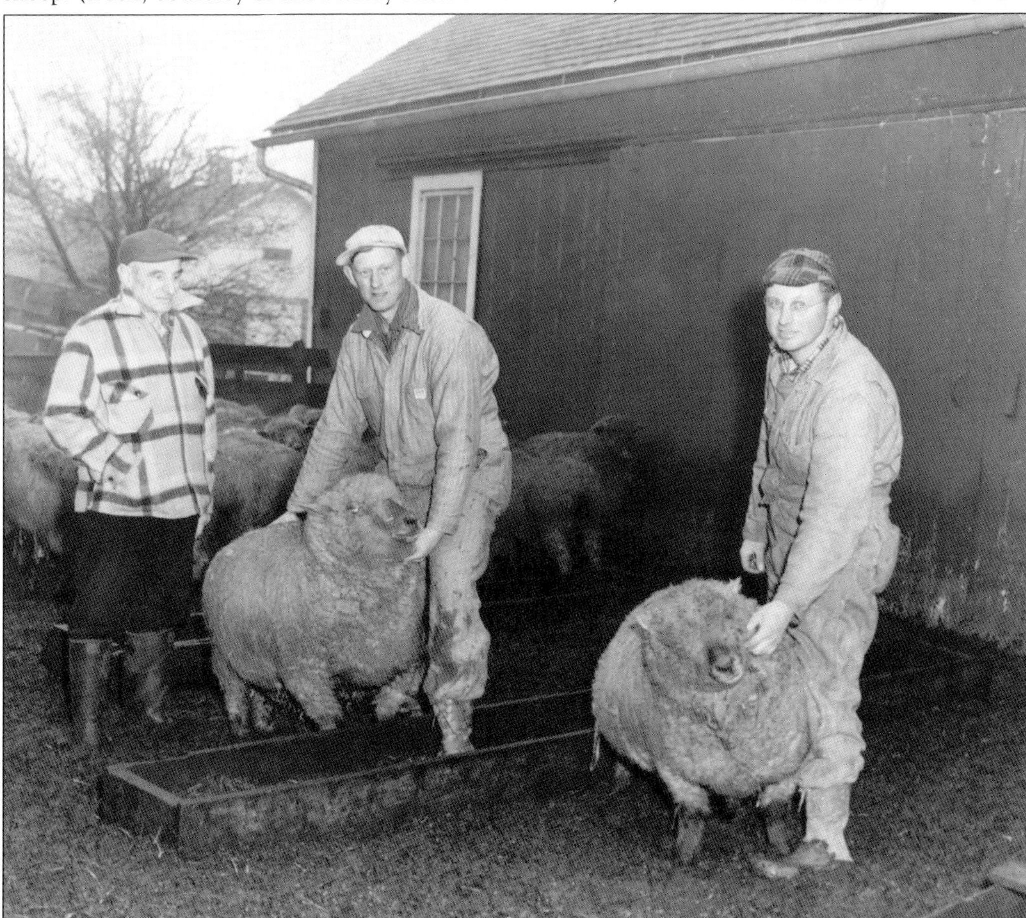

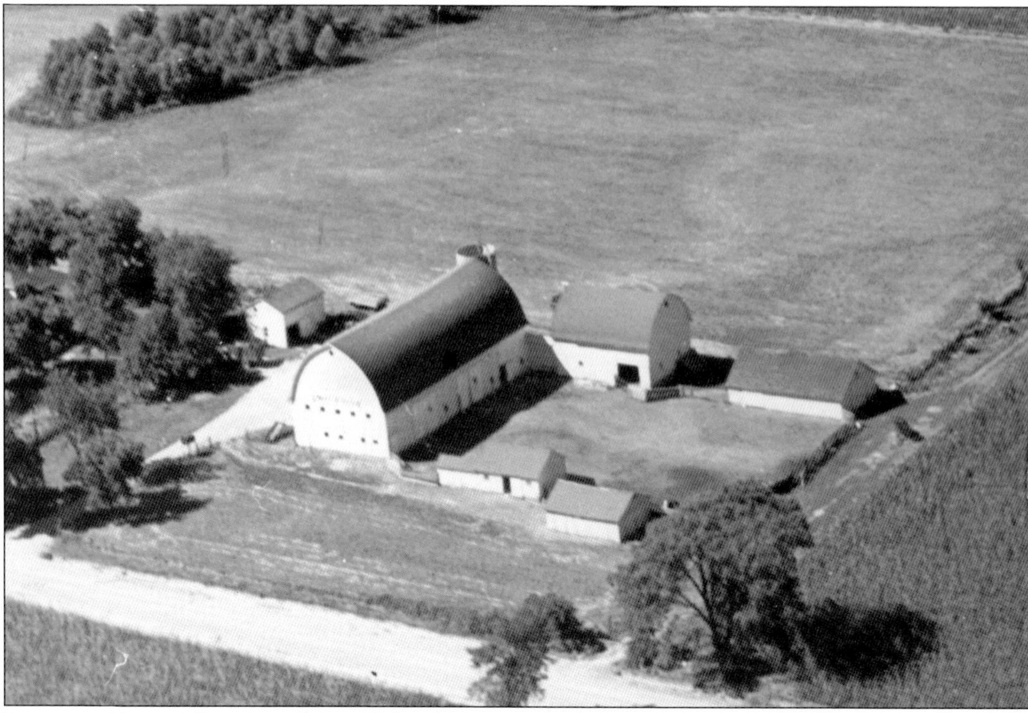

Ingleside Farm. Elmore Higby was born in 1930 and spent all his life in the Romeo area, graduating high school in 1947 and Michigan State University (MSU) in 1949. He married Joann Rountree in 1950, and they raised three daughters on their farm property called Ingleside Farms, located on 36 Mile Road in Bruce Township. The operation consisted of a peach orchard, chickens, cattle, sheep, and a few pigs. During the 1950s, most of the produce was sold at the Eastern Market in Detroit. Elmore passed away in 1999, and Joann still lives at the north end of the family farm. Seen below are Elmore and Joann Higby. (Both, courtesy of the Connie Schapman collection.)

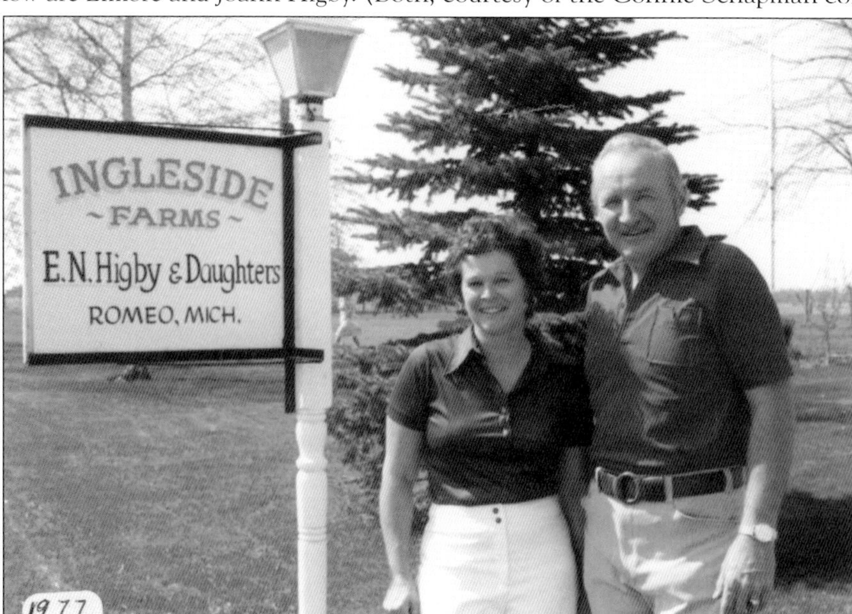

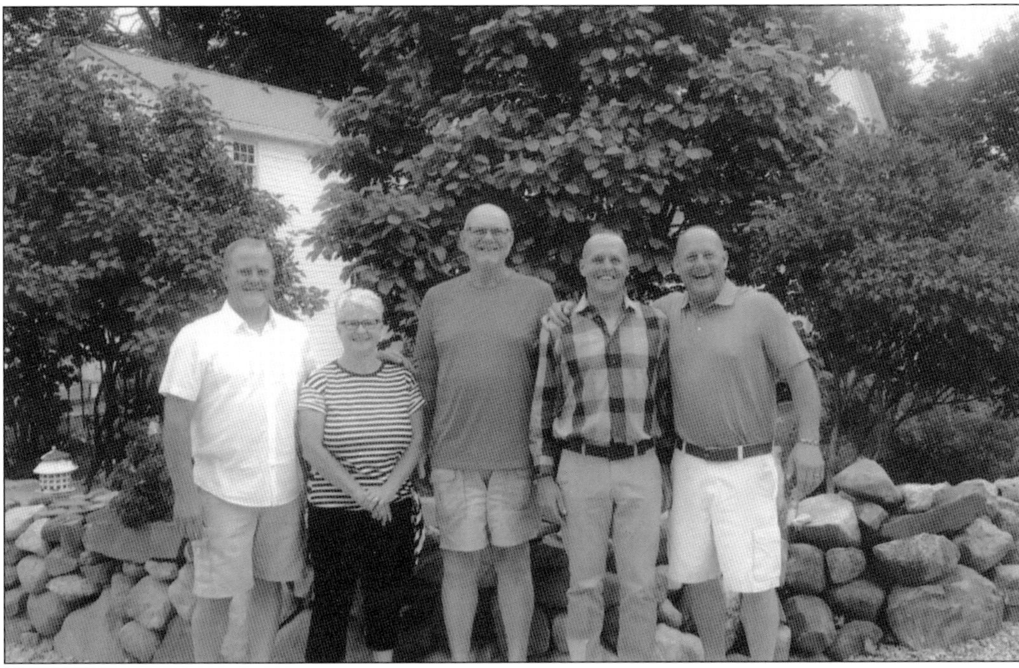

A Partnership Forms. In 1973, a family partnership was formed with their daughter Connie and son-in-law Rick Schapman. In 2021, the present operation consists of a partnership with Rick and Connie Schapman; their three sons, Todd, Jeremy, and Brett; and their families. The business centers around beef cattle and the cropping operation raising corn, soybeans, hay, and straw to maintain the livestock. (Both, courtesy of the Connie Schapman collection.)

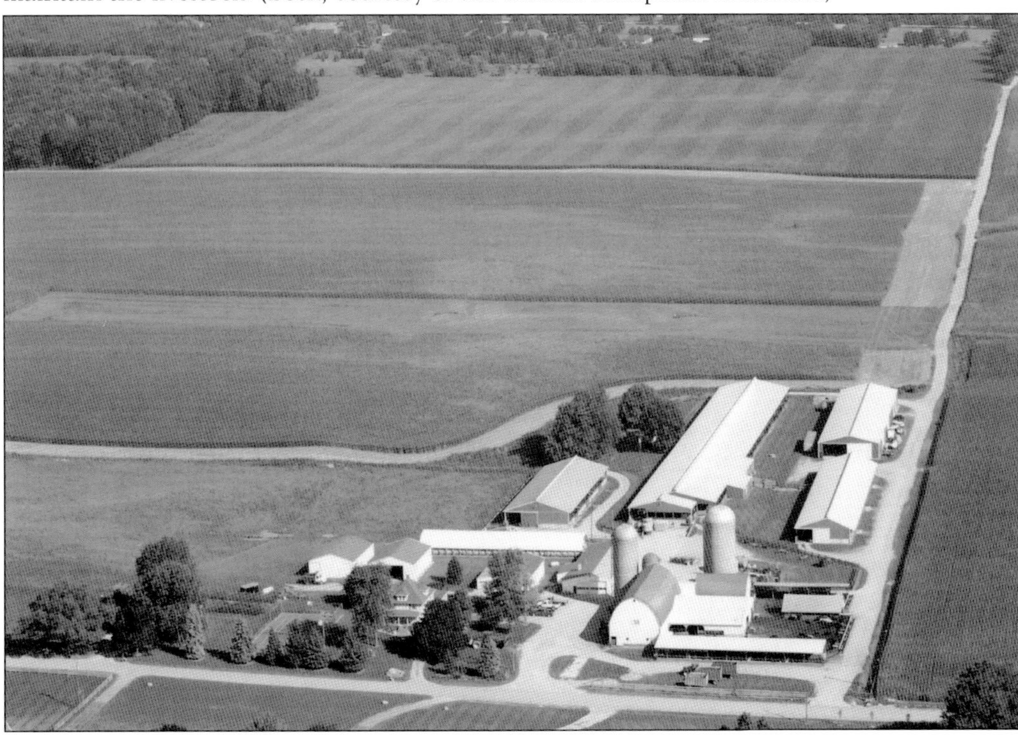

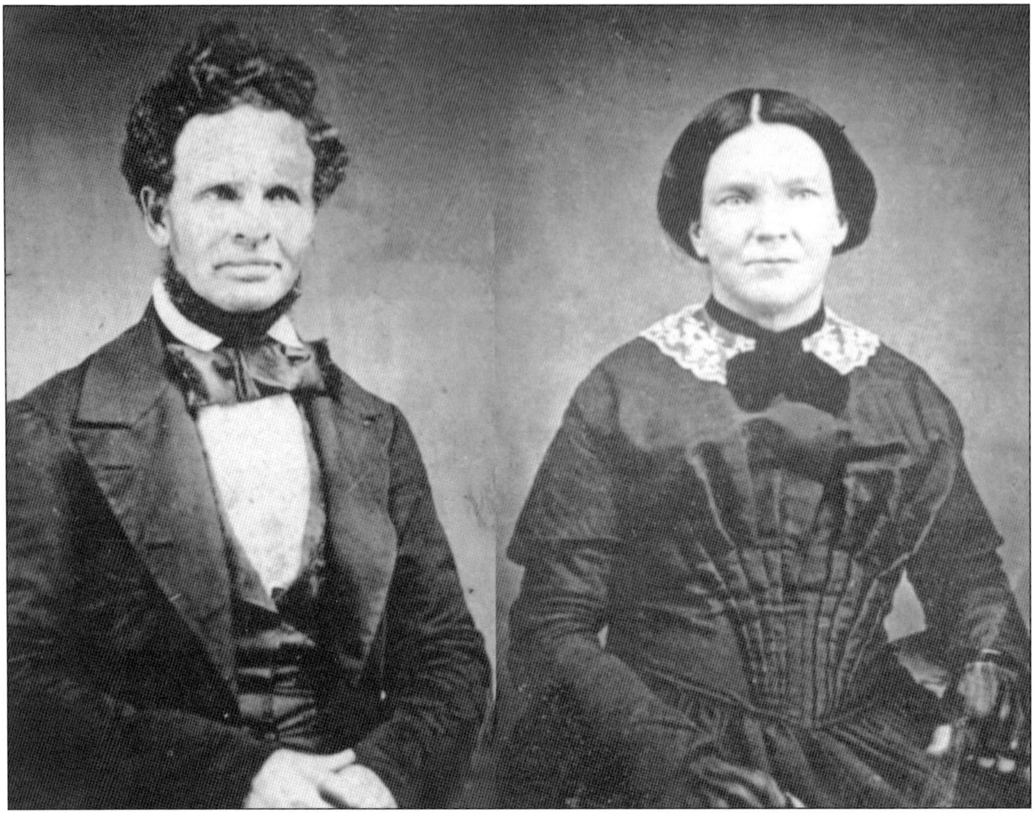

Bishop Farm. Truman Bishop (1806–1859) moved to Bruce Township from Richmond, Ontario County, New York, in 1833. He settled on the south side of the 6930 Boardman Road property, where his wife, Mary Sherman Bishop (1811–1859), soon followed. The Bishops raised three daughters and a son, Gilbert Sherman Bishop (1841–1917). Truman died tragically in 1859 after a farming accident in which he was run over by a horse. Mary also died months later from an illness. Gilbert, the 18-year-old son of Truman and Mary, assumed ownership and management of the farm. Gilbert later married Angeline Patch (1843–c. 1910–1917), and they raised their four daughters and a son, Frank L. Bishop, who helped run the farm from 1859 until Gilbert's death in 1917. Pictured below, Gilbert salvages the wheat from a barn on the property that burned down in 1915. (Both, courtesy of the John Bishop II collection.)

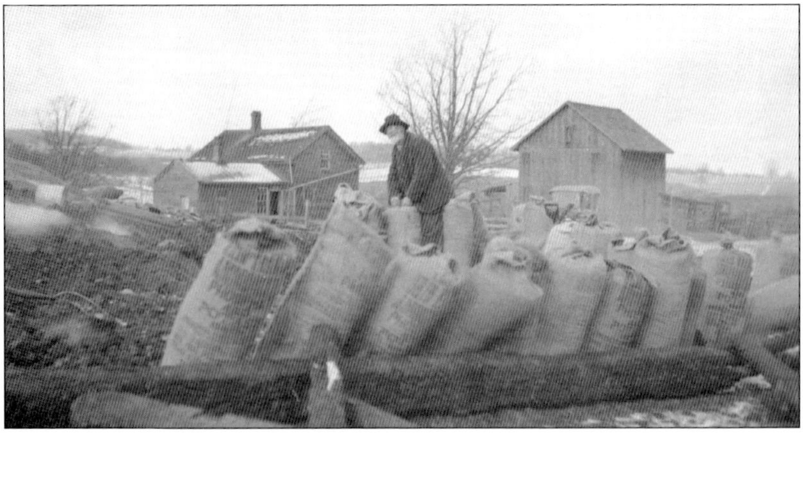

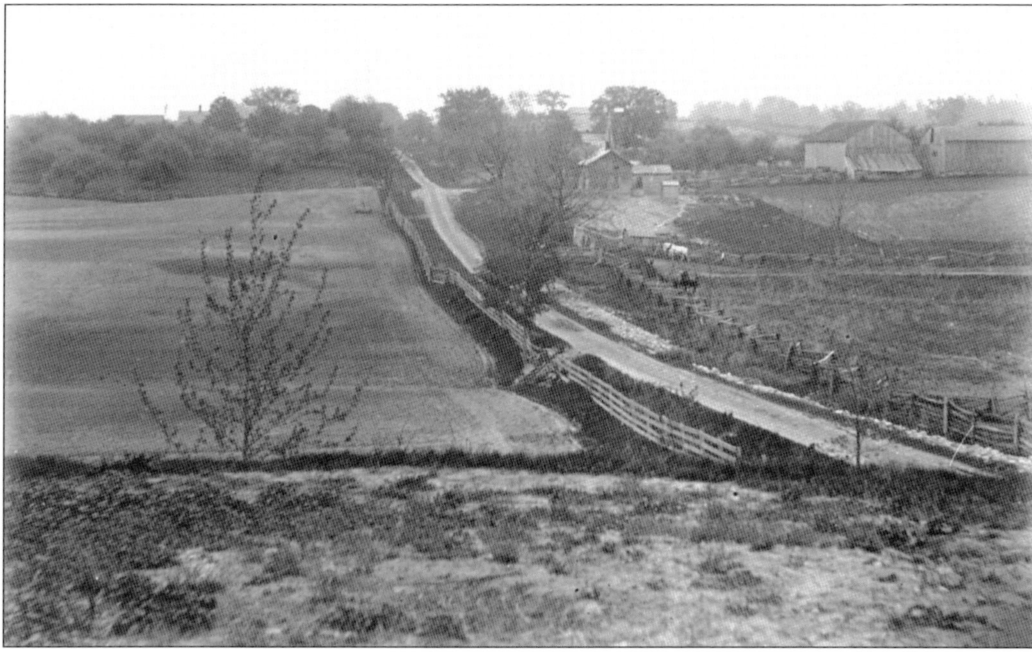

Boardman Road. The farm on Boardman Road began with 200 acres and progressed to 250 acres over the years. During Truman and Gilbert's time with the farm, they raised livestock, various produce, and wheat. From the 1940s through the 1980s, it was used as a dairy. Pictured below, this does become the story of two Bishops farms across the street from one another. But here, one would have to cross Boardman Road into Lapeer County for a short bit of time. Around 1900, the property across the street from the original homestead was purchased, and Frank Bishop, Gilbert and Angeline's son, lived on and managed the farm at 6939 Boardman Road, on the north side of the street. (Both, courtesy of the John Bishop II collection.)

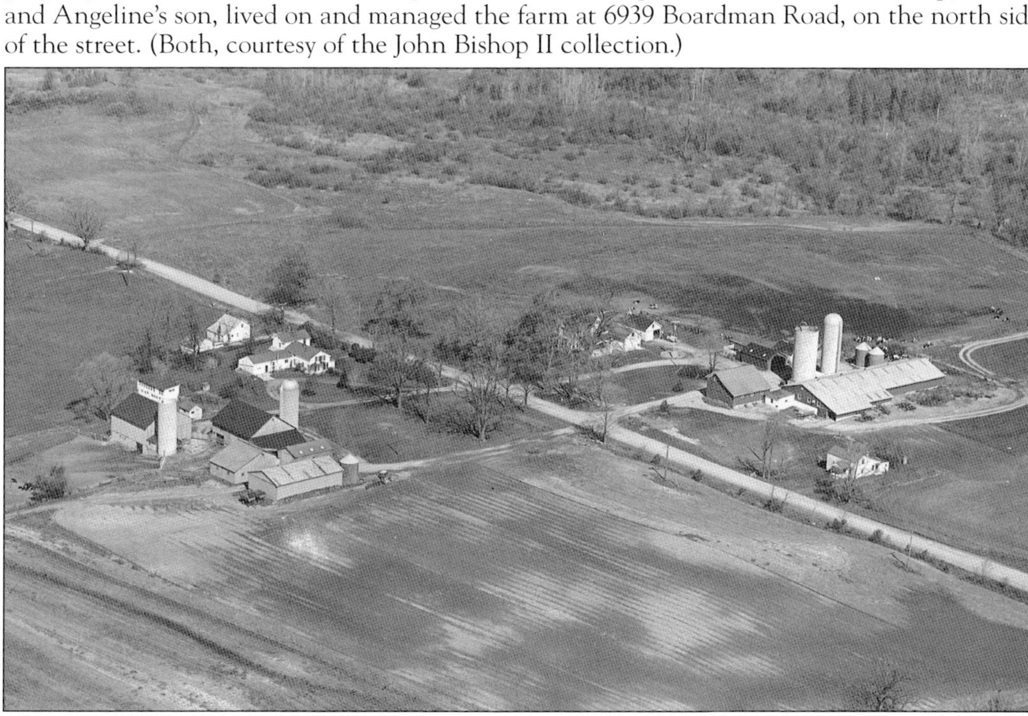

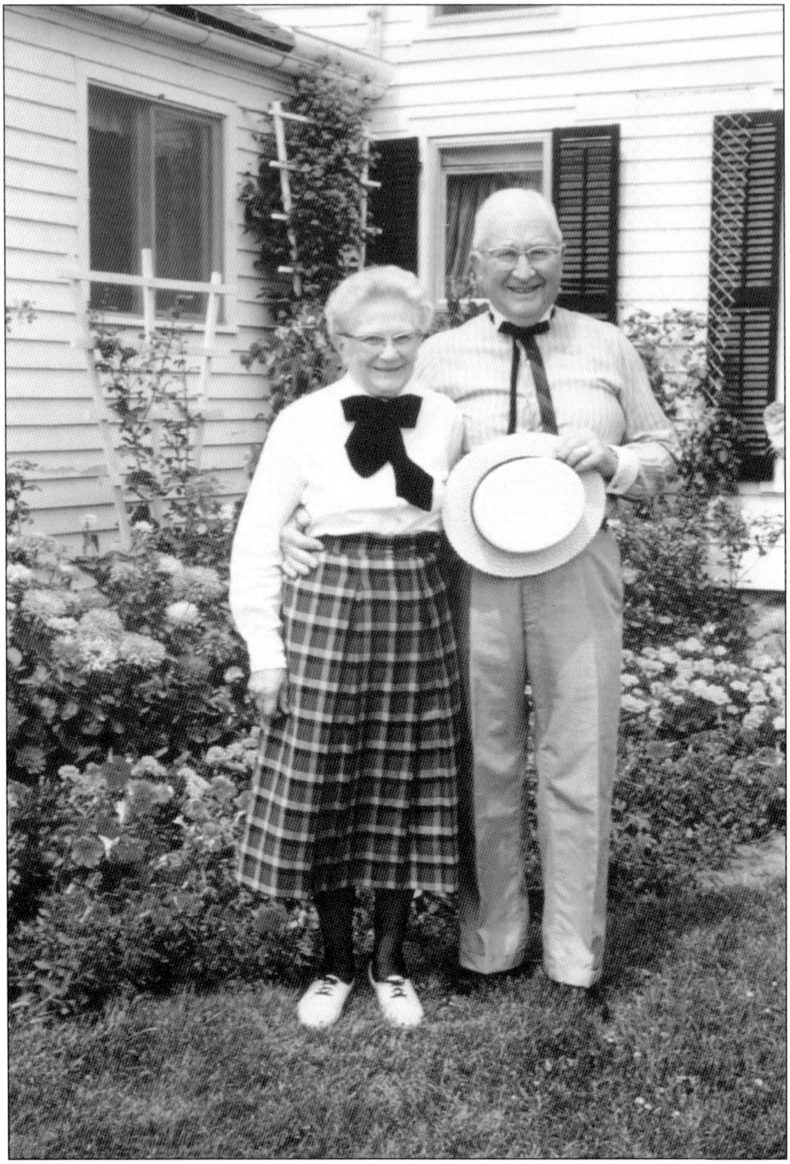

Almont's Homecoming Festivities. Frank's son Leon Bishop (1894–1989) grew up on the north-side farm on Boardman Road with his siblings and traveled to school in Almont, approximately four miles away, by horse and buggy. After Leon attended and graduated from Michigan Agricultural College, now Michigan State University, he returned home to live on the "home farm," as he referred to 6939 Boardman Road. In March 1918, he was appointed as the first extension agent for the new Lapeer County Farm Bureau. He worked in that job for a number of years while he and his wife, Emma Borland (1891–1976), raised their family of six children (two daughters and four sons). Leon and Emma left the farm at 6939 Boardman Road in 1925 to live "in town." In the early 1960s, they returned to live at the farm at 6930 Boardman Road, the south-side farm, until they passed away. The farm then passed onto their son John and Geraldine Bishop, keeping the farm in the Bishop family for over 165 years. Pictured above, Leon and Emma are outside of the farmhouse in the 1970s dressed in period clothing for Almont's homecoming festivities. (Courtesy of the John Bishop II collection.)

Eight

Armada Township

Armada Township was a brushy, low-lying swampland when the governmental surveyors came to the area in 1821. The Indians settled around the streams and bottomland that was flush with game, but few white settlers had found their way this far north in the county just yet. There would soon be a very rapid growth during the years of 1831–1836. There were early settlements started in the township at Selleck's Corners, located at Romeo Plank and 32 Mile Roads, and Berry's Corners, at Omo and 32 Mile Roads.

Hosea Northrup is given credit for coming up with the name of Armada while at a meeting for the purpose of separating the new township from Ray Township. One of the villages to survive during this time was the village of Armada, originally known as Burke's Corners. The village began to prosper in the early 1830s when the old Indian trail was laid out as a road now called Armada Ridge Road. The road became a major route for travelers between the village of Romeo and the area of Port Huron. The village became incorporated with the arrival of the railroad to the area in 1869.

The village soon prospered and was home to a sash and blind factory, a cheese industry, a flour mill, blacksmith shops, hardware stores, banks, and drugstores. It was home to the National Hotel, a library, and a newspaper. By 1885, an additional area was added to the village, and it was soon reincorporated. It would eventually have an opera house and a theater and become a cultural center for the area.

A large fire in 1899 destroyed many of the wooden buildings along Armada's Main Street, where the Armada residents went on to rebuild more permanent buildings and continue to make the area thrive. Andrew Carnegie, the Scottish industrialist, donated $8,000 toward the permanent building of a township library. With the help of the township to make up for the shortage, the Armada Free Public Library was erected in 1915.

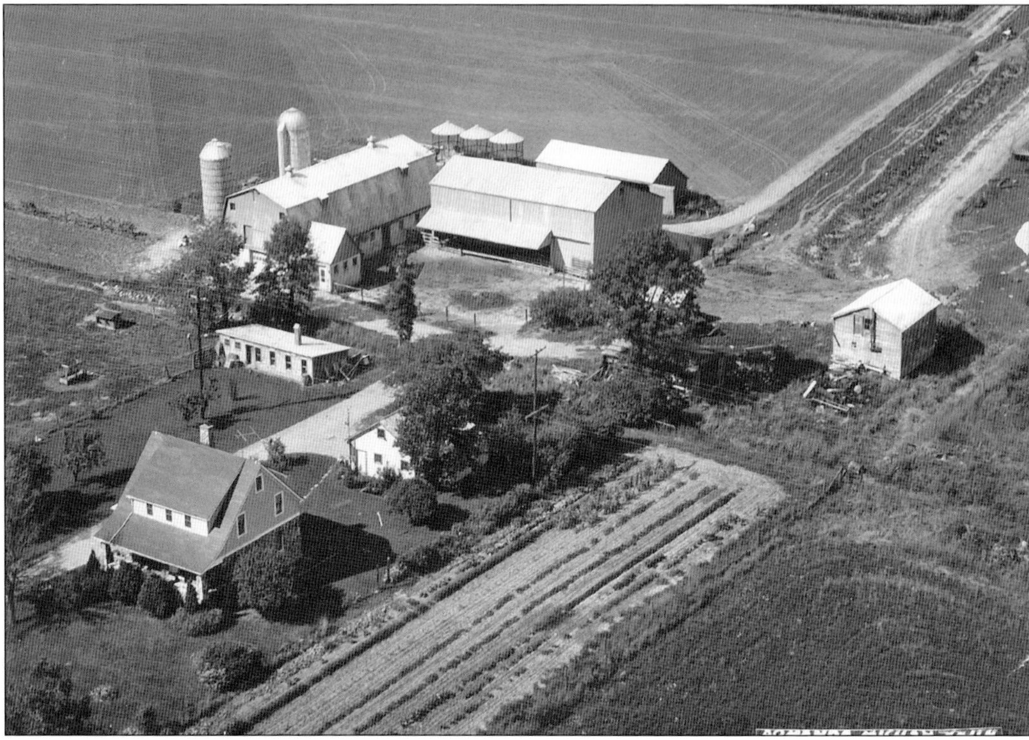

Enright Farm. The farm on the northeast corner of Capac and Armada Center Roads belonged to Carl Frederick Henry Christopher Enright (1902–1986) and his wife, Effie Sophia Wilbur (1902–1986). They married at the First Baptist Church in Romeo, and over the years, they became a family of eight with the addition of six children (two sons and four daughters). The farm had about 150 dairy cows that needed milking twice a day, along with the care in raising pigs, chickens, and ducks. The Enrights grew and baled hay, oats, wheat, and corn and then took their crops to the Armada elevator to be sold. Pictured below, grandson Steven milks the cows. (Both, courtesy of the Steven LeFever collection.)

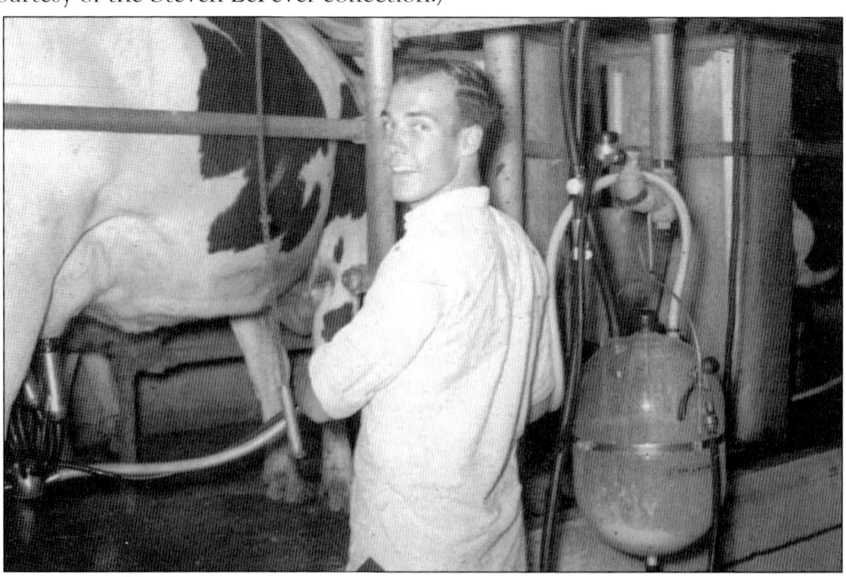

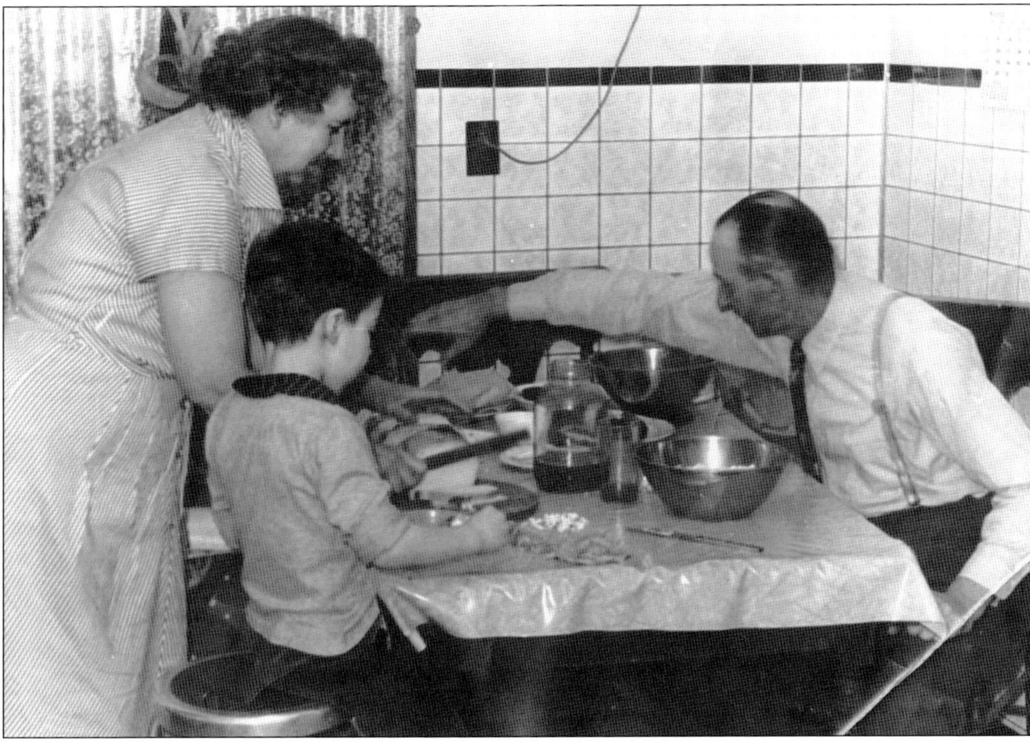

A Grandson Remembers Lunch on the Farm. One of the Enrights' sons, Lyle, purchased a farm across from his parents when he came home from the Korean War, serving with the 101st Airborne. Lyle passed away after a farm accident in 1968 at only 32 years of age. He was clearing some grain in the blue-glass silo so it would go down into the built-in auger, and even though he had opened vents, he was deprived of oxygen for a few minutes. He was found 10 minutes later. Carl came out of retirement and helped Lyle's wife and five children run the farm until the house and barns could be sold; however, a major portion of the farm is still in family hands. Above, Effie Enright, grandson Steven, and Carl Enright eat lunch in Effie's kitchen on the farm around the late 1950s. Carl and Effie were both buried in the Bruce Armada Cemetery after their deaths in 1986. (Both, courtesy of the Steven LeFever collection.)

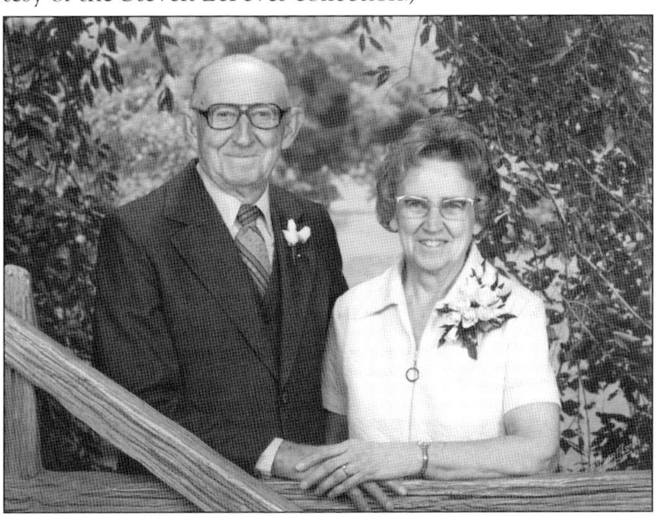

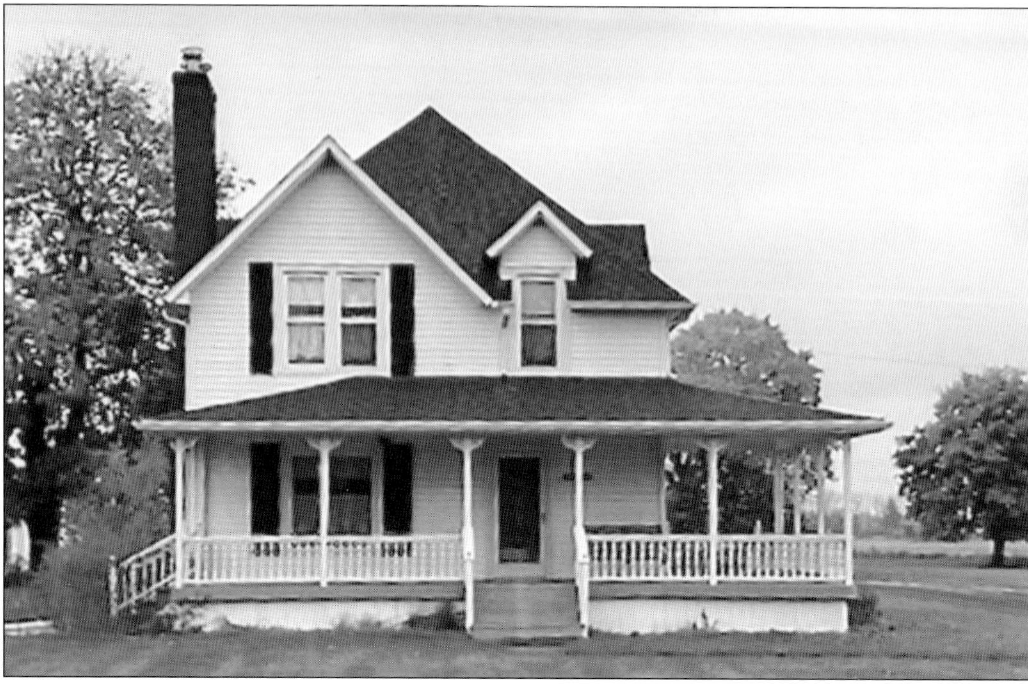

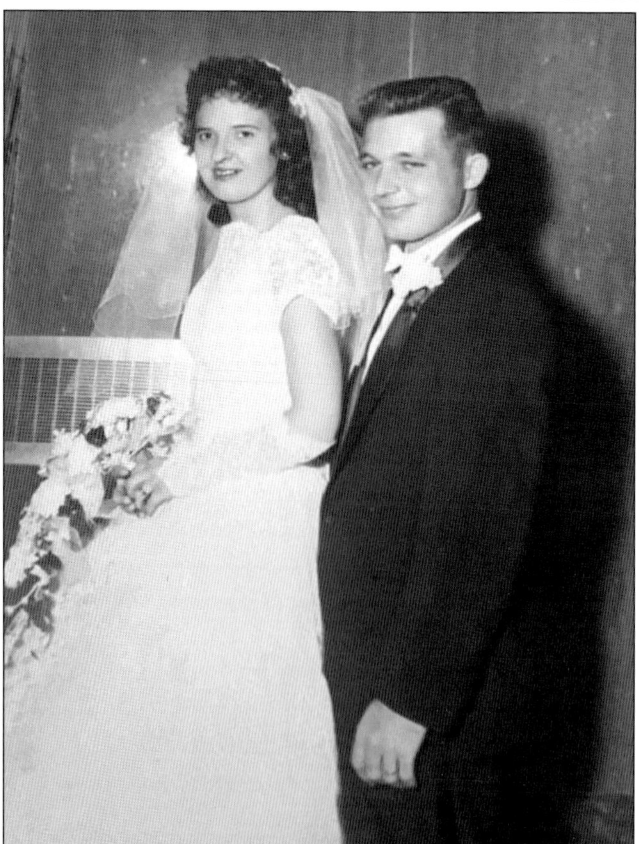

Fairbanks Farm. Jim Fairbanks was a Korean War veteran who worked at Chrysler as a boiler operator. Jim and his wife, Nancy, while living in the 9 Mile Road and Van Dyke Avenue area, would drive out most weekends to the Armada area looking for a farm. They ended up purchasing the farm their real estate agent had been living in. So, on August 5, 1968, the Fairbanks family, with two adults and four children, settled in Armada to a vastly different but highly enjoyable new life. The new life started at 24691 33 Mile Road in Armada, with horses and rabbits and eventually feeder pigs and beef cattle. Jim planted soybeans and corn and loved to work the farmland around the property. (Both, courtesy of the Kathy Dunlap collection.)

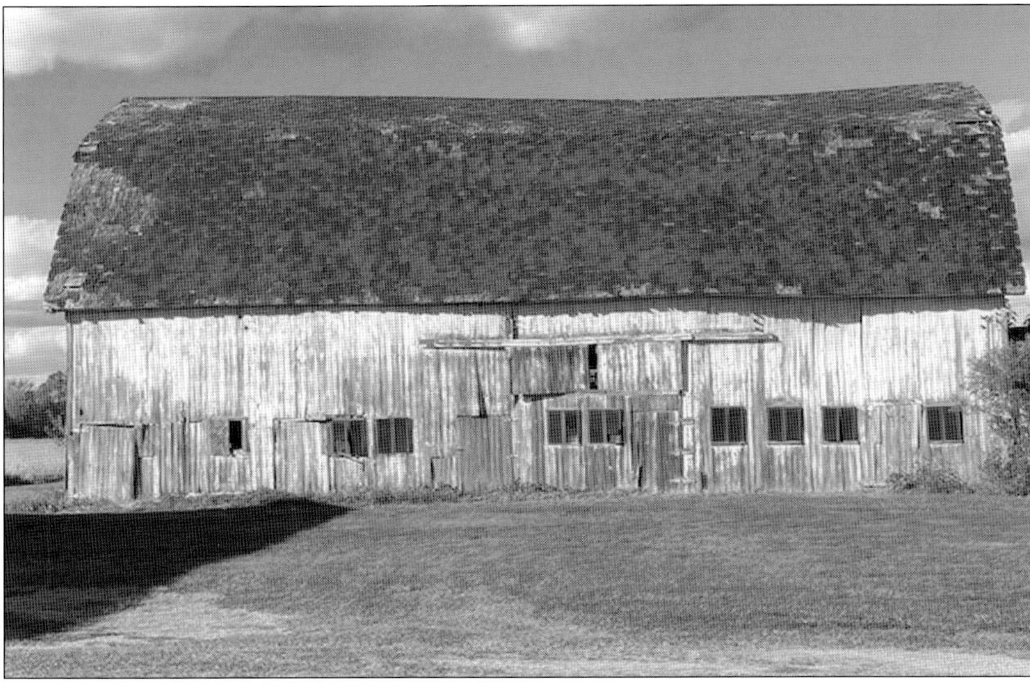

The Armada Fair. When younger, the Fairbanks children loved playing in the loft of the barn. While there were tractors, combines, and other farm equipment, the children helped with the baling of the hay and getting it into the barn. The Armada Fair was the big event that was looked forward to each year. Life was simpler then, and they all came to love the move that had changed their lives so much. (Courtesy of the Kathy Dunlap collection.)

Remembering a Special Birthday. Pictured is a note that Nancy Fairbanks wrote to her daughter Kathy in 1984 to remind her that their move in 1968 from the suburbs to this new farm had really been worth it—after all the tears that had occurred while looking for a farm. Kathy was teased throughout her life that the farm was her birthday present, as they had moved on her birthday. (Courtesy of the Kathy Dunlap collection.)

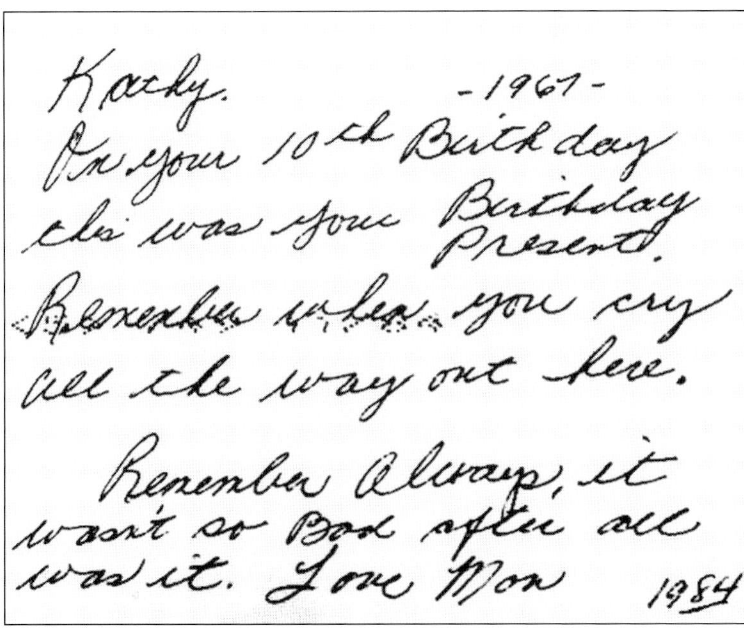

Kathy. -1967-
On your 10th Birthday
this was your Birthday
Present.
Remember when you cry
all the way out here.

Remember Always, it
wasn't so Bad after all
was it. Love Mom 1984

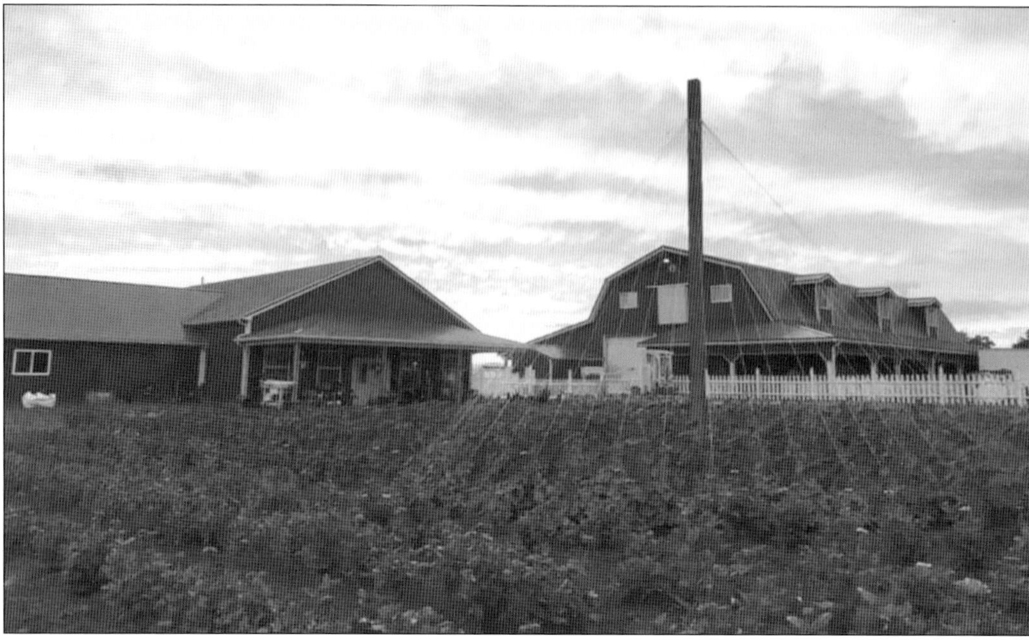

Don Van Houtte Farm. At 69475 Romeo Plank Road in Armada Township is Van Houtte's Farm Market, on 50 acres bought in 1991 and run by the father-and-son team of Don and Donny Van Houtte, as pictured below. The Van Houtte family has been farming since the 1920s. The family homestead on 34 Mile Road was started in 1969, and family members have been vendors at the Oakland County Farmers Markets since 1968. (Both, courtesy of the Don Van Houtte collection.)

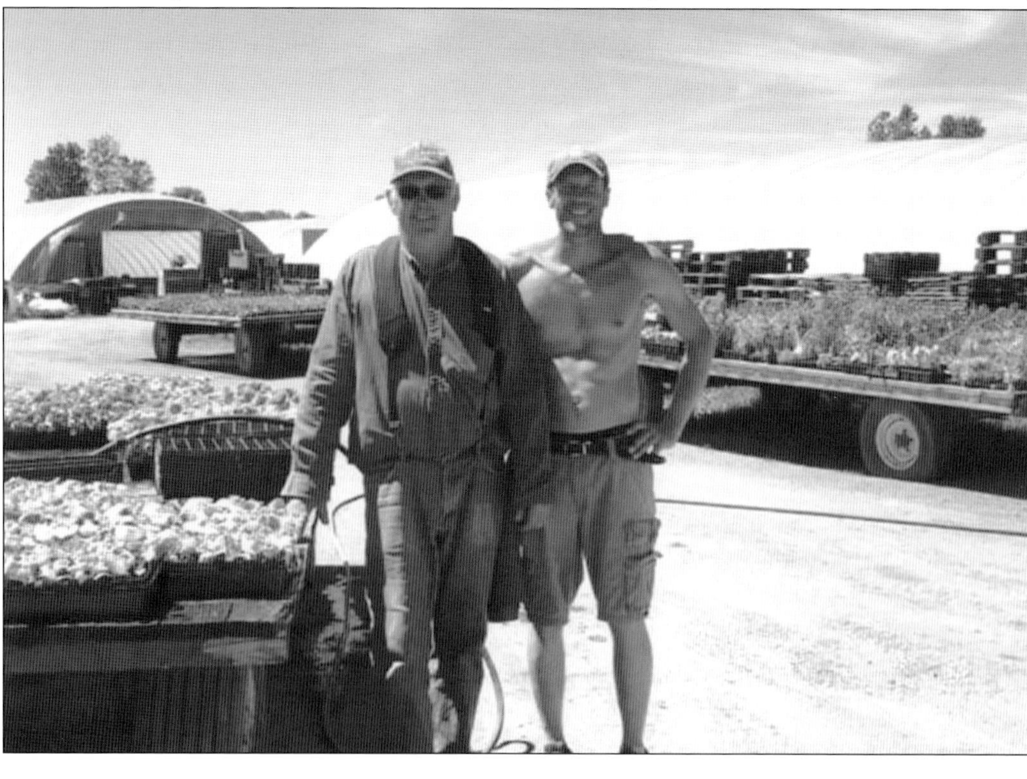

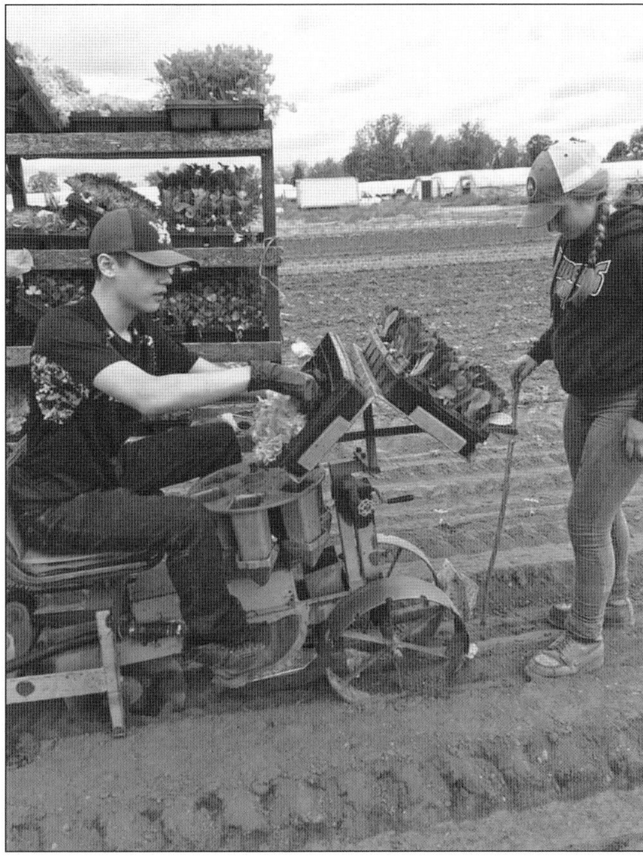

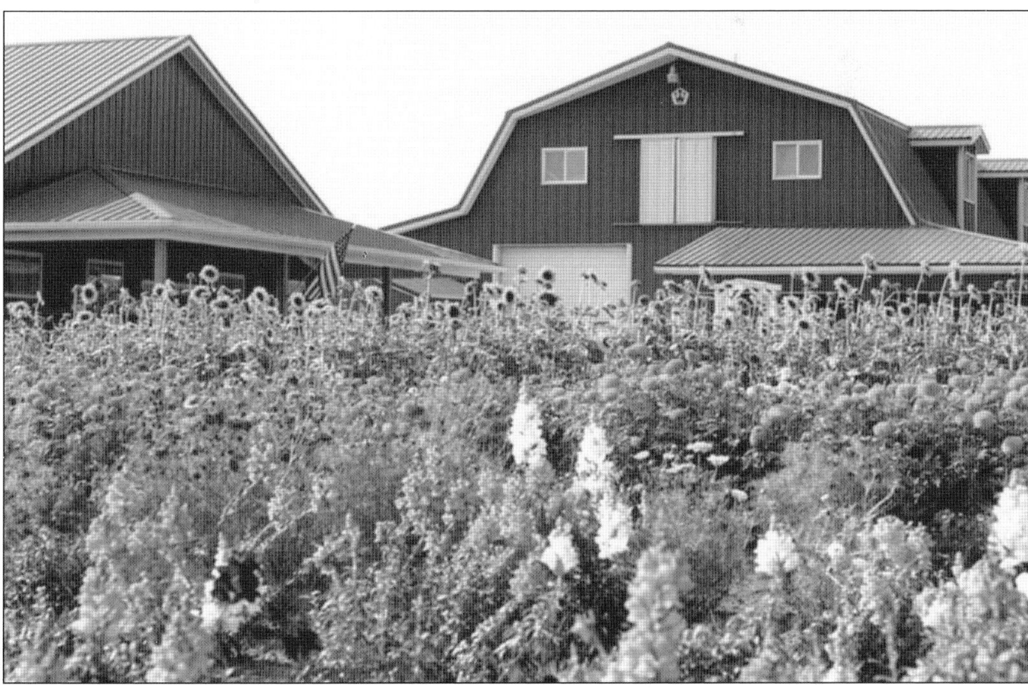

Planting Time. Pictured here are the Van Houttes getting the plants into the ground. Don and his three sons—Donnie, Michael, and Kyle—made Van Houtte's Farm Market known for its spring flowers and vegetables. In addition, the market's giant 50- to 150-pound pumpkins can be etched and personalized. (Both, courtesy of the Don Van Houtte collection.)

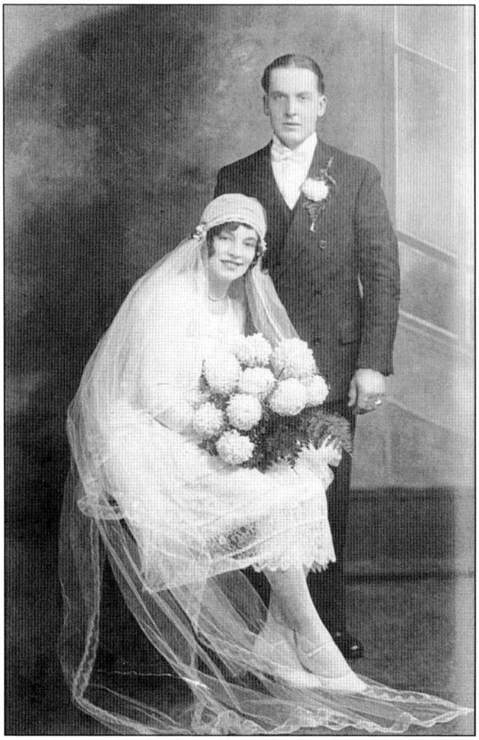

Jenuwine Farm. Leo (1902–1970) and Ethel Schoenherr Jenuwine (1905–1995) moved from their farm on 15 Mile Road in Warren to their 120-acre farm at 15670 33 Mile Road in Armada Township in 1957. Leo and Ethel raised 10 children: Shirley, Donna, Joseph, Thomas, Gary, Urban, Dale, Mark, Norman, and Lois. When they moved to Armada, there were six still at home who helped work the farm. The Jenuwine farm was mainly a dairy farm, but it also raised chickens, hogs, and sheep. The farm also grew hothouse rhubarb, and some of this produce was sold at Detroit's Eastern Market. Pictured are Leo and Ethel when they married. (Both, courtesy of the Dale Jenuwine collection.)

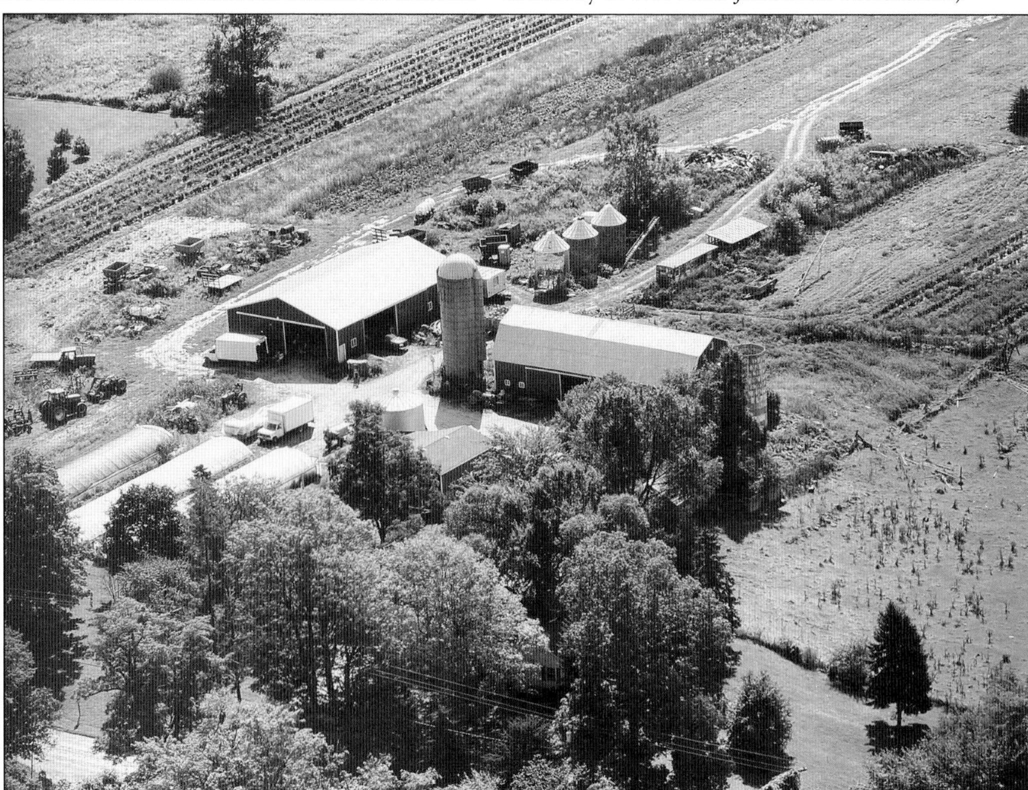

SELLING THE PRODUCE. Dale stayed on the farm and continued to farm with Leo until his death in 1970. Dale; his wife, Thomasine (Leto); and their children Jim, Mary, and JoEllen continued to farm with Ethel until 1986, when they purchased the farm from her. Afterward, the farm transitioned from dairy to other livestock and more produce in greenhouses. The family continues to sell produce at the Mount Clemens Farmers Market, Oakland County Market, and from their farm. Pictured at right is Leo with his son Dale. (Both, courtesy of the Dale Jenuwine collection.)

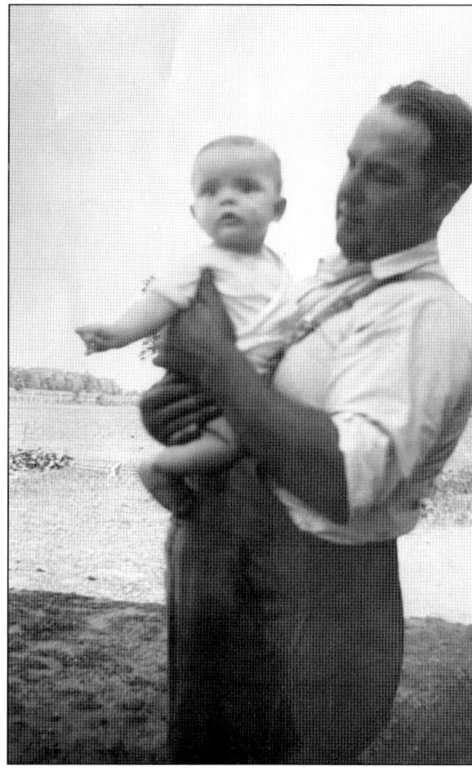

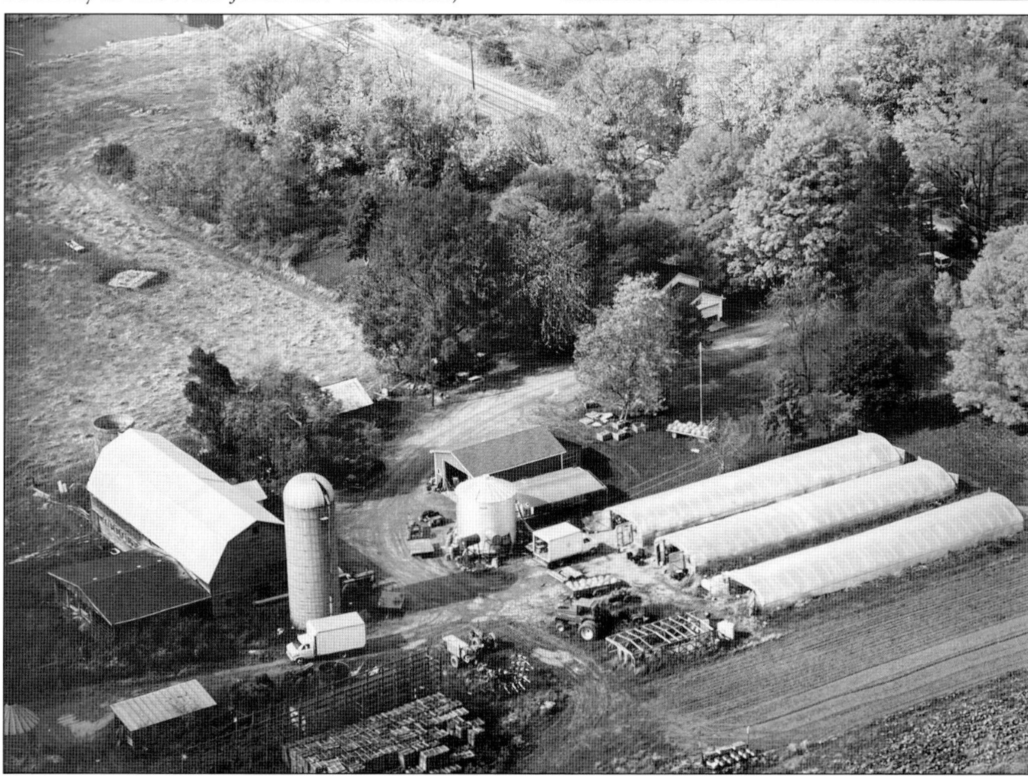

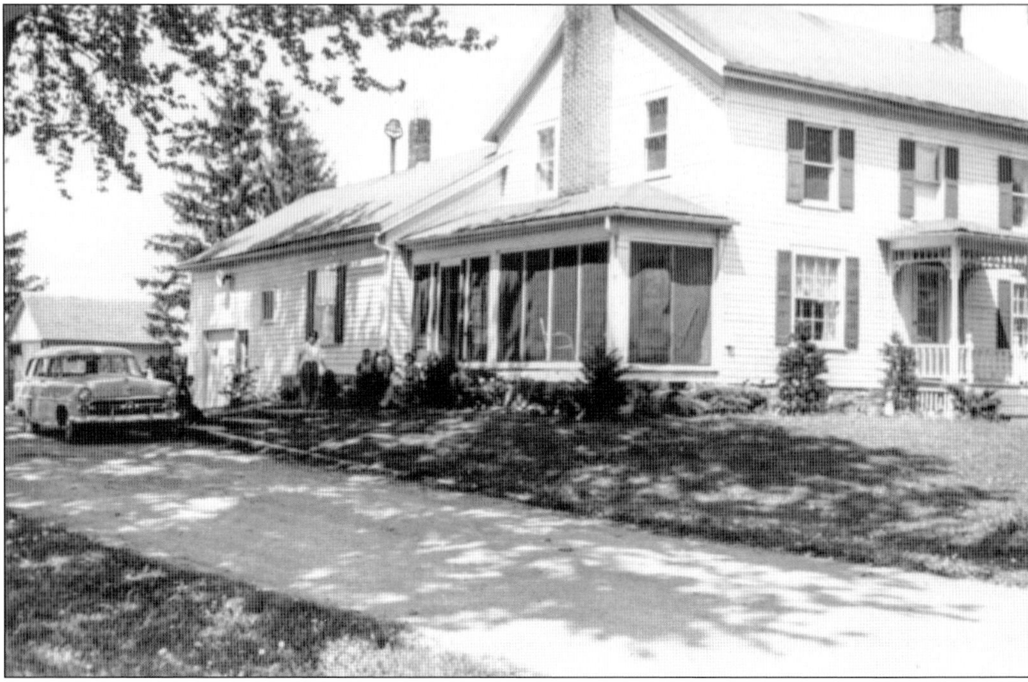

Blake's Orchard and Cider Mill. Founded in 1946 by Gerald and Lovely Blake, the Blake farm was built on hard work with help from family. Gerald moved the family out of the suburbs and onto a 100-acre property in Armada Township and raised 13 children in a three-bedroom farmhouse. The farm grew to an 800-acre working farm and orchards, growing over 40 different apple varieties for over 70 years. (Both, courtesy of the Blake's Orchard and Cider Mill collection.)

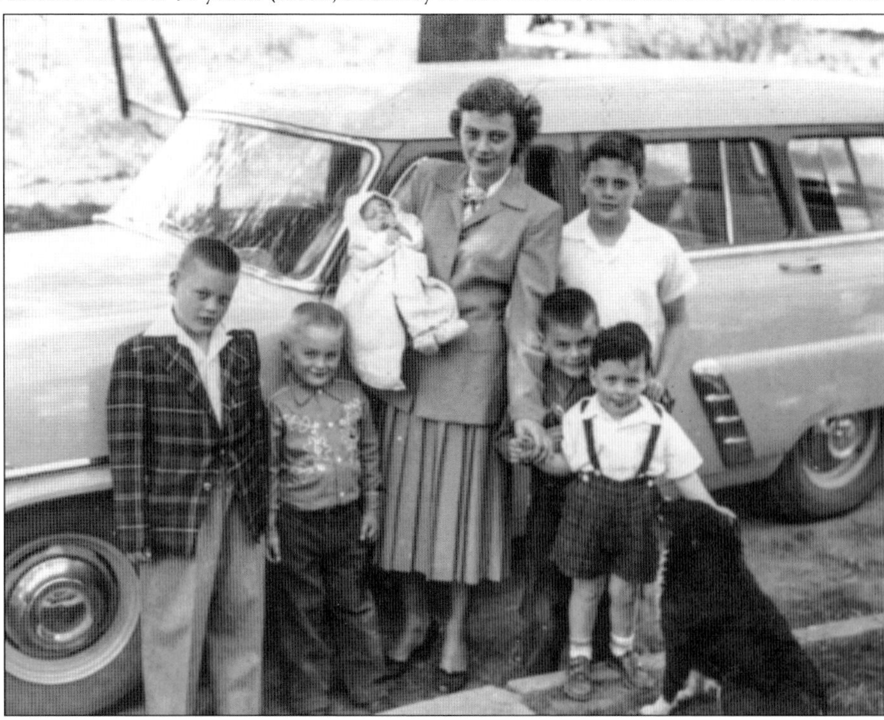

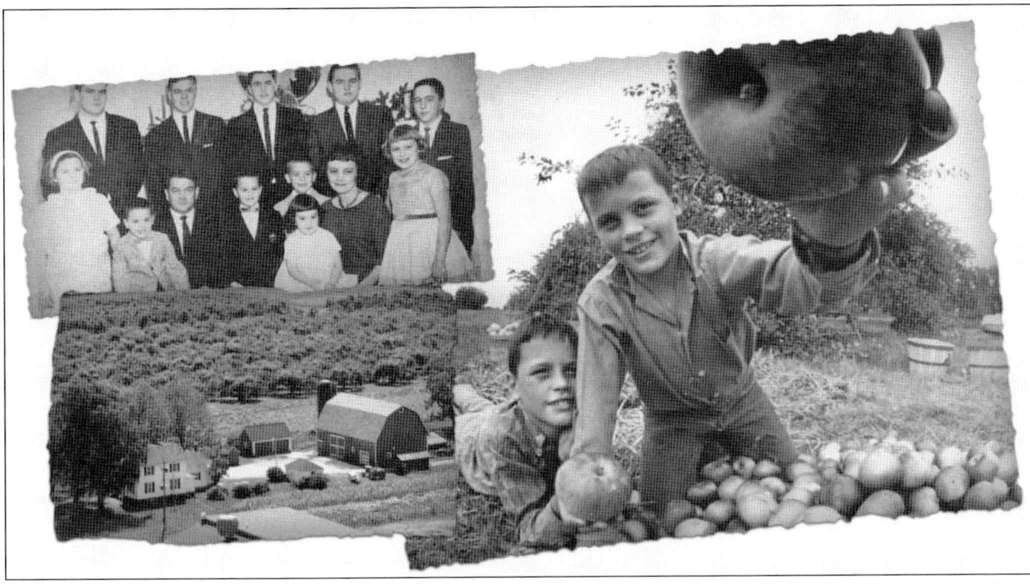

Growing a Business. Twins Pete and Paul Blake returned after graduating from Michigan State University with an interest in growing what their family had built over the years and adding more diverse experiences for visitors. Years later, Paul's son Andrew Blake, who had grown up working the farm with his family, returned to Armada after graduating from Michigan State University with a desire to explore hard cider. With his family's blessing and support, Andrew founded Blake's Hard Cider in 2013. (Both, courtesy of the Blake's Orchard and Cider Mill collection.)

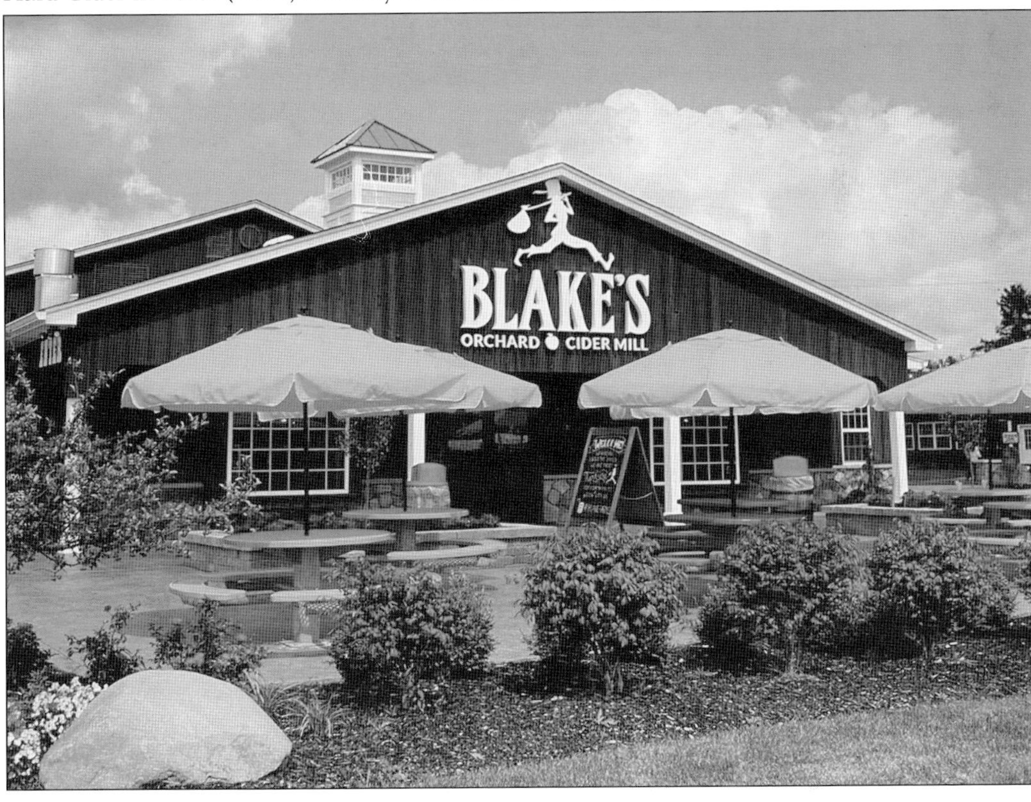

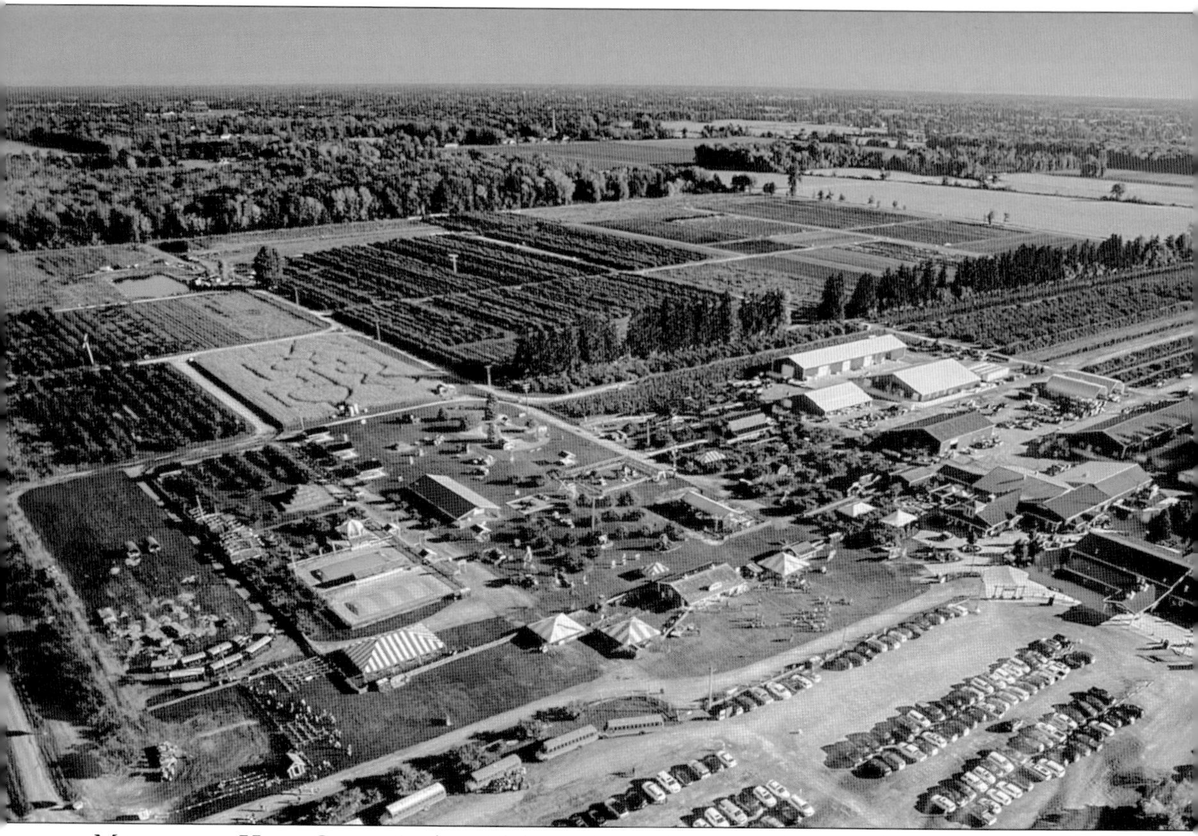

Making the Hard Cider. Andrew Blake made his first batch of hard cider in his college garage while attending MSU and would take it around to parties for friends to enjoy, but he admits it was not his best work and that he did not know what he was doing at first. After coming back home, Andrew was determined to craft an uncompromised line of all-natural hard ciders that were not overly sweet like the competitors. Andrew says the unique profile is attributed to a blend of five apple varieties grown on the Blake farms with an added proprietary wine yeast. The apple base used is pure cider and not from concentrate, resulting in the purest profile, creating a bright, clean, and flavorful line of products. This has led to one of the fastest-growing companies in the industry, with distribution in 18 states. (Courtesy of the Blake's Orchard and Cider Mill collection.)

Nine

Richmond Township

Richmond is the northernmost township in Macomb County; it was settled later than most of the other townships that are nearer to Mount Clemens and the Clinton River. The township was first organized under legislation authority on March 6, 1838. Phillip Cudworth suggested the name of Richmond after a town in Ontario County, New York, with the same name. It was 1884 before the last of the governmental lands were purchased by Richard Ball in section 16. Another village in Richmond is Memphis, although it lies partly in St. Clair County. It would become an incorporated village in 1865. A portion of the city of Richmond is adjacent to the township but administratively separate.

The land where the village of Richmond now stands was called Beebe's Corners after Erastus Beebe first bought the land from the government in 1835. Being the area where the ridge running east and west joined the ridge running north and south, with the importance of highlands for roadways, it seemed the perfect area to grow a community. It soon had a general store and a blacksmith shop, run by H.P. Beebe, and it remained Beebe's Corners until the area was granted a village charter in 1879. In 1878, it joined with the two nearest neighboring communities of Ridgeway and Cooper Town to form the village of Richmond. The portion of the township known as "the Ridge" was the first to see new settlers from the trail and from the settlement of Armada and then between the villages of Richmond and Memphis farther north. The Muttonville community was so named because of its predominance as a sheep-raising area.

With the building of the Grand Trunk Railroad, the village began to grow and expand, and with the large agricultural interests of the township, Richmond formed a very important portion of the county. The Richmond Post Office was established in 1840 with Phillip Cudworth as the first postmaster. The village of Richmond has seven churches: Baptist, Roman Catholic, Congregational, German Evangelical, Methodist Episcopal, German Lutheran, and German Methodist.

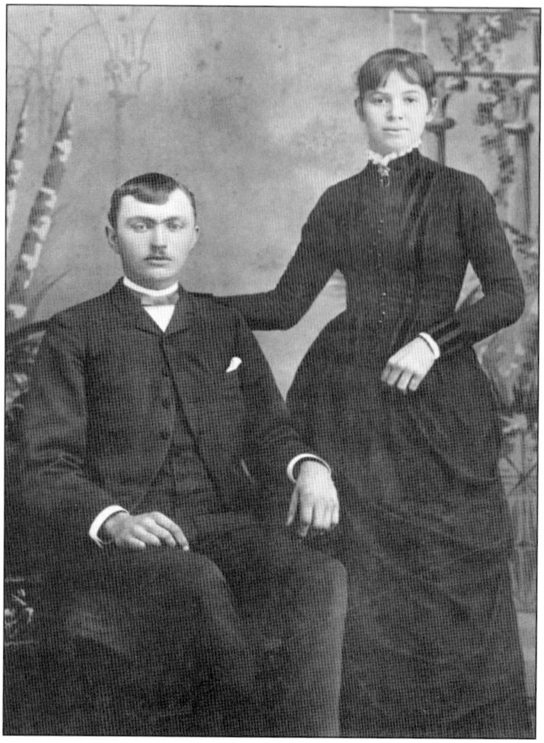

Fuerstenau Farm. In 1902, Charles William Fuerstenau (1864–1956) and his wife, Minnie Caroline Kemp (1864–1919), purchased the 160-acre farm on the southeast corner of Lowe Plank and Fuerstenau Road where they raised five children. The Fuerstenaus favored purebred Holsteins for their dairy farm. They also grew a small area of wheat and beans for cash crops. Charles and Minnie's son Roy (1891–1966) and his wife, Frances Kooiker (1899–1982), were the next generation to become the farm owners. Roy was a soil conservation enthusiast and a crop reporter in the township for over 20 years as part of the Farm Bureau. Roy and Frances raised a daughter, Ruth, and son, Gordon, on the farm. Gordon continued working the farm after the death of his father in 1956. (Both, courtesy of the Phyllis Fuerstenau collection.)

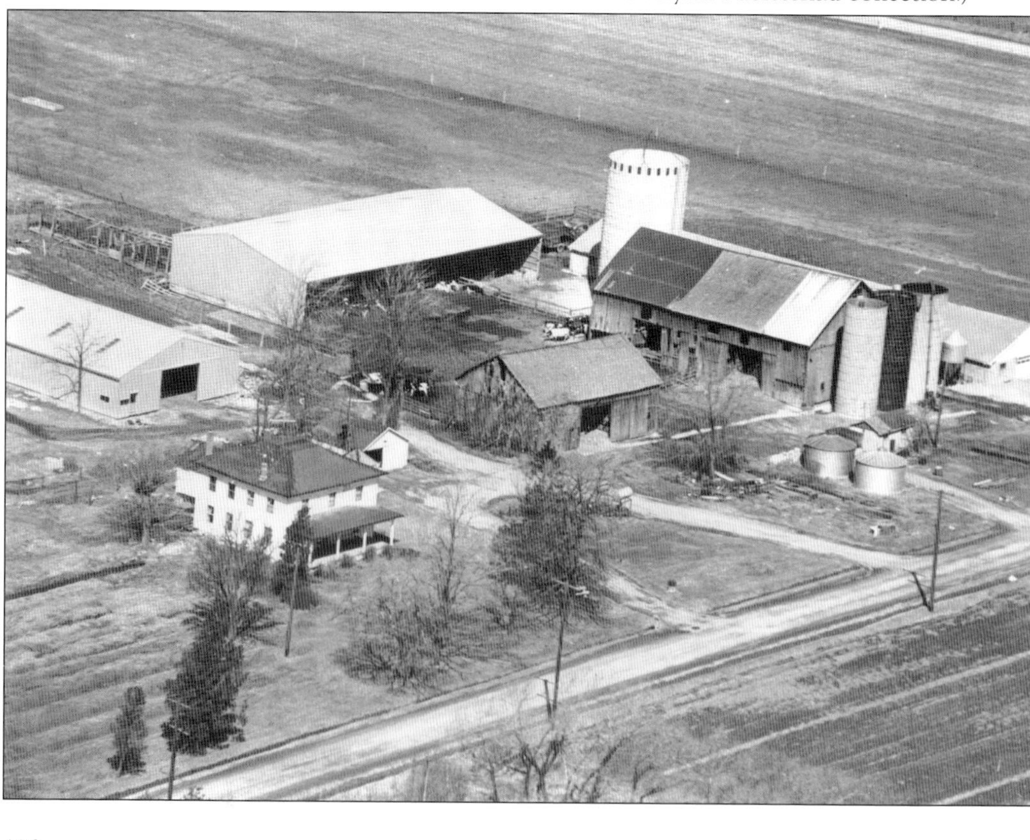

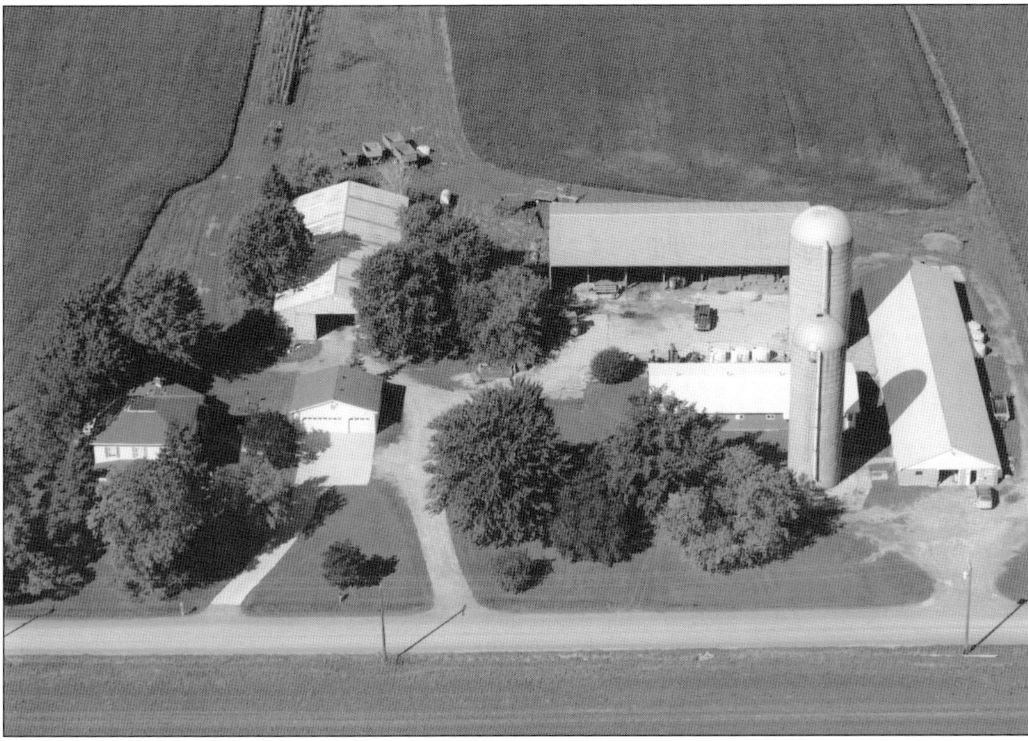

The Third Generation Continues the Farm. Gordon Fuerstenau (1932–2015) and Phyllis Brueninger (1934–) married in Dexter, Michigan, in 1957. Gordon obtained a two-year degree from Michigan State University in agriculture. While enjoying the farming life, he also became a longtime Richmond Township clerk and supervisor; member of the Michigan Farm Bureau, Michigan Holstein Association, Michigan Milk Producers Association, and Michigan Dairy Herd Association; and state board member of the Greenstone Farm Credit Services. Gordon and Phyllis had two children and numerous grandchildren. It was while serving on the township board that he worked with the administration to preserve the farmland in the Richmond Township area. (Both, courtesy of the Phyllis Fuerstenau collection.)

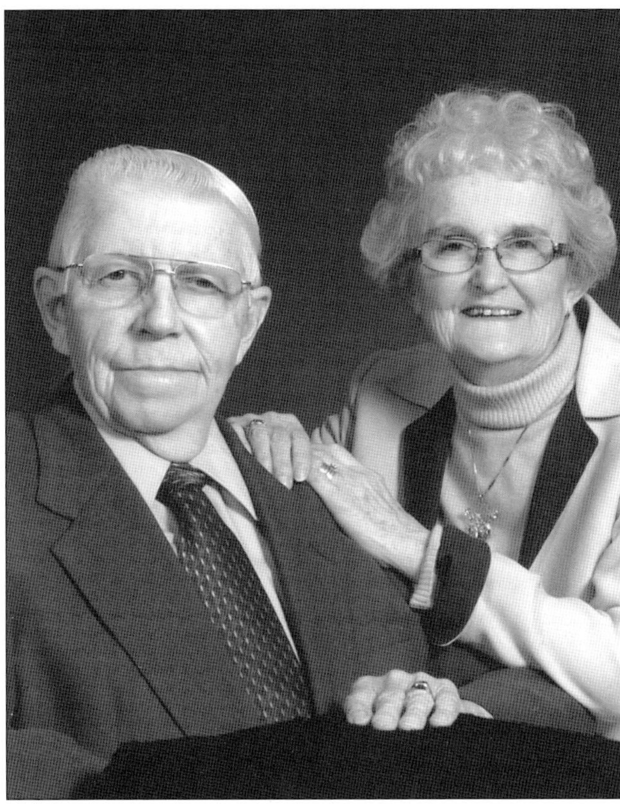

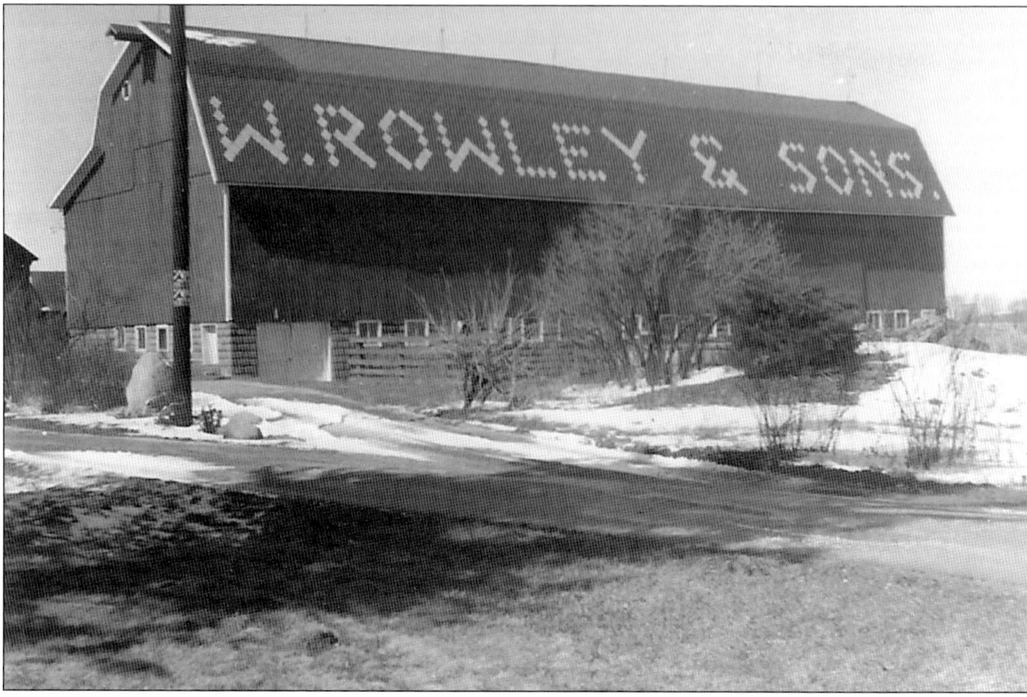

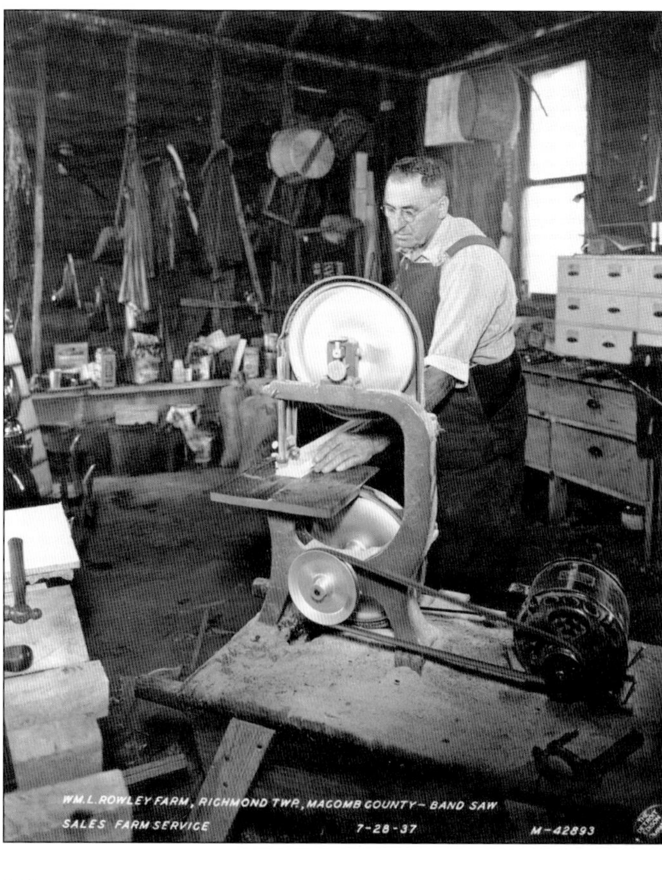

ROWLEY FARM. The Rowley farm was established in Richmond Township in 1914 by William L. "Will" Rowley (1874–1960). The farm was located on the corner of Main Street and School Section Road. In addition to a dairy herd, Rowley & Sons had a threshing and a milk-hauling business. By 1916, there were 160 acres that the Rowley family is still managing today. Will's wife, Mary Ward Rowley, passed away in 1931. (Both, courtesy of the Christine Rowley collection.)

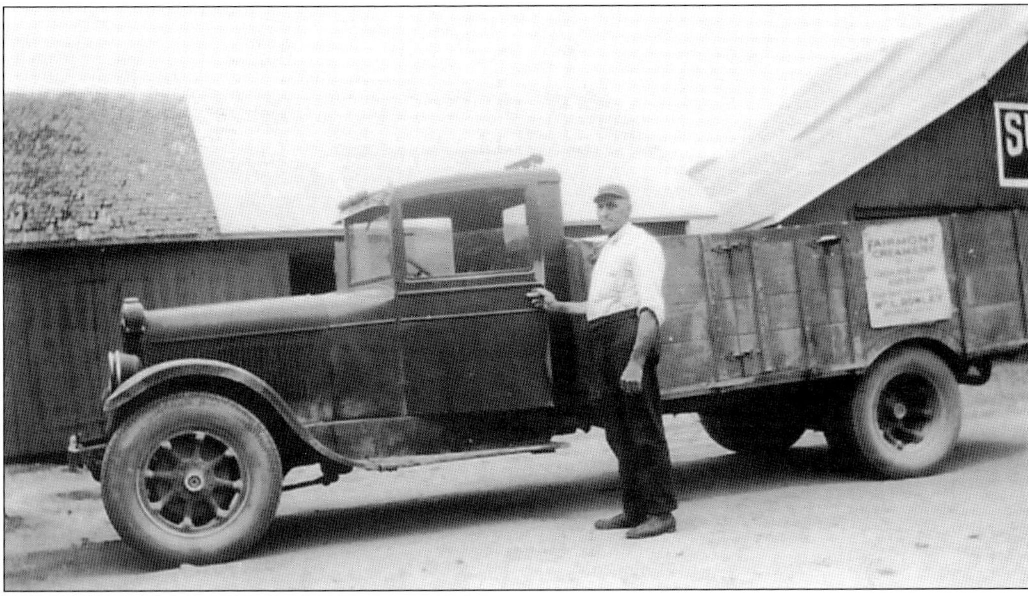

Four Generations. Will's son William Arthur "Art" (1912–2005) worked on the family farm his entire life. Art's wife, Arleen Hartway Rowley (1908–1990), was an area schoolteacher. Art and Arleen's sons, Bill (1943–2005), Bob (1944–2016), and John (1946–2001), followed the family tradition and continued with the dairy and milk-hauling business. Art and Arleen's daughters, Christine (1950–) and Barbara (1953–2007), followed their mother's path as schoolteachers. Today, the fourth generation of Rowleys continues to own and operate the Rowley farm. (Both, courtesy of the Christine Rowley collection.)

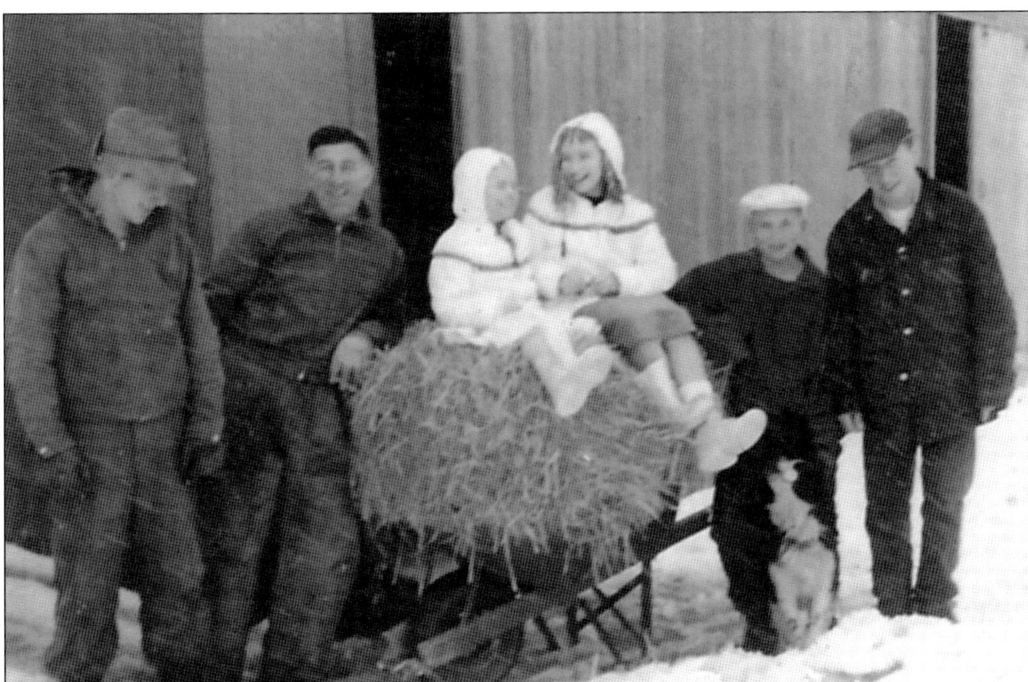

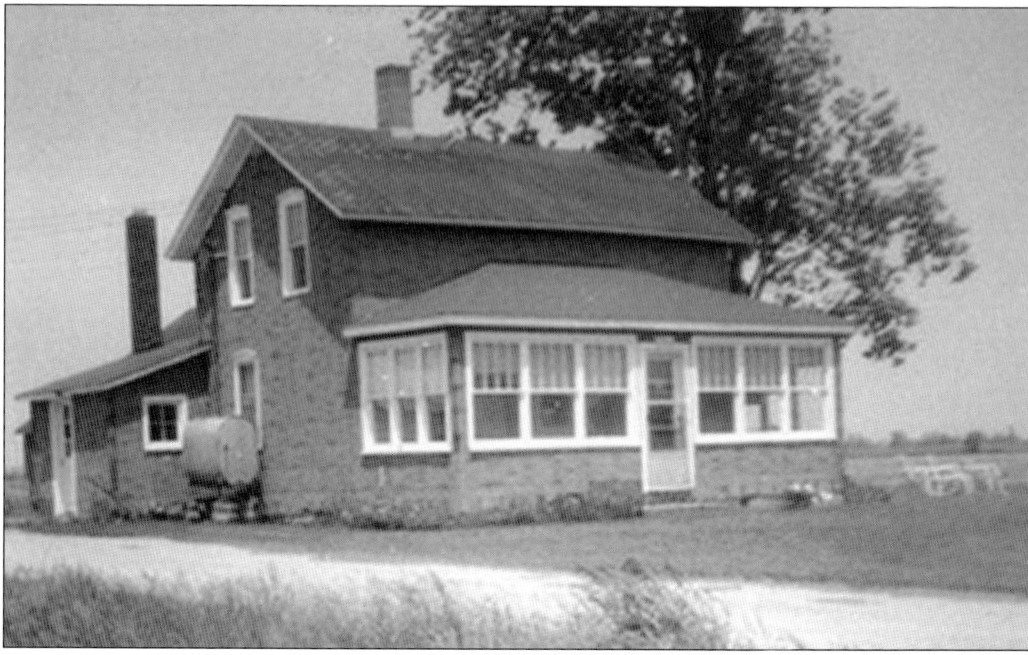

Arthur Plagens Farm. Arthur Karl Plagens (1894–1972) and Ethel May Shue (1894–1984) married in 1916. Growing up on a farm during the Great Depression meant that everyone had to pitch in with the chores. The children (there were eight of them on the Dayton Road farm) tended the cows while they grazed along the roadside and worked the fields, hoeing thistles and weeds. It was also the children's job to help plant the potatoes: they cut each potato into four, always making sure there was at least one potato eye in each piece, and then dipped them in a solution to keep them from rotting before they could grow. The potato planter was pulled by a horse, and the width of the rows was determined by the width of the horse's rear end. The Eastern Market in Detroit was of great importance to these farmers in getting their produce out to the public. (Both, courtesy of the Deborah Leach Doyle collection.)

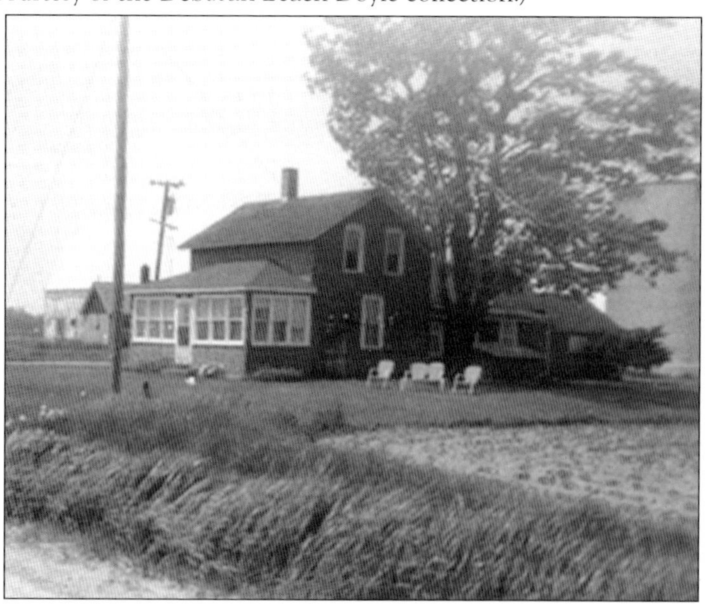

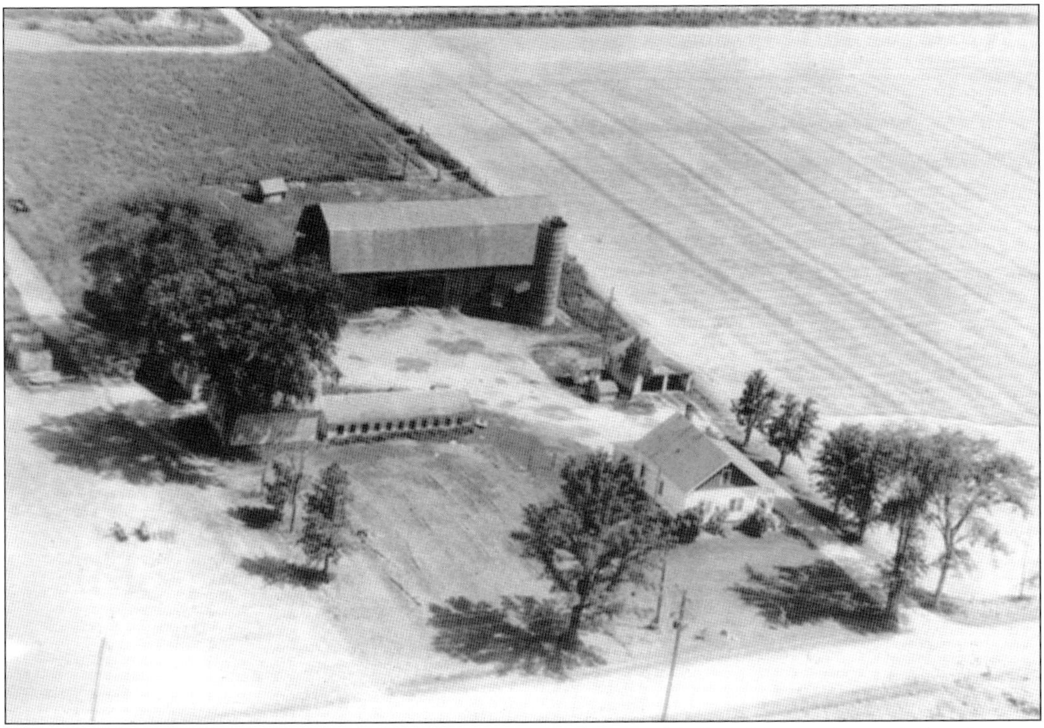

Truck Farming at Detroit's East Market. Arthur and Ethel Plagen farmed the Dayton Road farm and later moved the family to a farm on 34 Mile Road. This aerial view shows all the outbuildings that were put to use in the running of the farm. Their daughter Grace and her siblings attended School Section School, a short half-mile walk from her home. She graduated from eighth grade in 1939. Grace had memories of the times she went to Detroit's Eastern Market with her parents when she was young; when it became her turn, her siblings stayed behind to do the household chores. The truck had to be loaded with eggs, potatoes, rabbits, and chickens, and the drive to Detroit started about 4:00 or 5:00 a.m. Pictured are Arthur and Ethel celebrating their 50th wedding anniversary. (Both, courtesy of the Deborah Leach Doyle collection.)

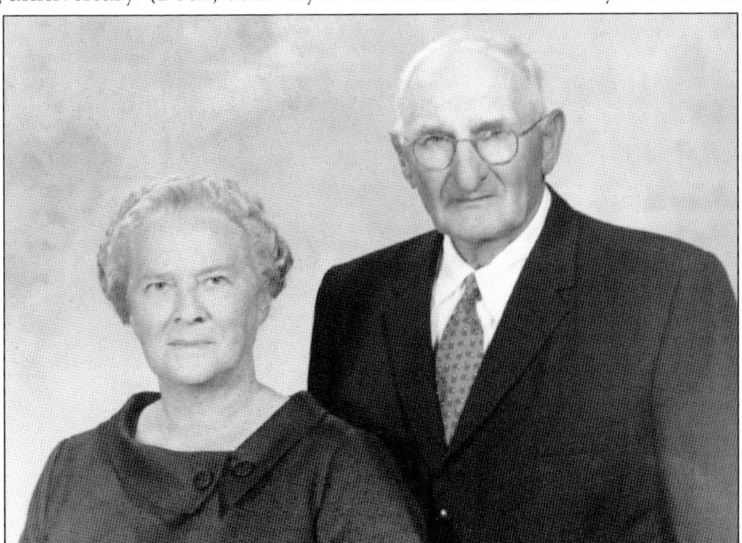

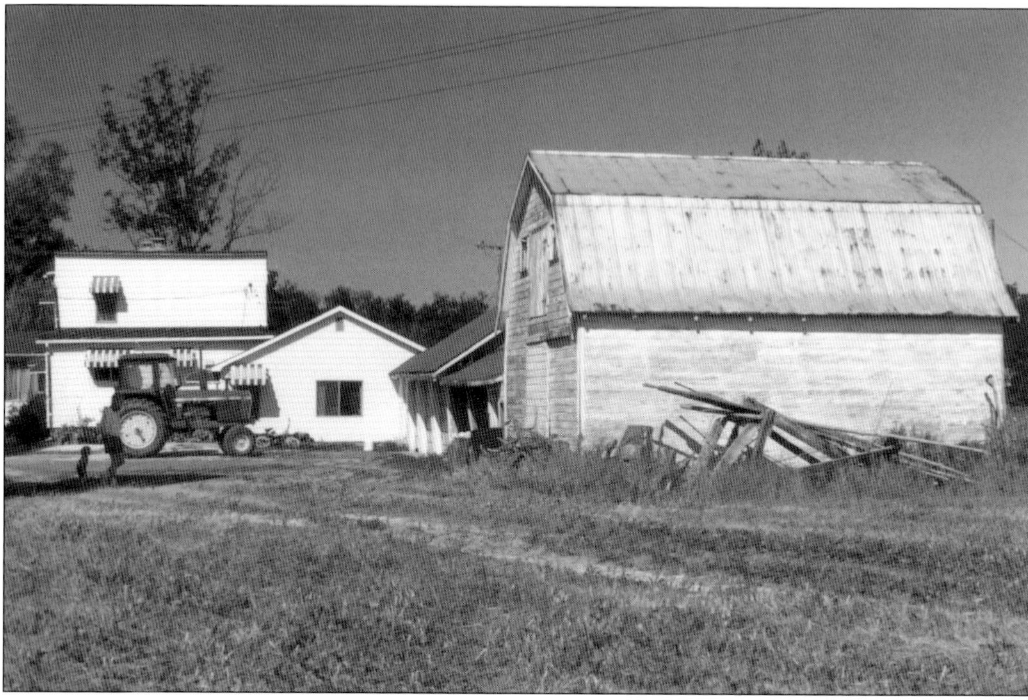

Leach Farm. Albert Lloyd Leach (1896–1972) and Ruth Jane Droulard (1896–1970) married in 1915 and bought a farm at 71260 Welding Road in Richmond Township. They had six children (four sons and two daughters), and all would help out with the farm. Albert was in the roofing business in Detroit in the early years of their marriage. In 1927, they bought their Welding Road farm from O.E. and Hattie Welding. Their son Nelson remembered times when hired hands were sometimes sailors from the Great Lakes freighters. Pictured are Albert and Ruth Leach around the 1920s. (Both, courtesy of the Deborah Leach Doyle collection.)

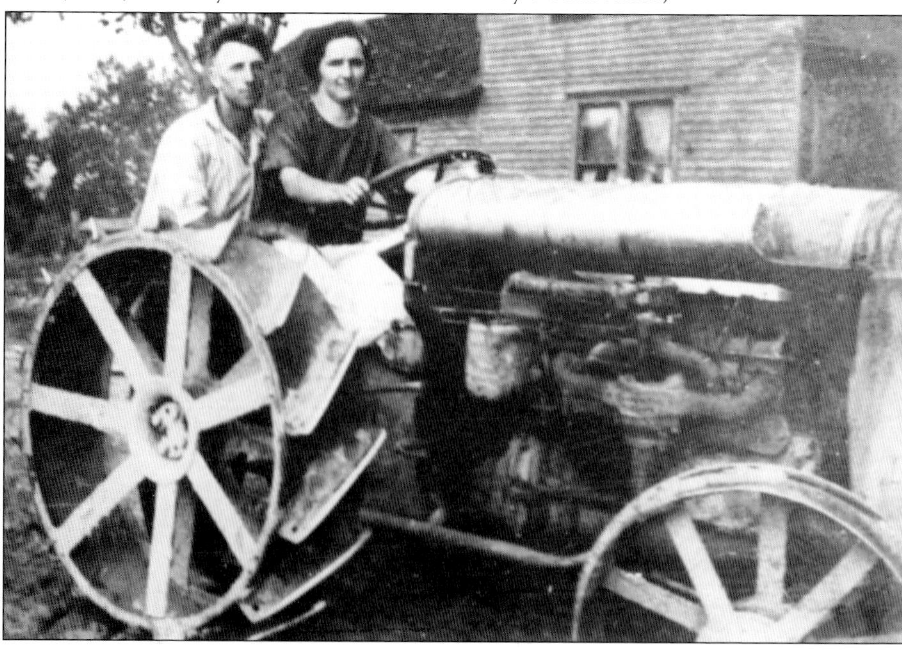

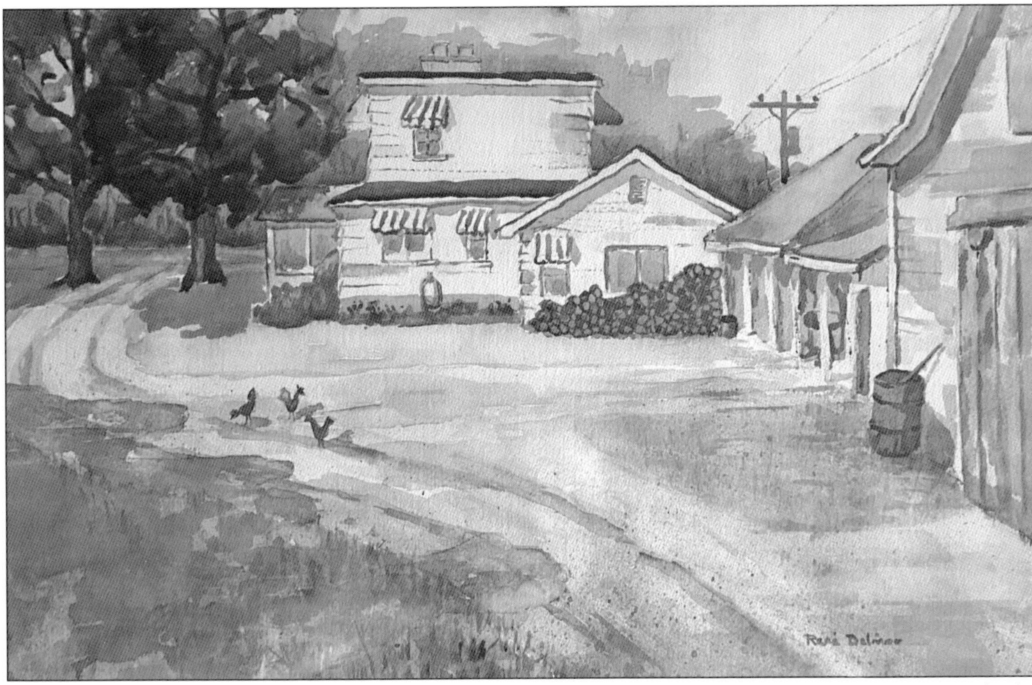

The Leach Family. In 1943, while still continuing to farm, Albert accepted a position with the Michigan Milk Producers Association. In 1953, he began work for German Farmers Mutual (which changed its name to Hastings), and by 1963, Albert purchased the Hastings Mutual Insurance office on Main Street in Richmond and operated his own insurance agency. Pictured below is a Leach family portrait from the early 1940s. From left to right are (first row) Ruth, Ruthann, Roy, and Albert; (second row) David, Stanley, Agnes, and Nelson. It was remembered that when Albert was courting Ruth they both lived near Belle River. Albert rode his horse to Ruth's house. When he went home, he would climb on his horse, hug its neck, and fall asleep. His horse would take him home along the river. (Both, courtesy of the Deborah Leach Doyle collection.)

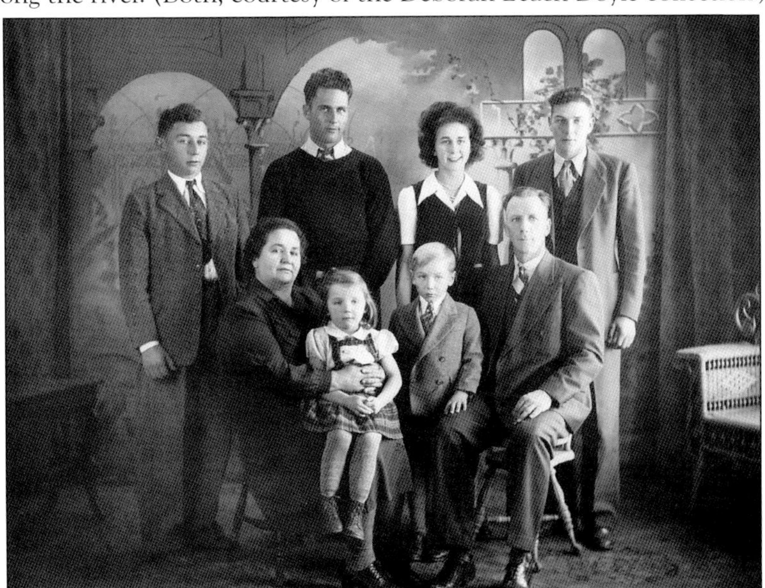

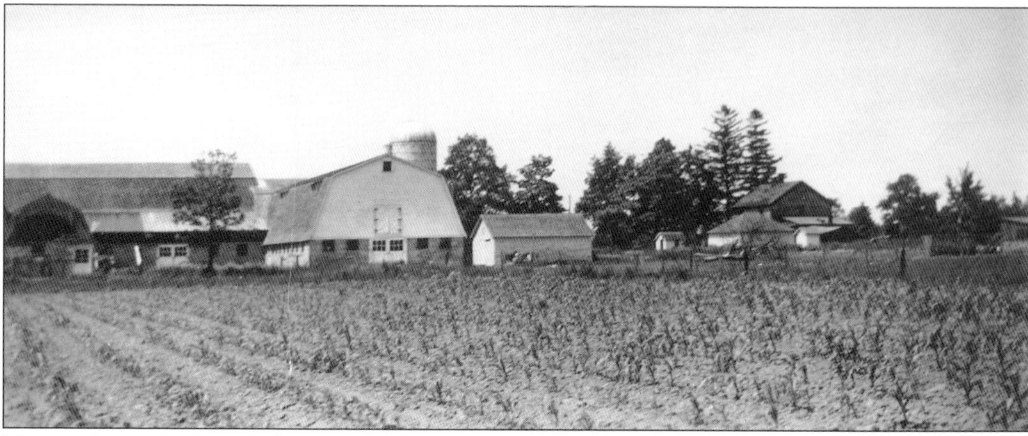

Nelson Leach Farm. Nelson John Leach (1922–2017), son of Albert and Ruth Leach, and Grace Marie Plagens (1925–2015), daughter of Arthur and Ethel Plagens, married on March 8, 1947. They purchased an 80-acre property next to Nelson's parents at 71900 Welding Road for $8,700 in August 1947. They continued to farm shares with his parents. They raised dairy cattle and planted wheat and corn for cash crops. There was always milk and eggs from the farm. In 1948, they split up the cows, and half were moved to Nelson and Grace's farm. (Both, courtesy of the Deborah Leach Doyle collection.)

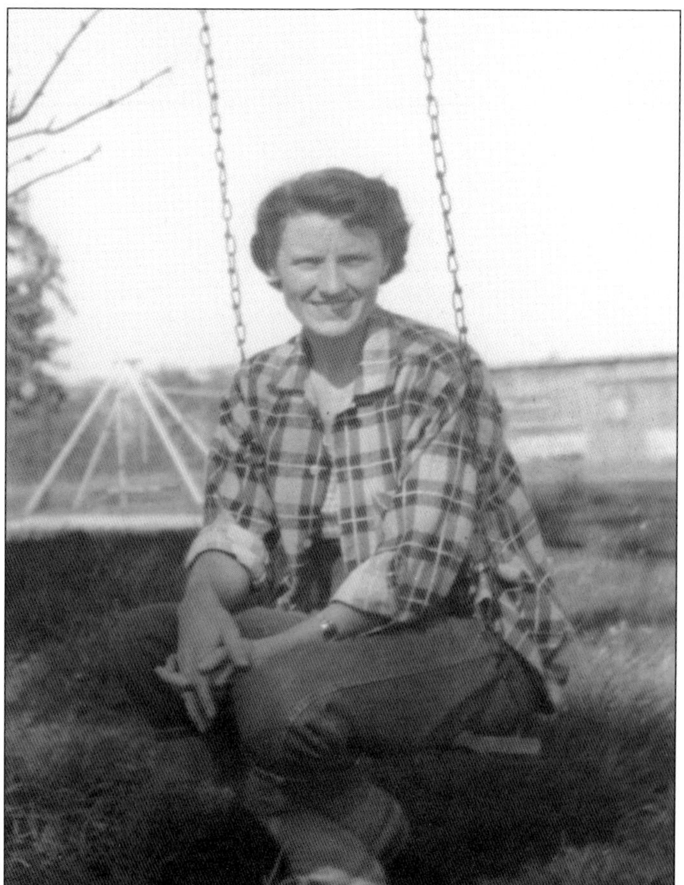

THE 71900 WELDING ROAD HOMESTEAD. In 1965, Nelson and Grace Leach bought the Hennigan farm on Furstenau Road, increasing the amount of land they could work. Dairy farming continued until the 1970s. After the death of Nelson's parents, they bought his childhood home farm. They continued to purchase additional land on School Section Road. They soon owned 350 acres and farmed even more due to rented acreage. Pictured to the right, Nelson Leach is on his tractor in 1956. Below is the homestead at 71900 Welding Road. Nelson and Grace sold the farm in 2004. (Both, courtesy of the Deborah Leach Doyle collection.)

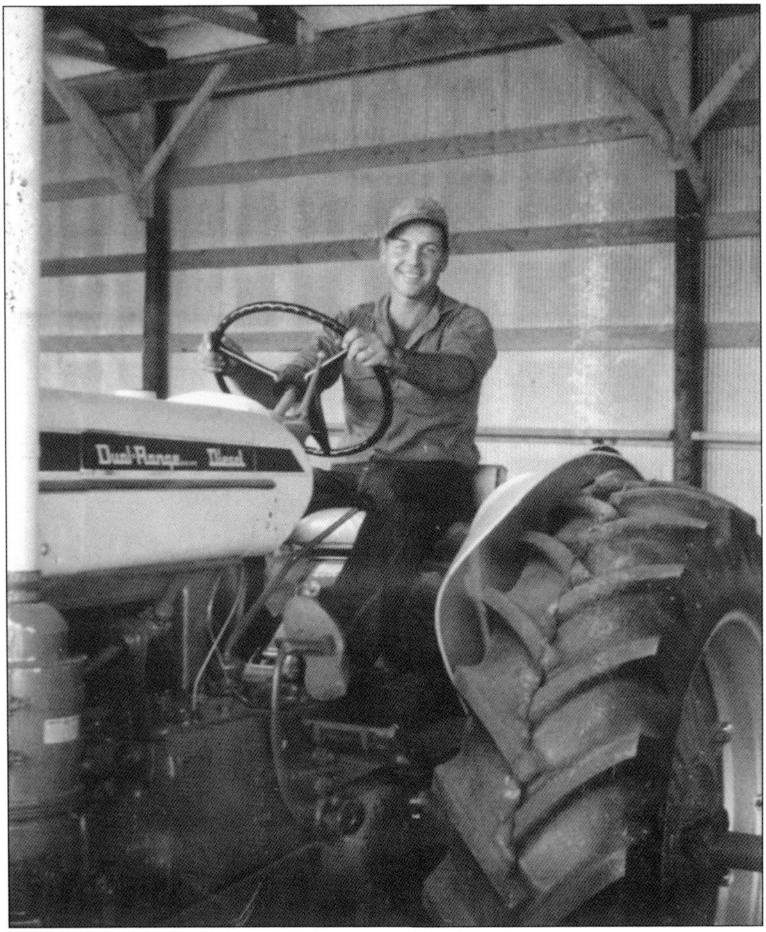

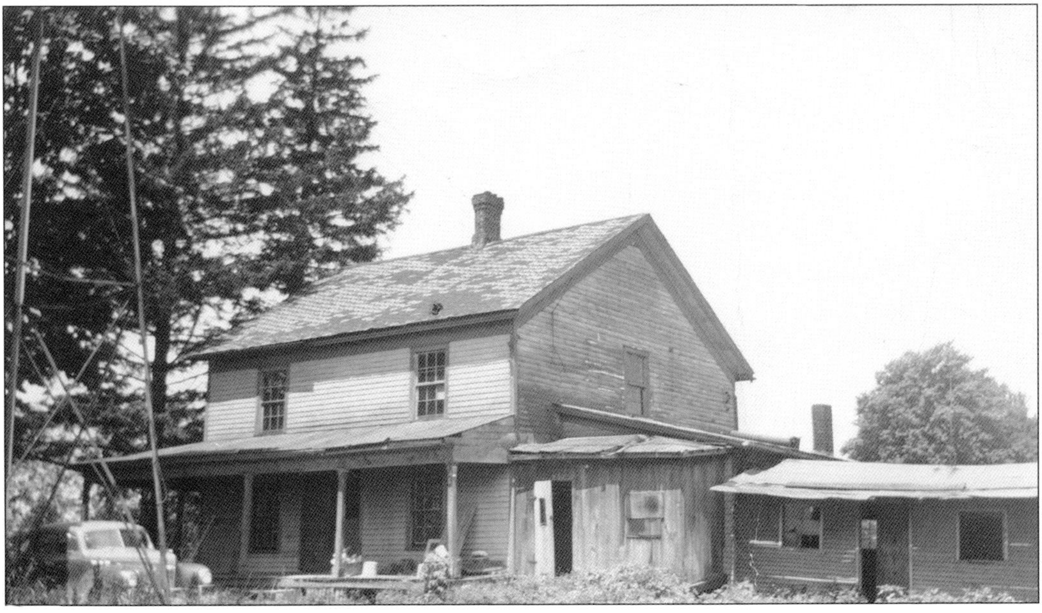

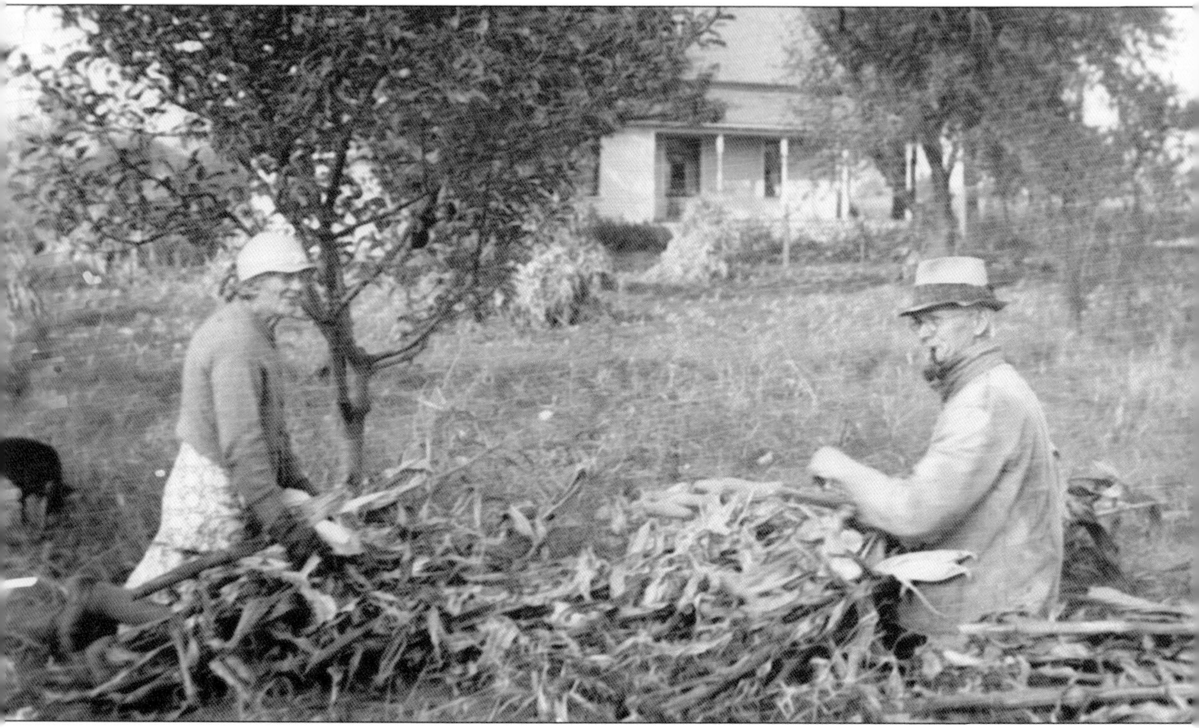

COTTON FARM. Grant Cotton, son of Leander and Maria Cotton, was born in 1871 in Lenox Township, a mile and a half from New Haven. The Cotton family came to Macomb County in 1832 from New York and settled on Gratiot Road at Chesterfield and Fairchild Roads. Jennie Cleveland was the daughter of Ambrose and Jane Cleveland. She was born on Plank Road, two and a half miles from New Haven, and her parents were also early pioneers of the area. Grant and Jennie married in 1891 and moved to Richmond to the corner of Maple Street and Hart Road, where they raised four children. They spent their years growing corn and chickens and were known for making their own cottage cheese. (Courtesy of the Michael Sullivan collection.)

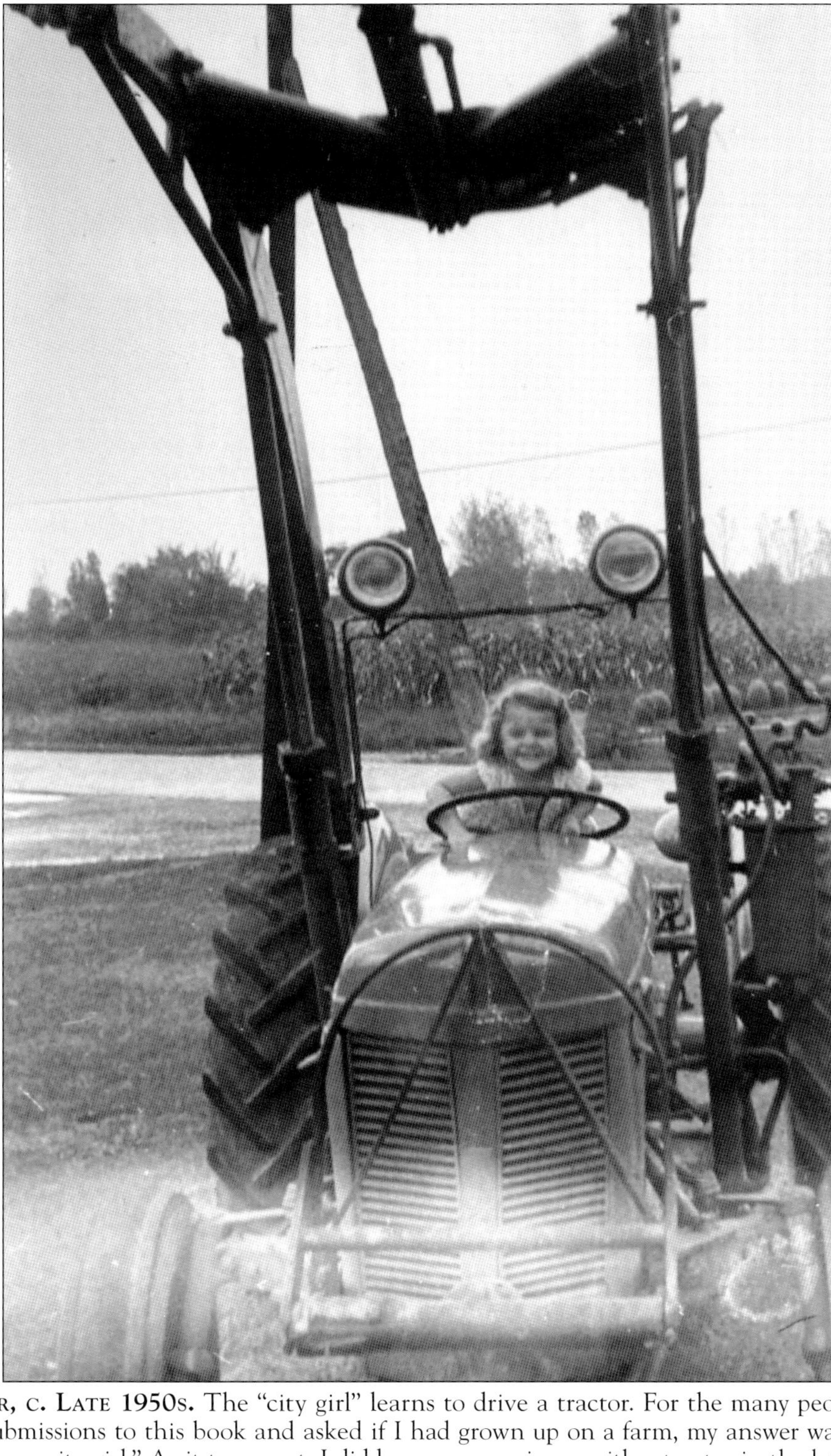

AUTHOR, C. LATE 1950S. The "city girl" learns to drive a tractor. For the many people who made submissions to this book and asked if I had grown up on a farm, my answer was always "No, I am a city girl." As it turns out, I did have an experience with a tractor in the late 1950s. (Author's collection.)

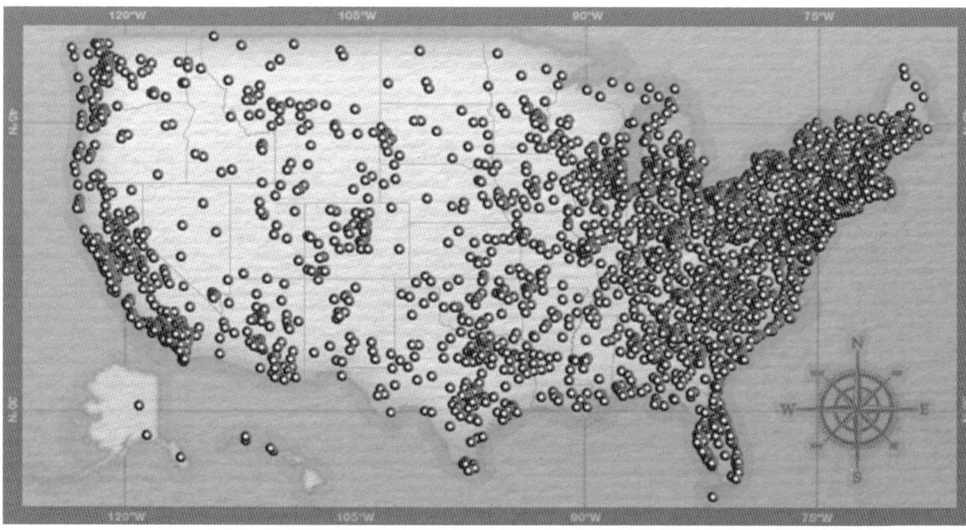